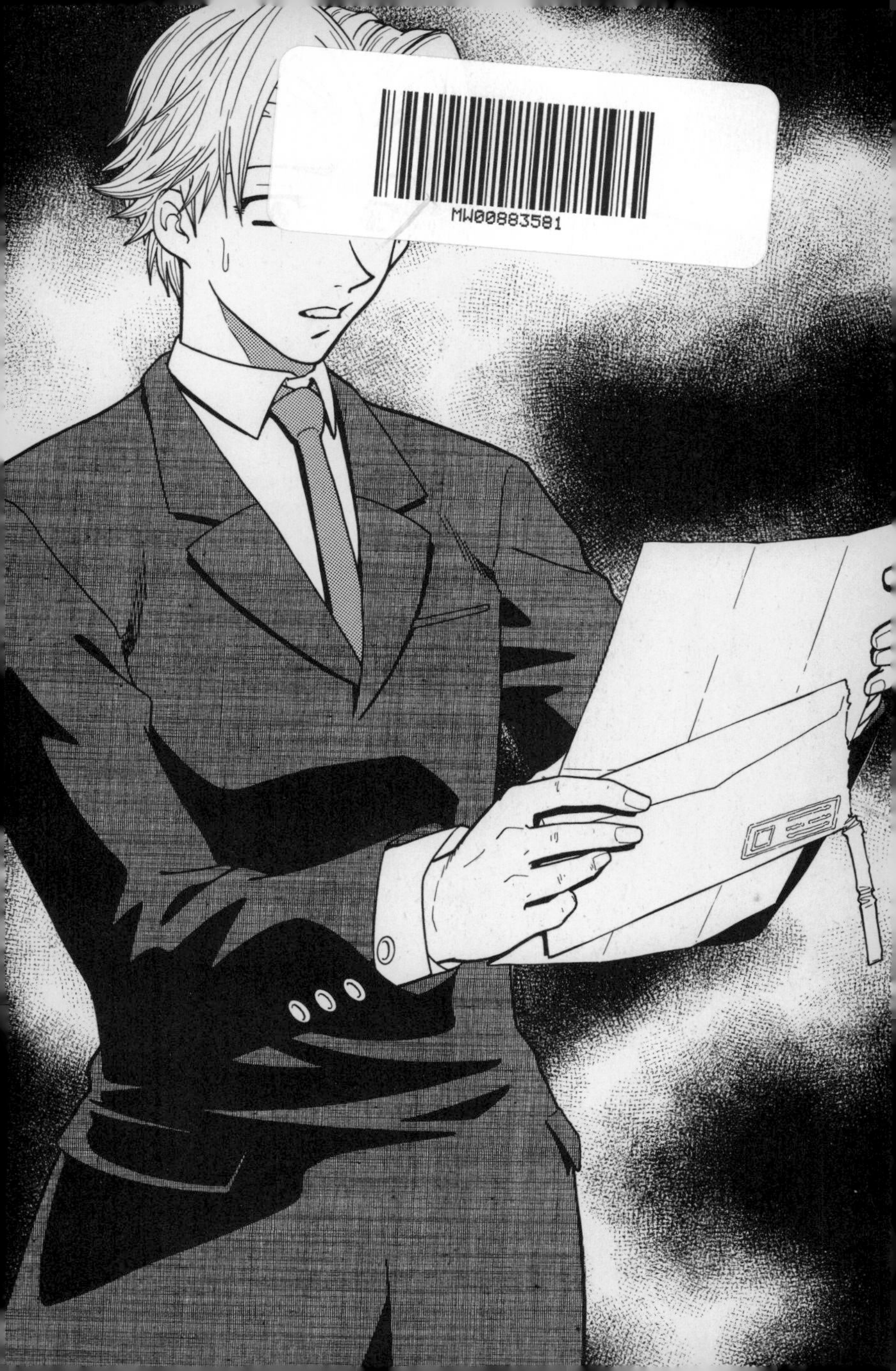

# Juror 13
## Story by D.J. Milky
## Art by Makoto Nakatsuka

Script Editor - Mark Paniccia
Retouch and Lettering - James Dashiell
Production Artists - Jason Milligan and Lucas Rivera
Cover Design - Christian Lownds

Editors - Rob Valois and Shun Nakazawa
Digital Imaging Manager - Chris Buford
Production Managers - Jennifer Miller and Mutsumi Miyazaki
Managing Editor - Lindsey Johnston
Editorial Director - Jeremy Ross
VP of Production - Ron Klamert
Publisher and E.I.C. - Mike Kiley
President and C.O.O. - John Parker
C.E.O. - Stuart Levy

A  Manga

TOKYOPOP Inc.
5900 Wilshire Blvd. Suite 2000
Los Angeles, CA 90036

E-mail: info@TOKYOPOP.com
Come visit us online at www.TOKYOPOP.com

ISBN: 1-59816-395-7
First TOKYOPOP printing: January 2006
10 9 8 7 6 5 4 3 2 1
Printed in the USA

# JuRor 13 ™

HAMBURG // LONDON // LOS ANGELES // TOKYO

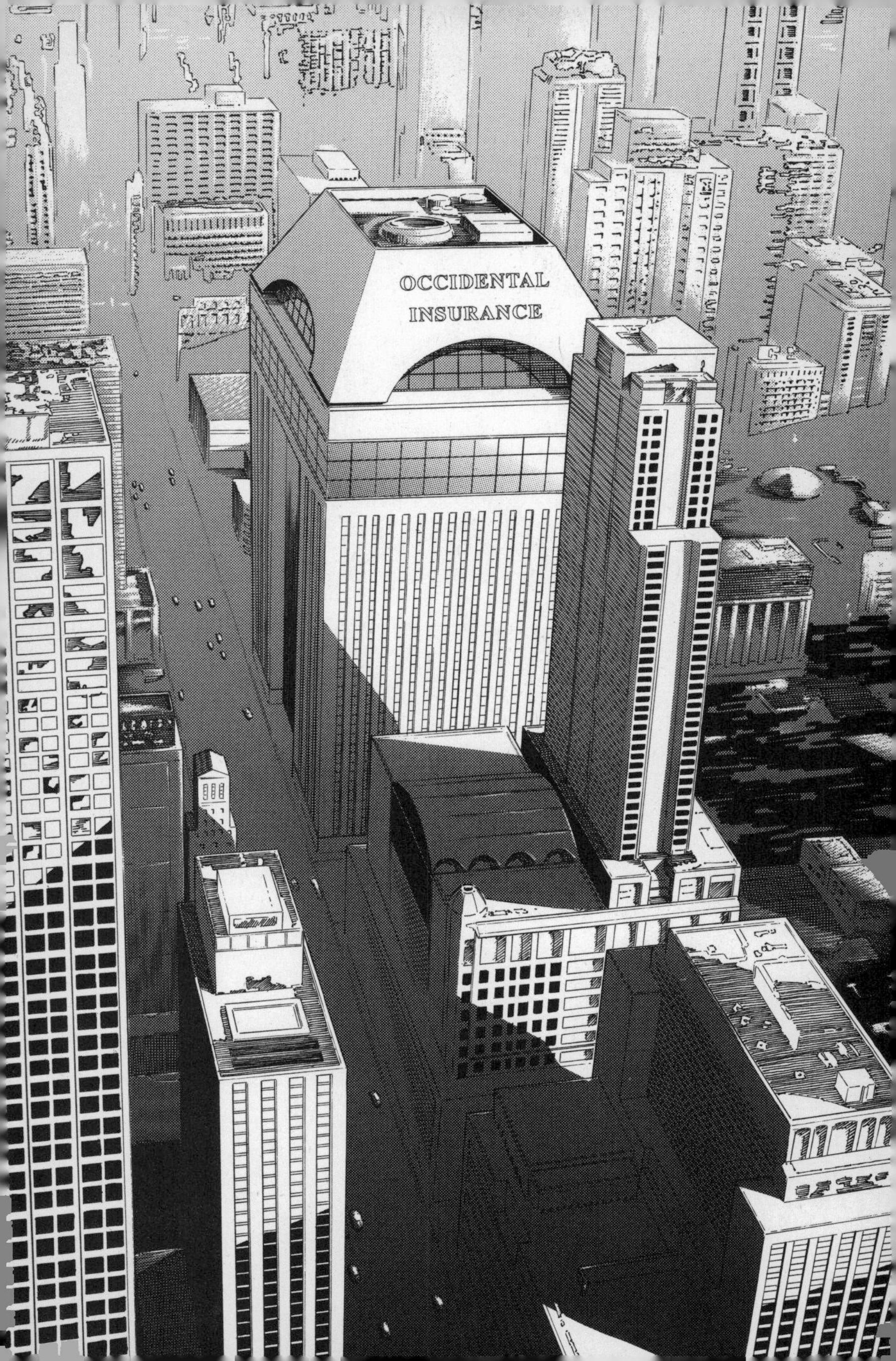
OCCIDENTAL
INSURANCE

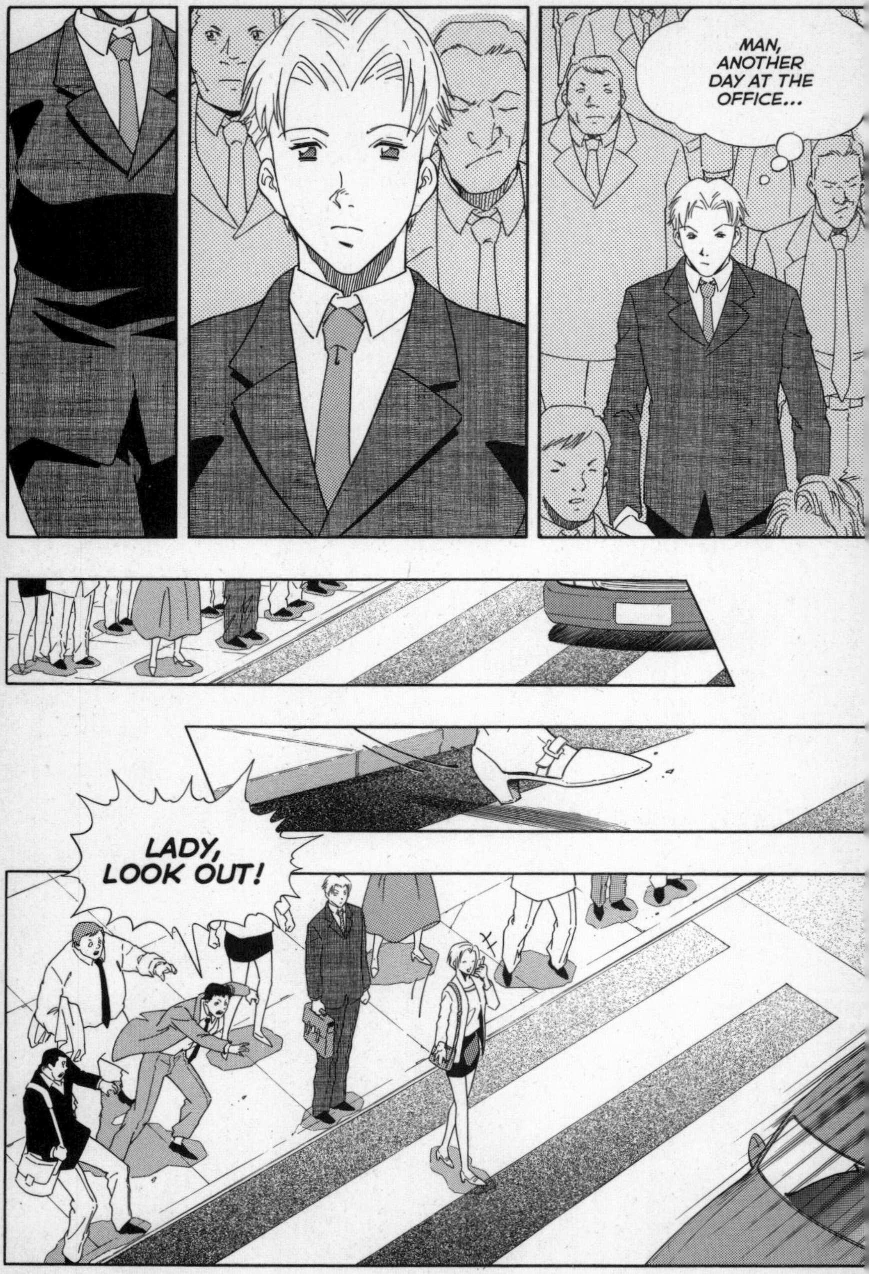
MAN, ANOTHER DAY AT THE OFFICE...
LADY, LOOK OUT!

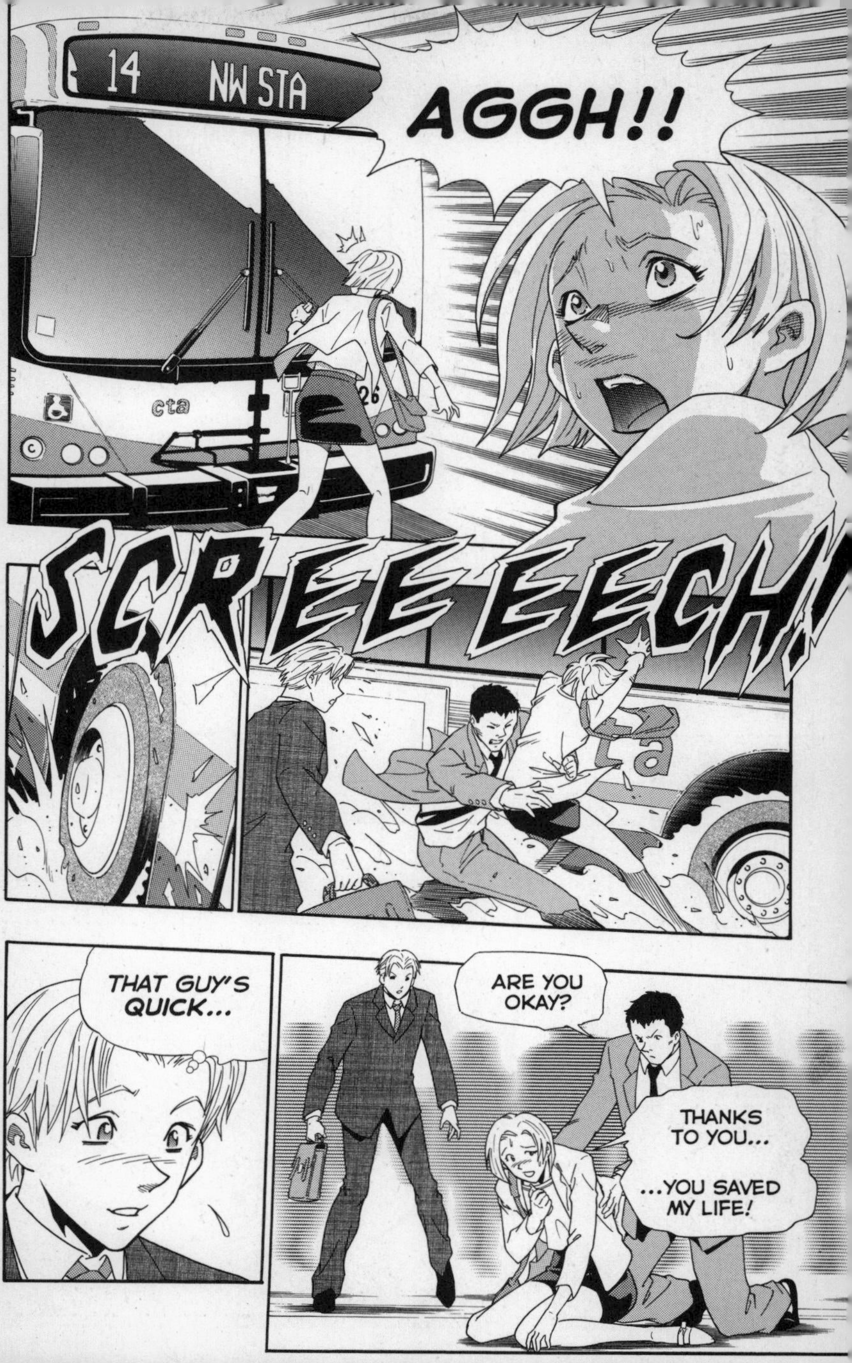
14 NW STA
cta
AGGH!!
SCREEEECH!
cta
THAT GUY'S QUICK...
ARE YOU OKAY?
THANKS TO YOU...
...YOU SAVED MY LIFE!

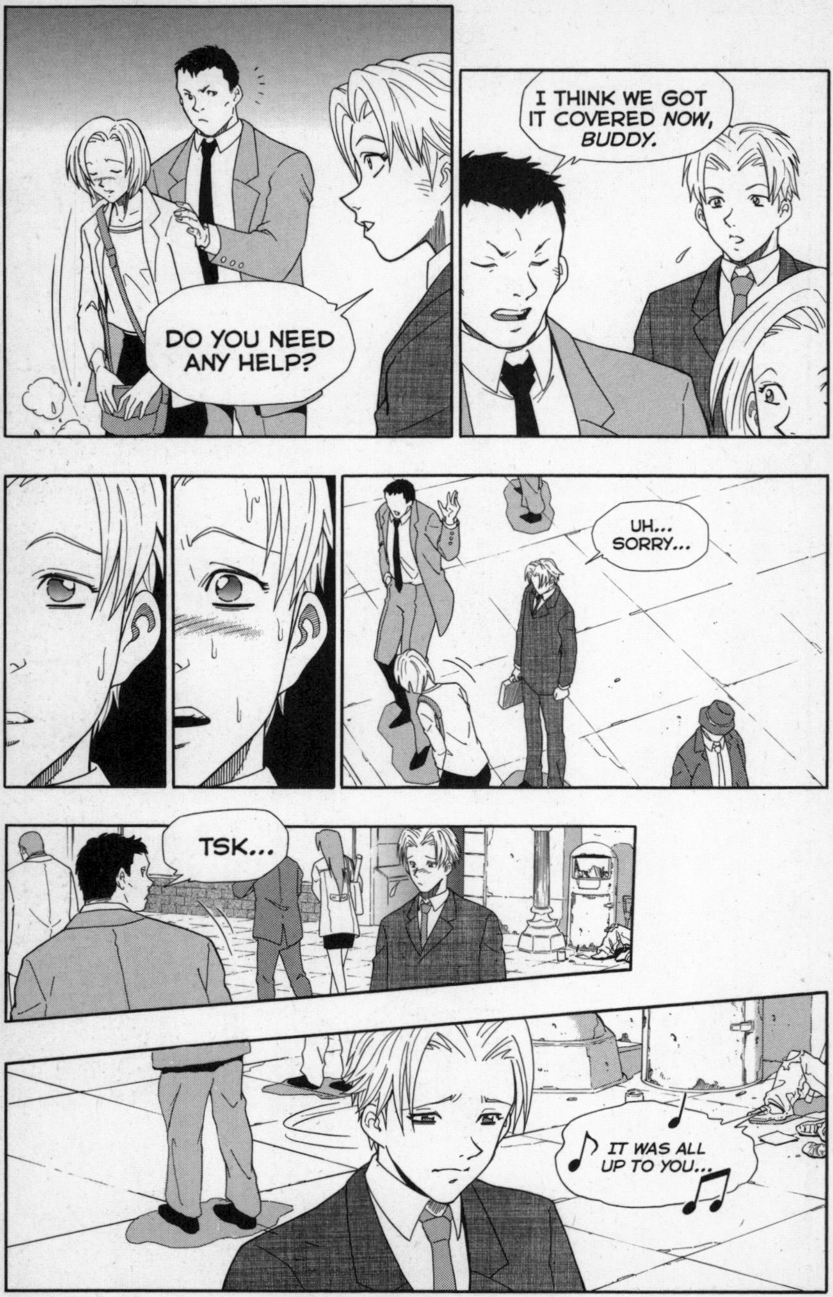
DO YOU NEED ANY HELP?
I THINK WE GOT IT COVERED *NOW*, *BUDDY.*
UH... SORRY...
TSK...
IT WAS ALL UP TO YOU...

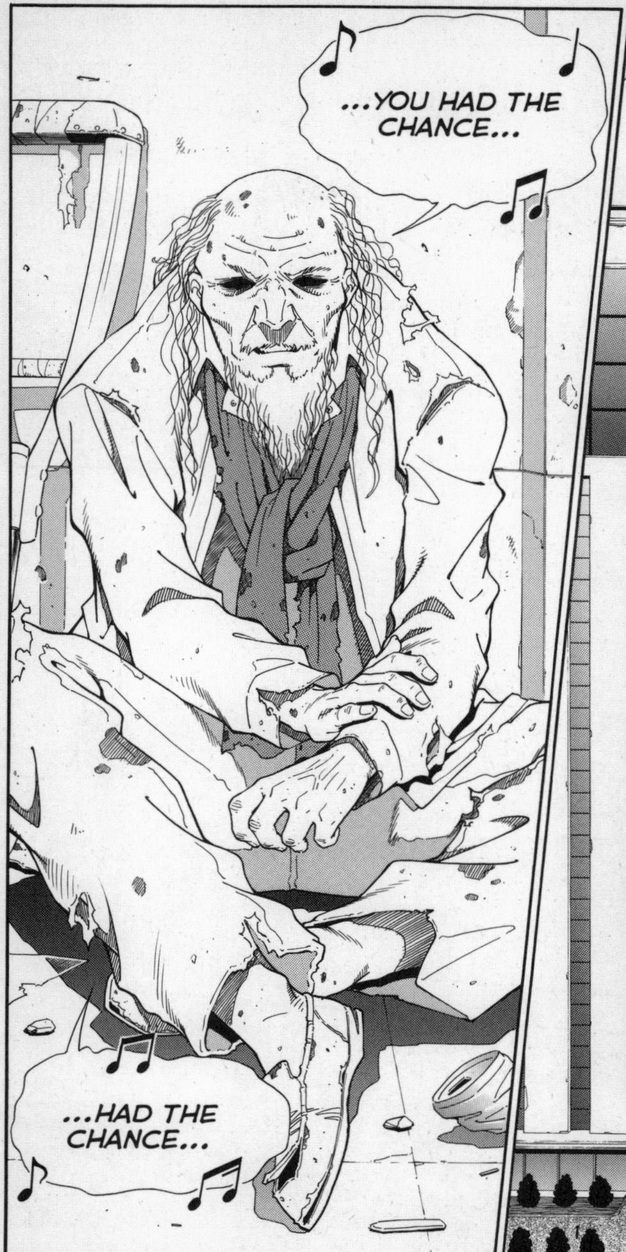
...YOU HAD THE CHANCE...
...HAD THE CHANCE...
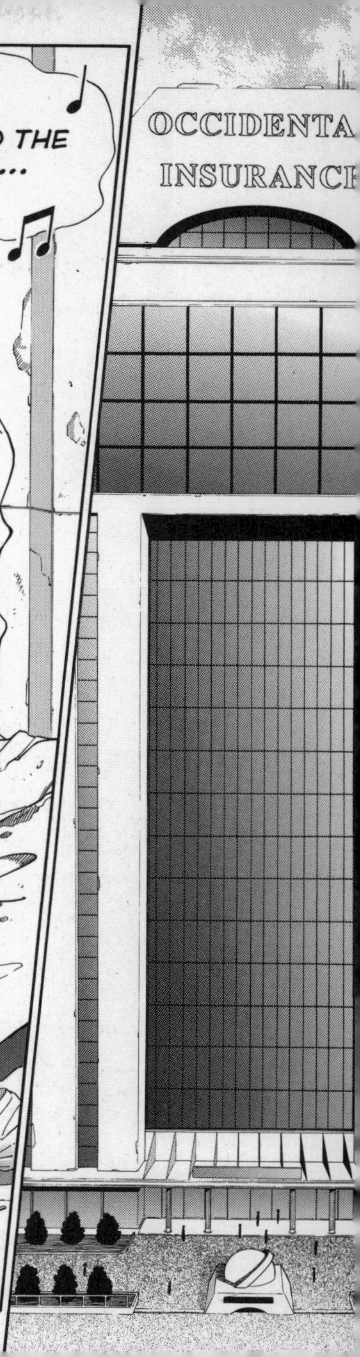
OCCIDENTA
INSURANC

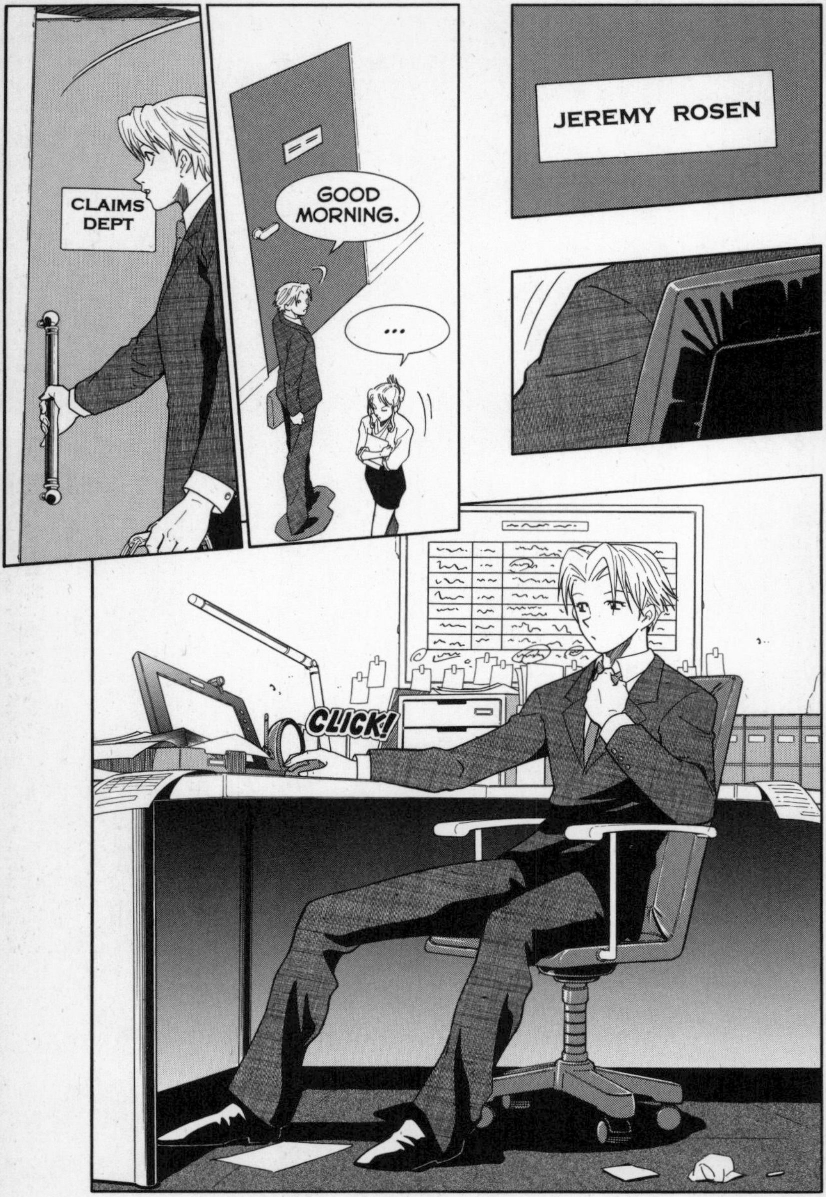
CLAIMS DEPT
GOOD MORNING.
...
JEREMY ROSEN
CLICK!

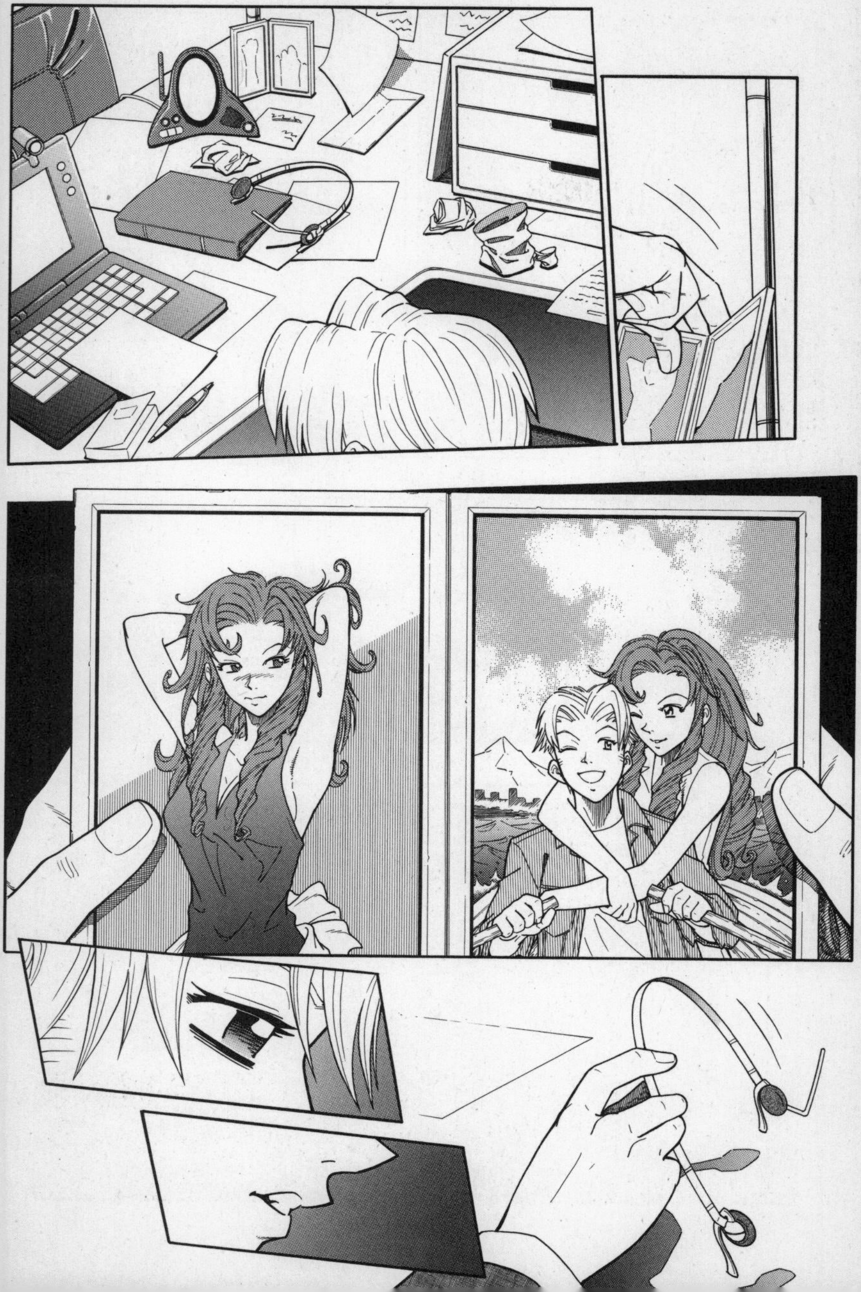

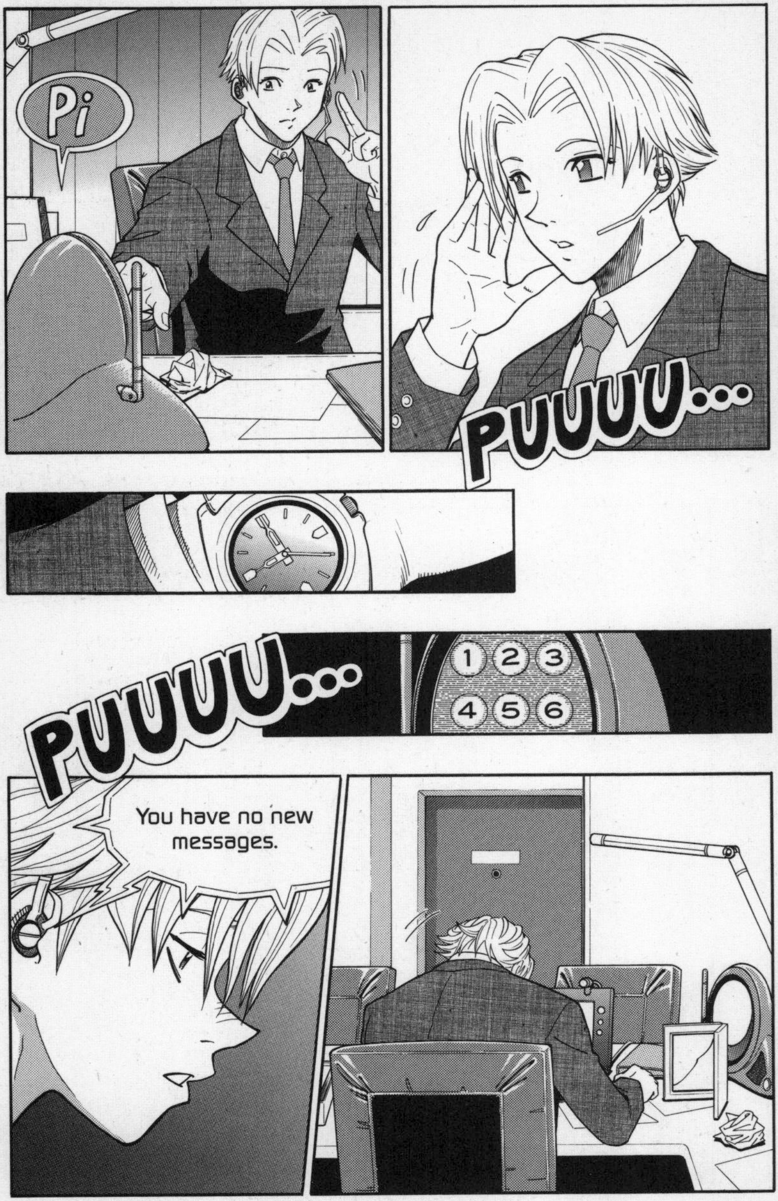
Pi
PUUUU...
1 2 3
4 5 6
PUUUU...
You have no new messages.

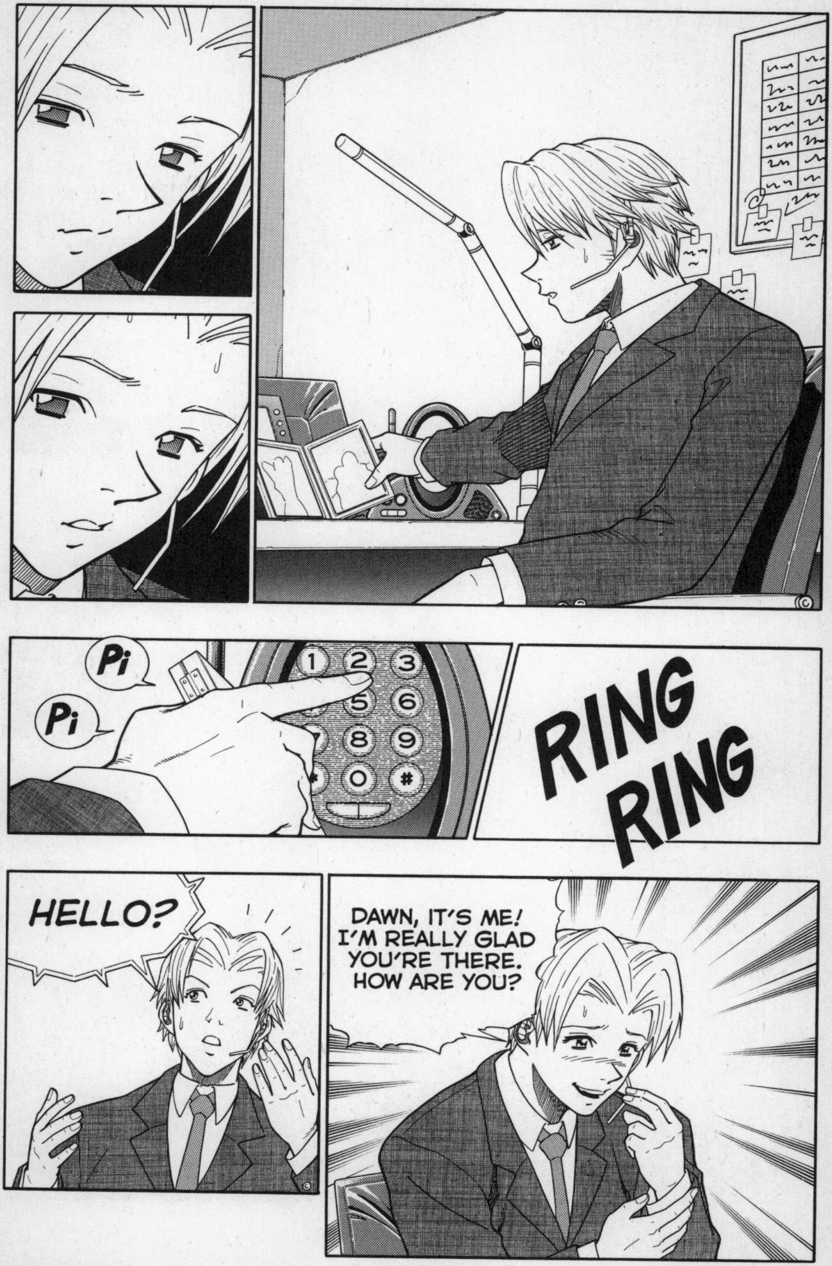
Pi
Pi
RING
RING
HELLO?
DAWN, IT'S ME! I'M REALLY GLAD YOU'RE THERE. HOW ARE YOU?

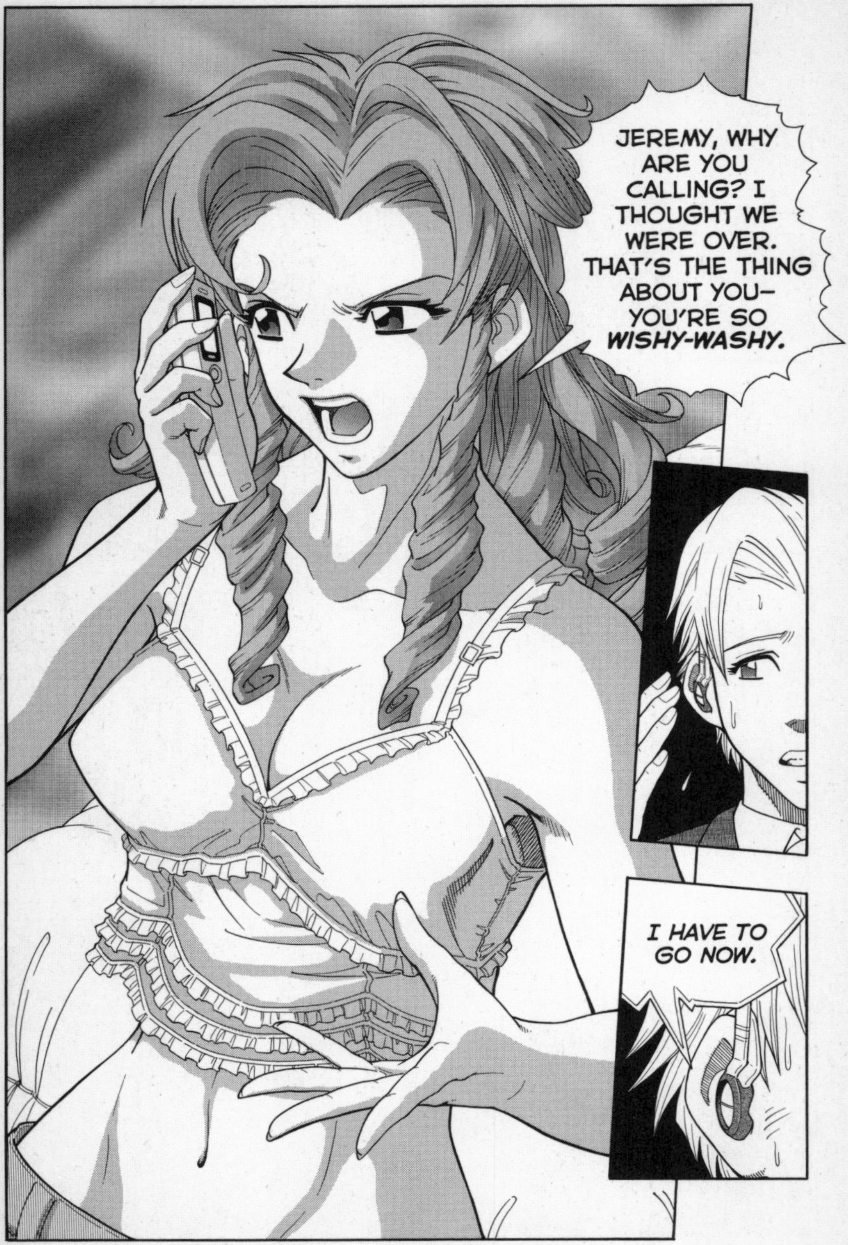
JEREMY, WHY ARE YOU CALLING? I THOUGHT WE WERE OVER. THAT'S THE THING ABOUT YOU— YOU'RE SO *WISHY-WASHY.*
*I HAVE TO GO NOW.*

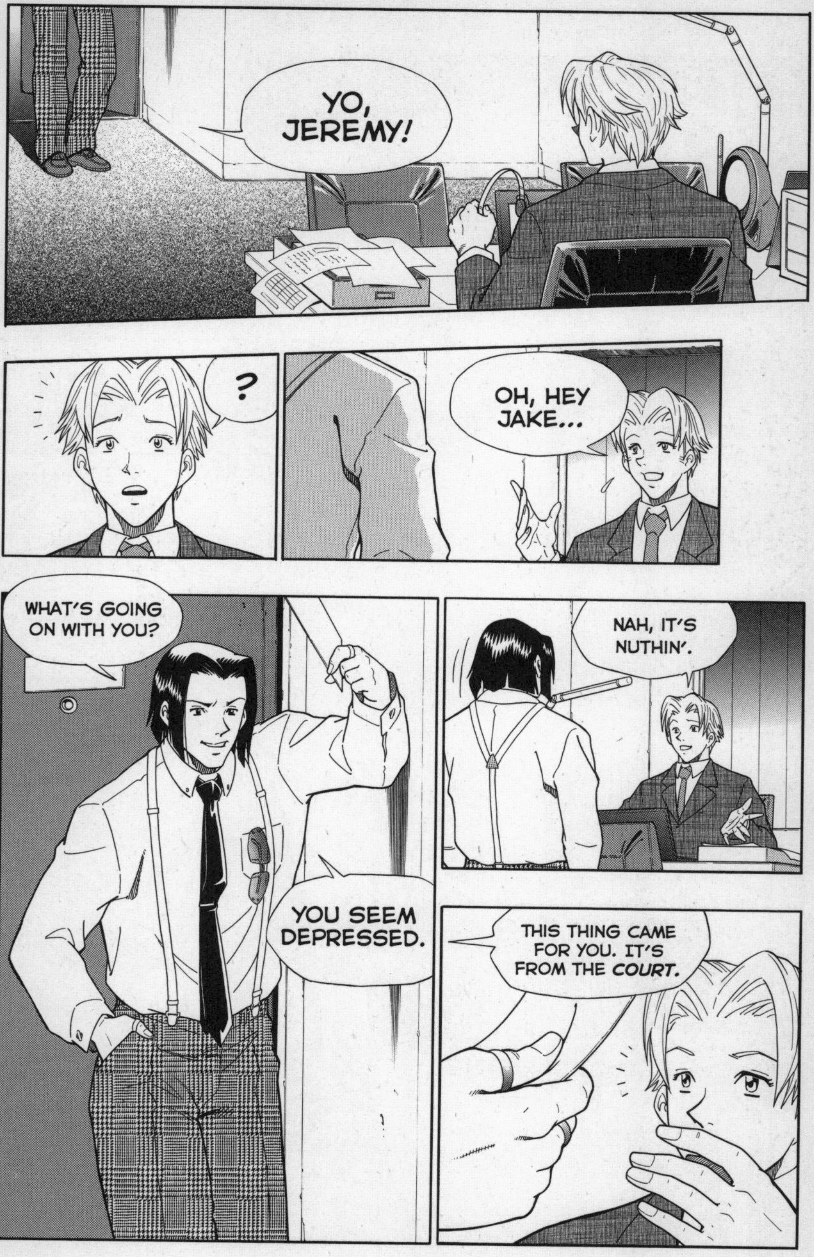
YO, JEREMY!
?
OH, HEY JAKE...
WHAT'S GOING ON WITH YOU?
YOU SEEM DEPRESSED.
NAH, IT'S NUTHIN'.
THIS THING CAME FOR YOU. IT'S FROM THE *COURT*.

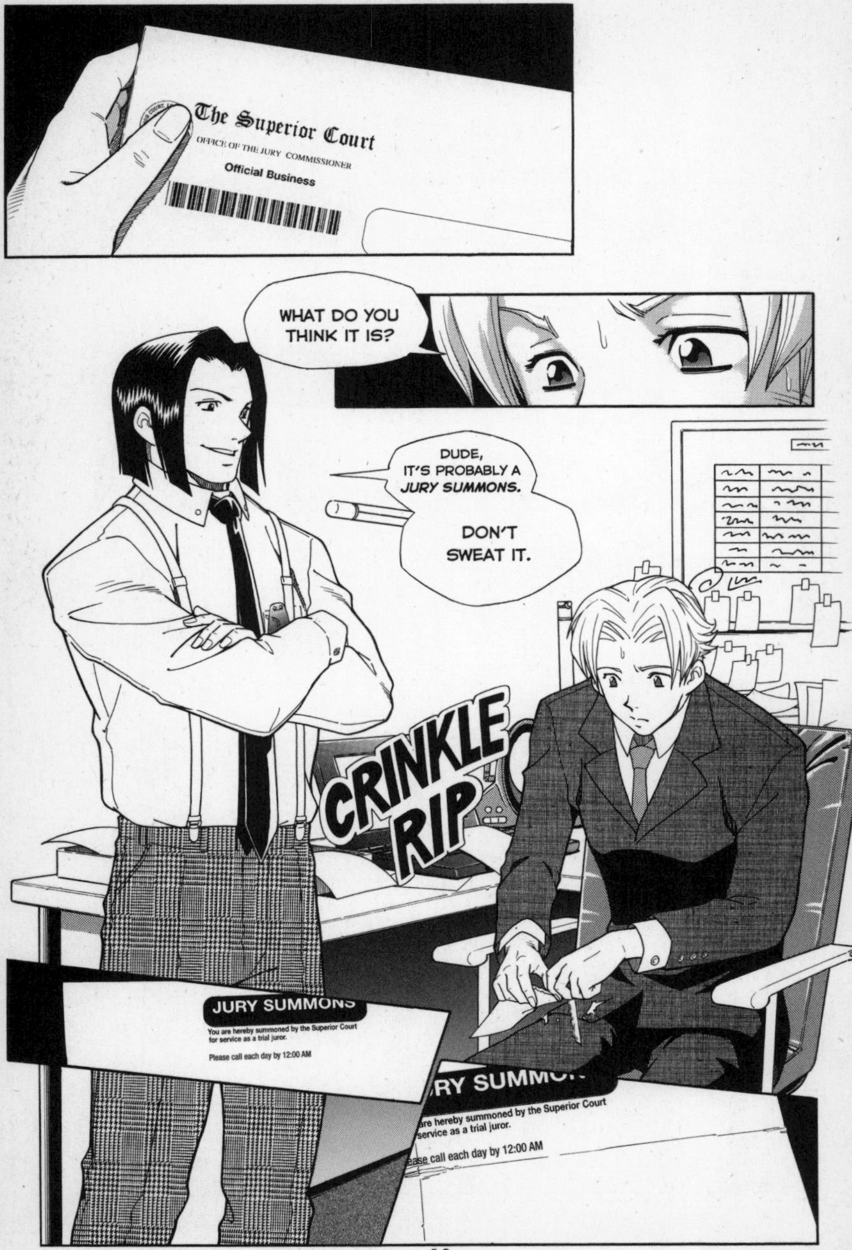
The Superior Court
OFFICE OF THE JURY COMMISSIONER
Official Business
WHAT DO YOU THINK IT IS?
DUDE, IT'S PROBABLY A *JURY SUMMONS.*
DON'T SWEAT IT.
CRINKLE
RIP
JURY SUMMONS
You are hereby summoned by the Superior Court for service as a trial juror.
Please call each day by 12:00 AM

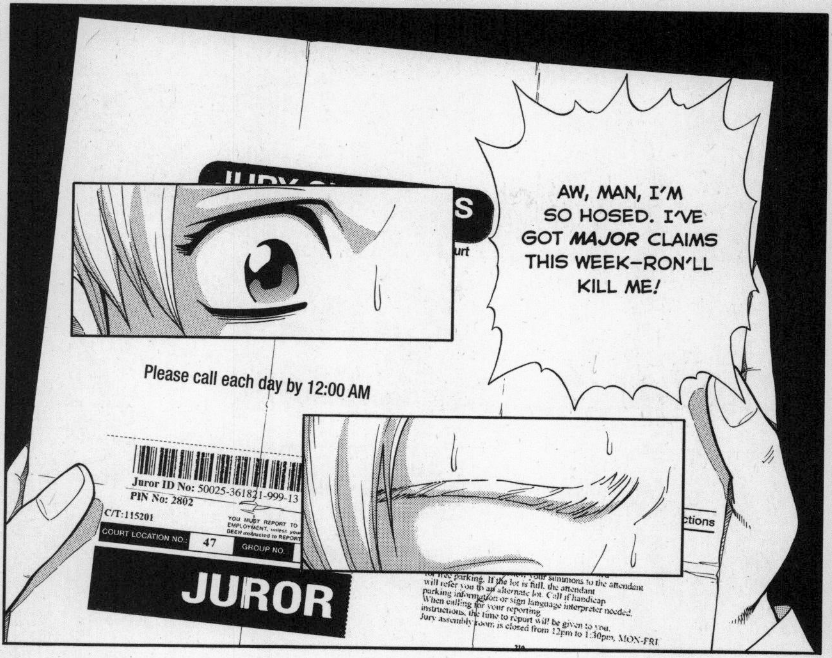
Please call each day by 12:00 AM
Juror ID No: 50025-361821-999-13
PIN No: 2802
C/T:115201
COURT LOCATION NO.: 47
GROUP NO.
JUROR
AW, MAN, I'M SO HOSED. I'VE GOT *MAJOR* CLAIMS THIS WEEK–RON'LL KILL ME!

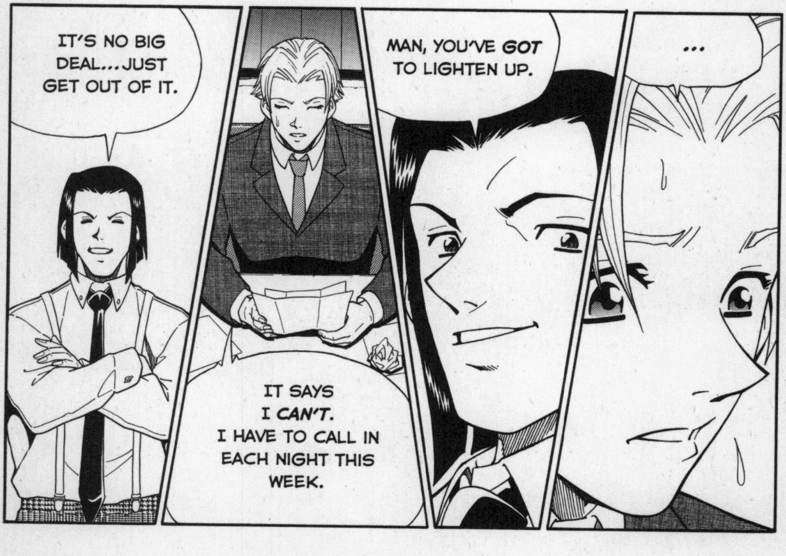
IT'S NO BIG DEAL...JUST GET OUT OF IT.
IT SAYS I *CAN'T*. I HAVE TO CALL IN EACH NIGHT THIS WEEK.
MAN, YOU'VE *GOT* TO LIGHTEN UP.
...

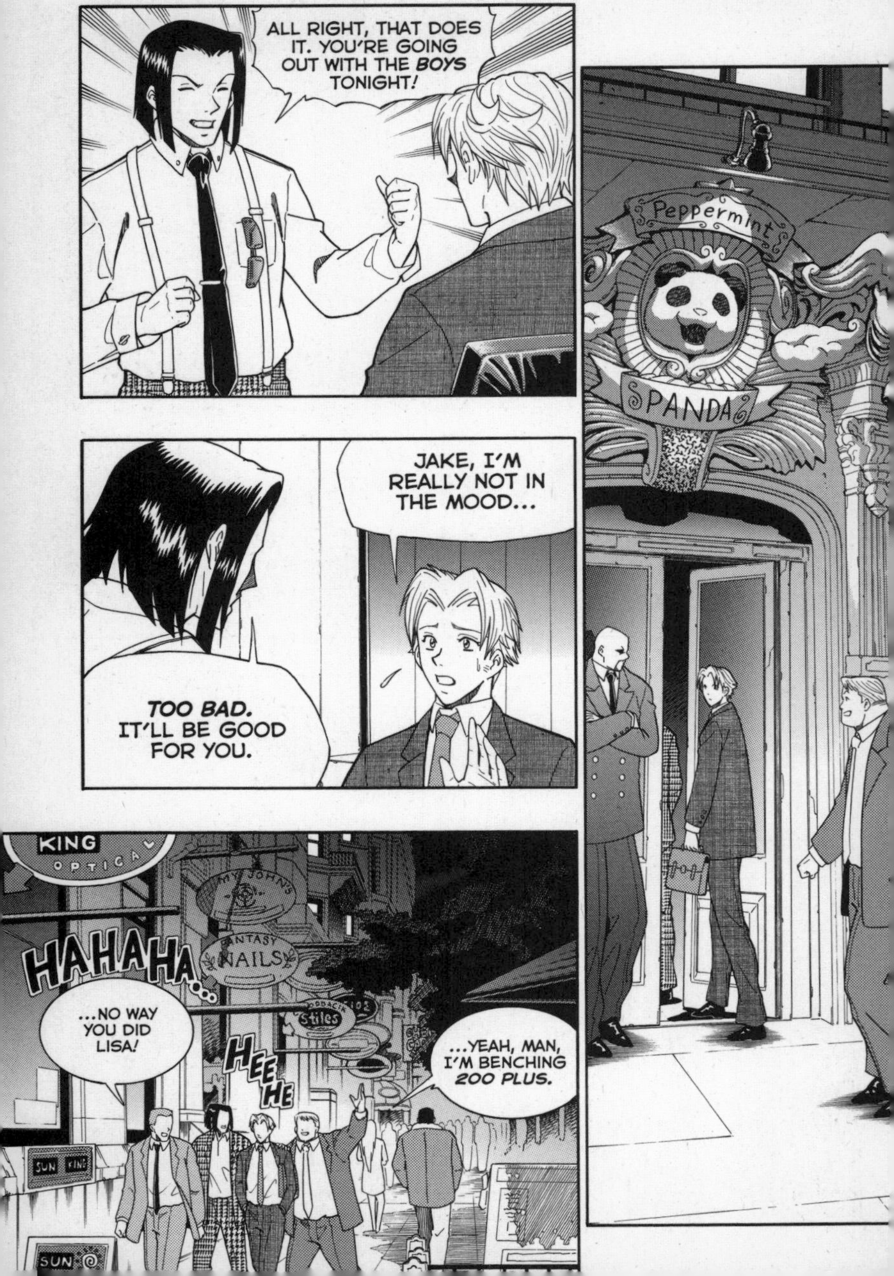
ALL RIGHT, THAT DOES IT. YOU'RE GOING OUT WITH THE *BOYS* TONIGHT!
JAKE, I'M REALLY NOT IN THE MOOD...
*TOO BAD.* IT'LL BE GOOD FOR YOU.
KING
OPTICA
FANTASY NAILS
HAHAHA...
...NO WAY YOU DID LISA!
Stiles
HEE HE
...YEAH, MAN, I'M BENCHING *200 PLUS.*
SUN KING
SUN
Peppermint
PANDA

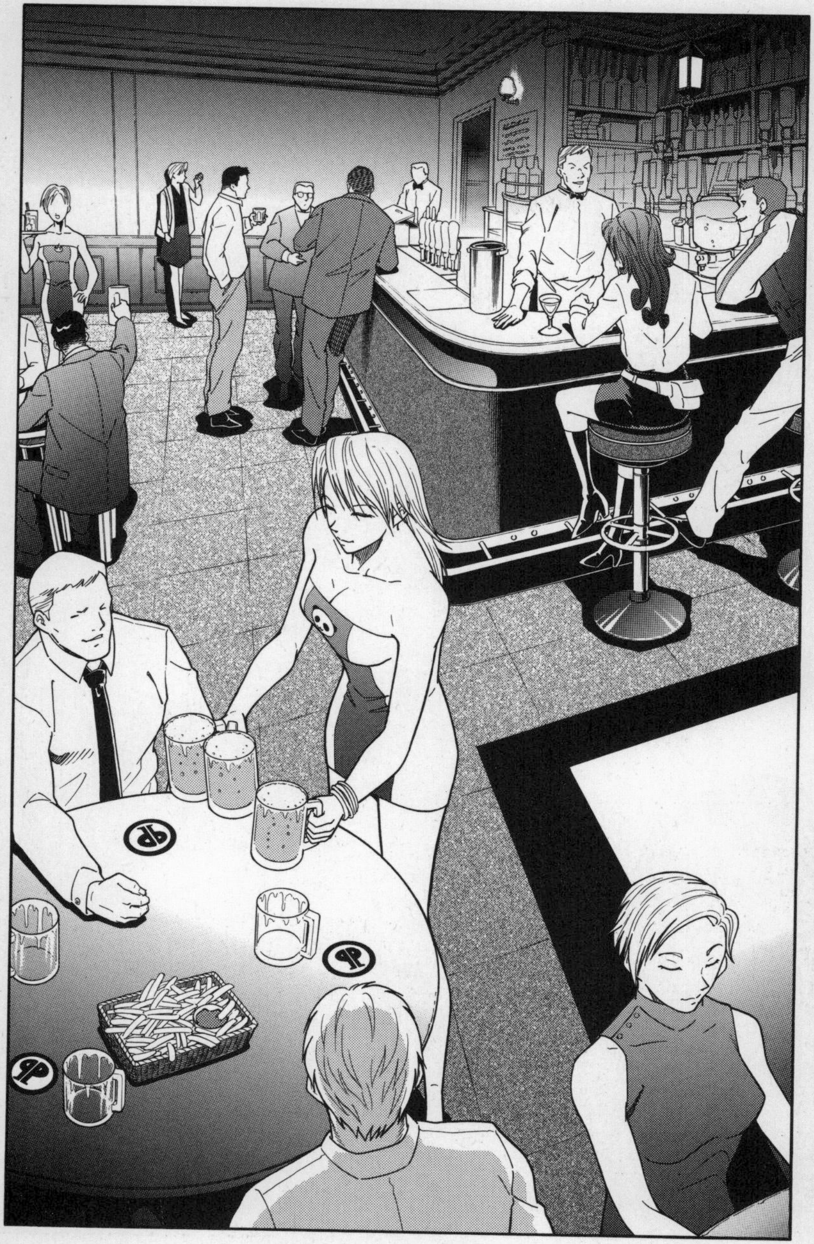

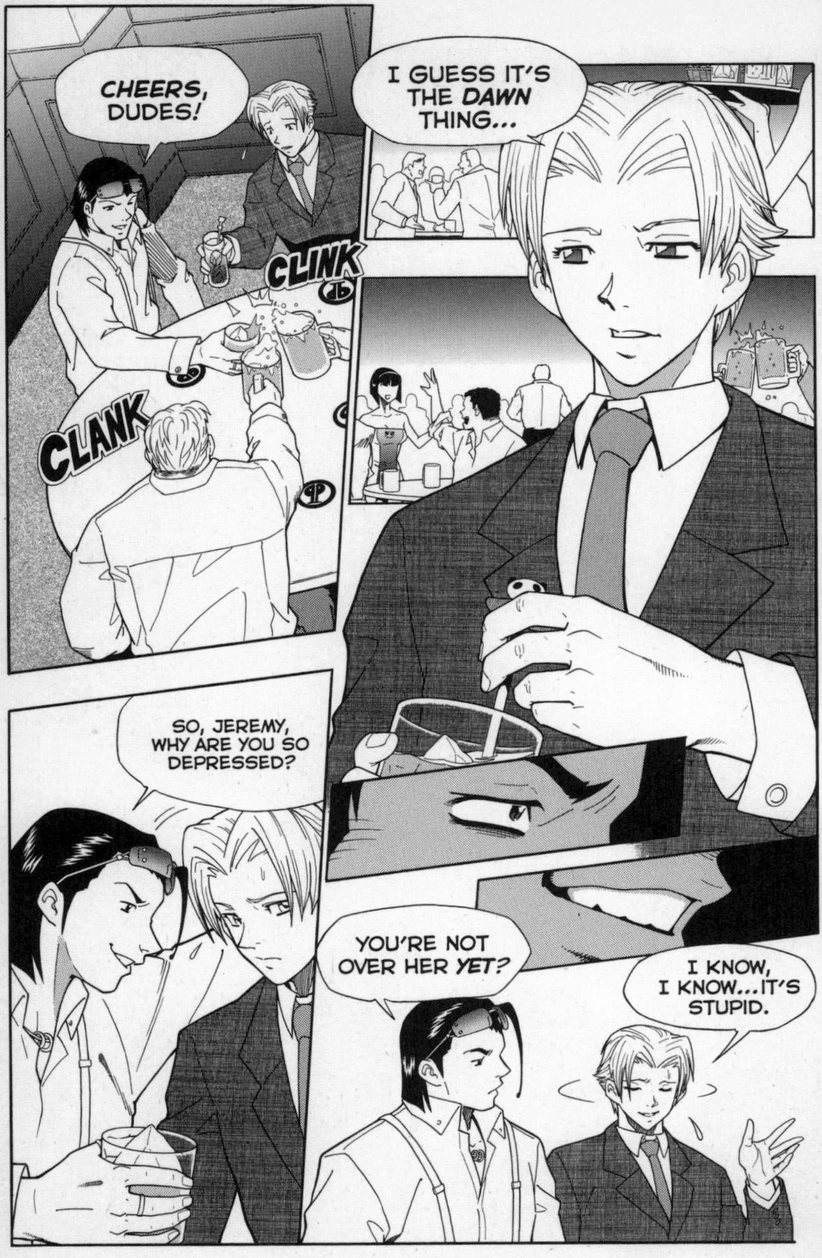
CHEERS, DUDES!
CLINK
CLANK
I GUESS IT'S THE *DAWN* THING...
SO, JEREMY, WHY ARE YOU SO DEPRESSED?
YOU'RE NOT OVER HER *YET*?
I KNOW, I KNOW...IT'S STUPID.

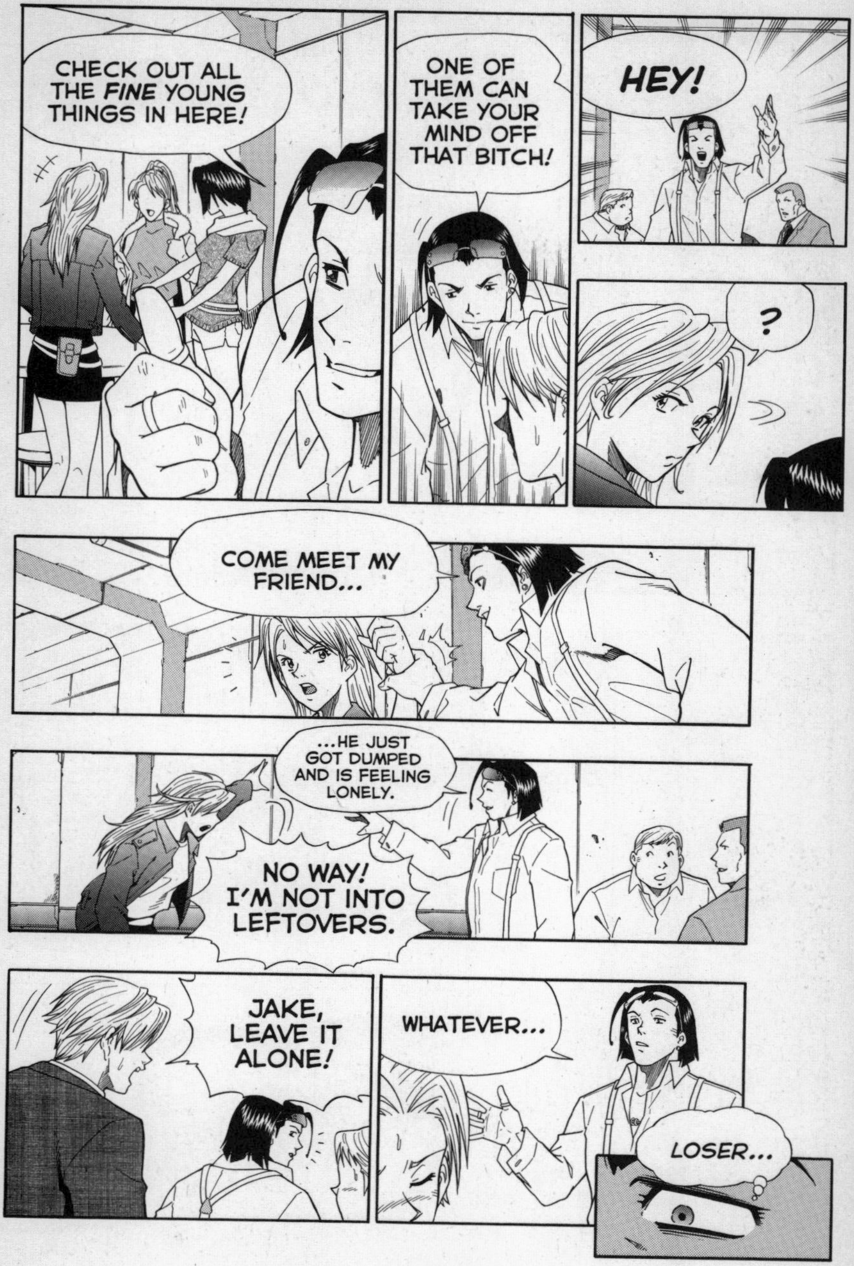
CHECK OUT ALL THE *FINE* YOUNG THINGS IN HERE!
ONE OF THEM CAN TAKE YOUR MIND OFF THAT BITCH!
HEY!
?
COME MEET MY FRIEND...
...HE JUST GOT DUMPED AND IS FEELING LONELY.
NO WAY! I'M NOT INTO LEFTOVERS.
JAKE, LEAVE IT ALONE!
WHATEVER...
LOSER...

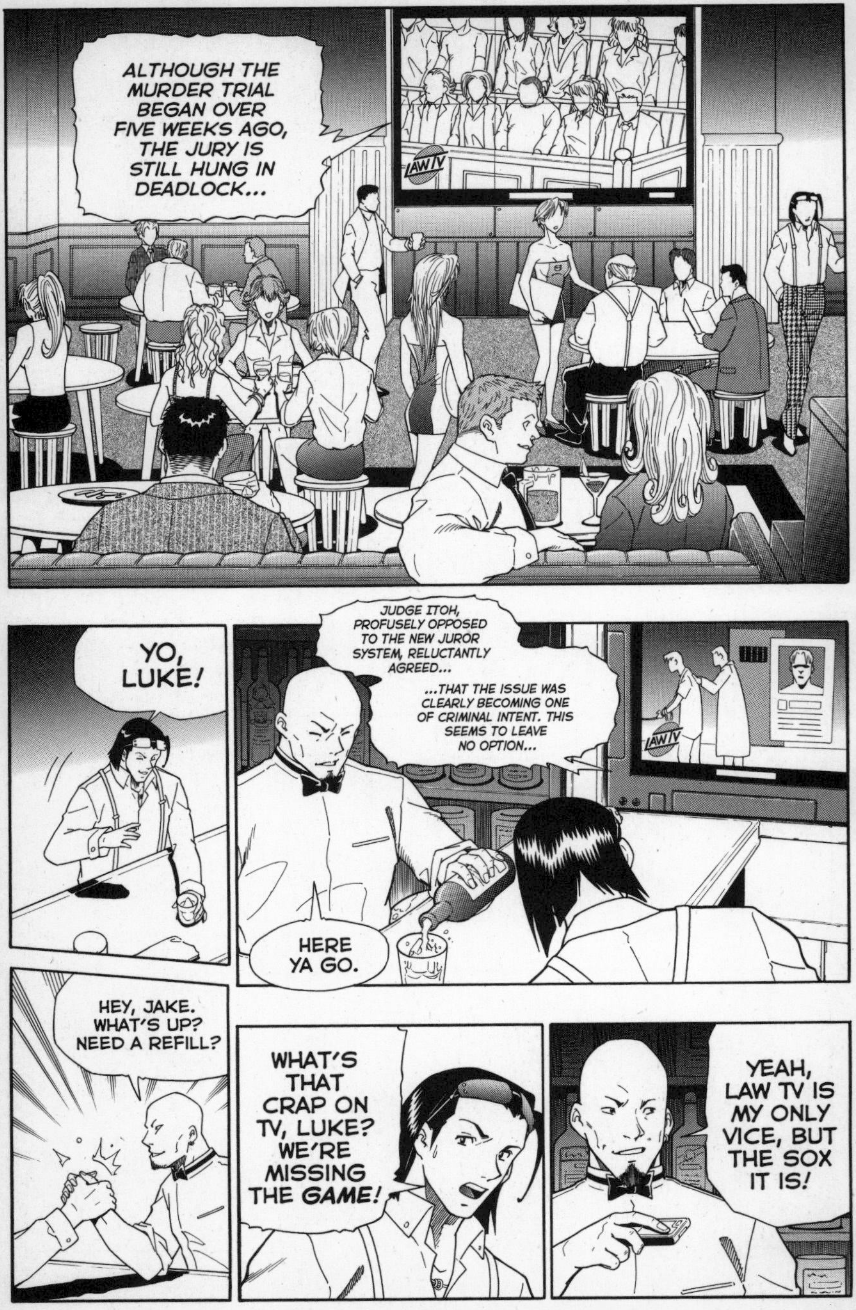
ALTHOUGH THE MURDER TRIAL BEGAN OVER FIVE WEEKS AGO, THE JURY IS STILL HUNG IN DEADLOCK...
LAW TV
YO, LUKE!
JUDGE ITOH, PROFUSELY OPPOSED TO THE NEW JUROR SYSTEM, RELUCTANTLY AGREED...
...THAT THE ISSUE WAS CLEARLY BECOMING ONE OF CRIMINAL INTENT. THIS SEEMS TO LEAVE NO OPTION...
LAW TV
HERE YA GO.
HEY, JAKE. WHAT'S UP? NEED A REFILL?
WHAT'S THAT CRAP ON TV, LUKE? WE'RE MISSING THE GAME!
YEAH, LAW TV IS MY ONLY VICE, BUT THE SOX IT IS!

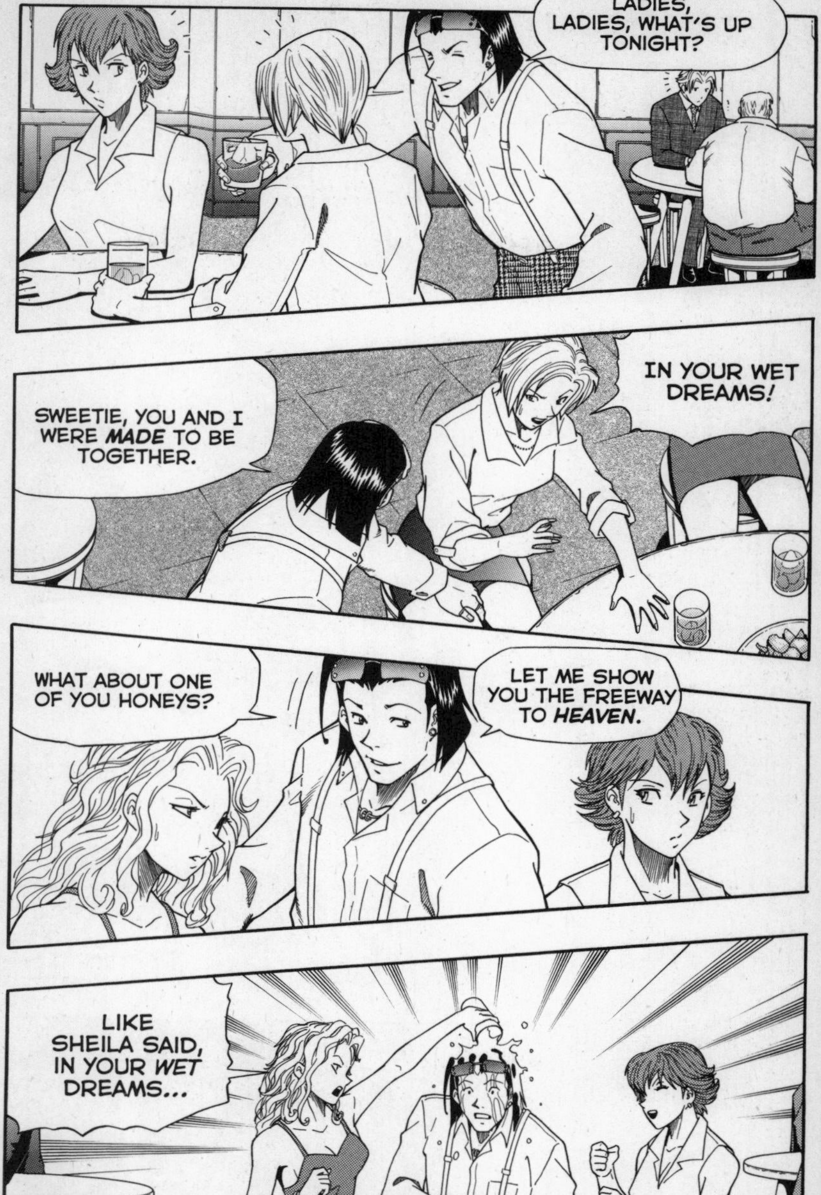
LADIES, LADIES, WHAT'S UP TONIGHT?
SWEETIE, YOU AND I WERE *MADE* TO BE TOGETHER.
IN YOUR WET DREAMS!
WHAT ABOUT ONE OF YOU HONEYS?
LET ME SHOW YOU THE FREEWAY TO ***HEAVEN***.
LIKE SHEILA SAID, IN YOUR *WET* DREAMS...

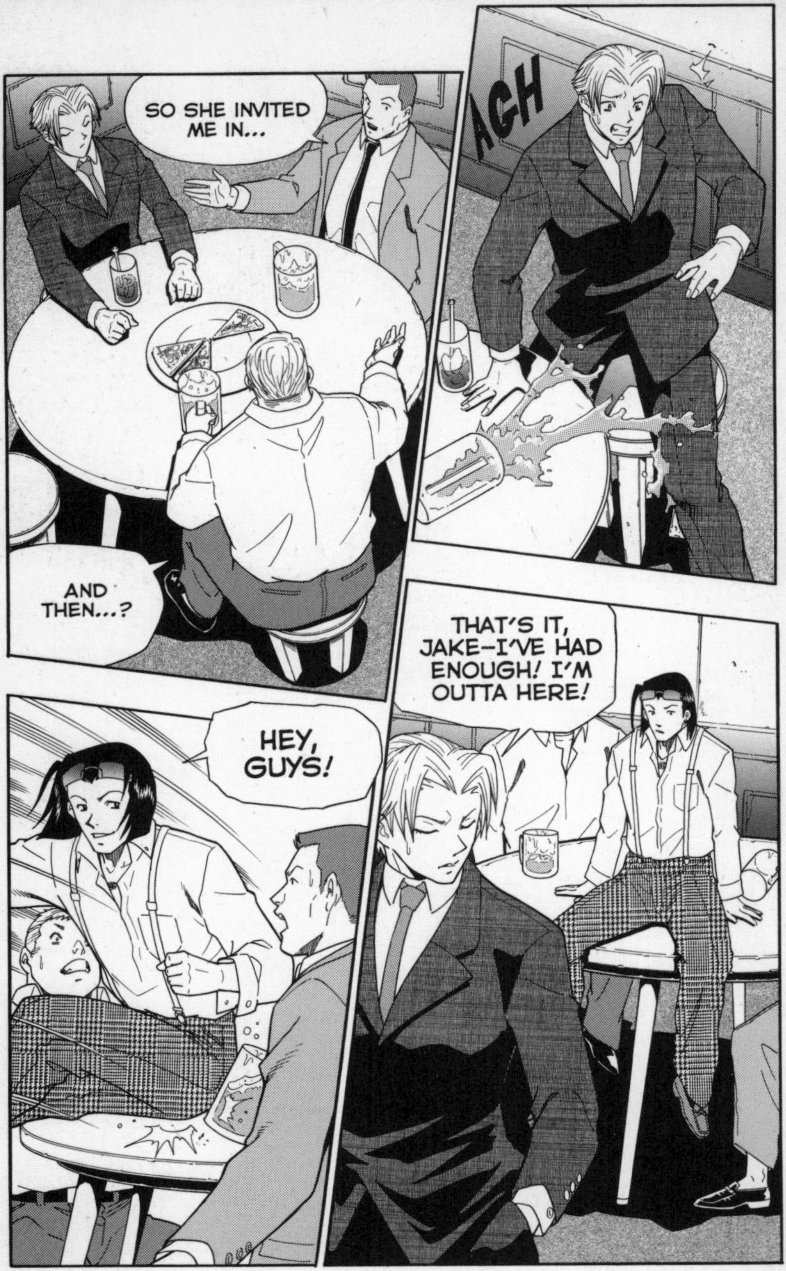
SO SHE INVITED ME IN...
AND THEN...?
ACH
HEY, GUYS!
THAT'S IT, JAKE–I'VE HAD ENOUGH! I'M OUTTA HERE!

Juror 13™

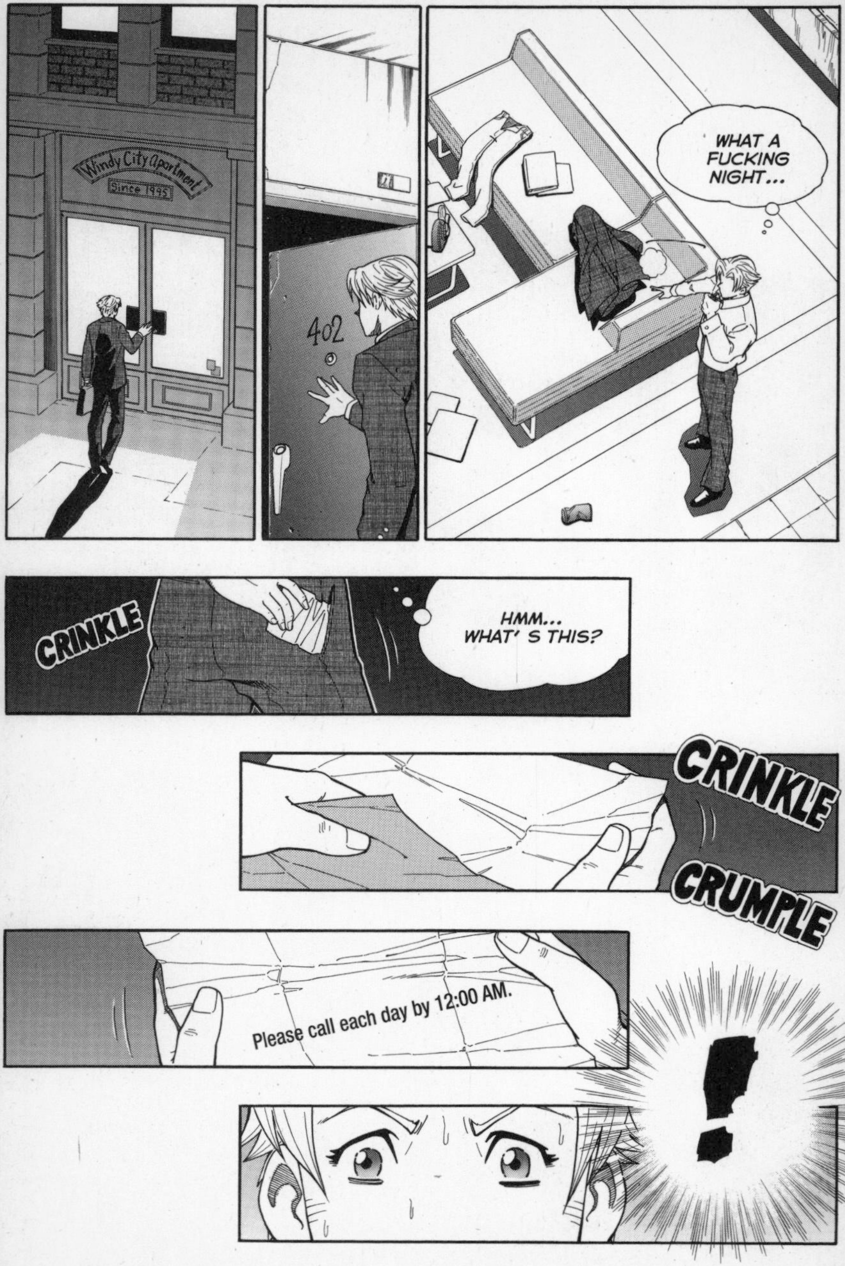
Windy City Apartment
Since 1995
402
WHAT A FUCKING NIGHT...
CRINKLE
HMM... WHAT' S THIS?
CRINKLE
CRUMPLE
Please call each day by 12:00 AM.
!

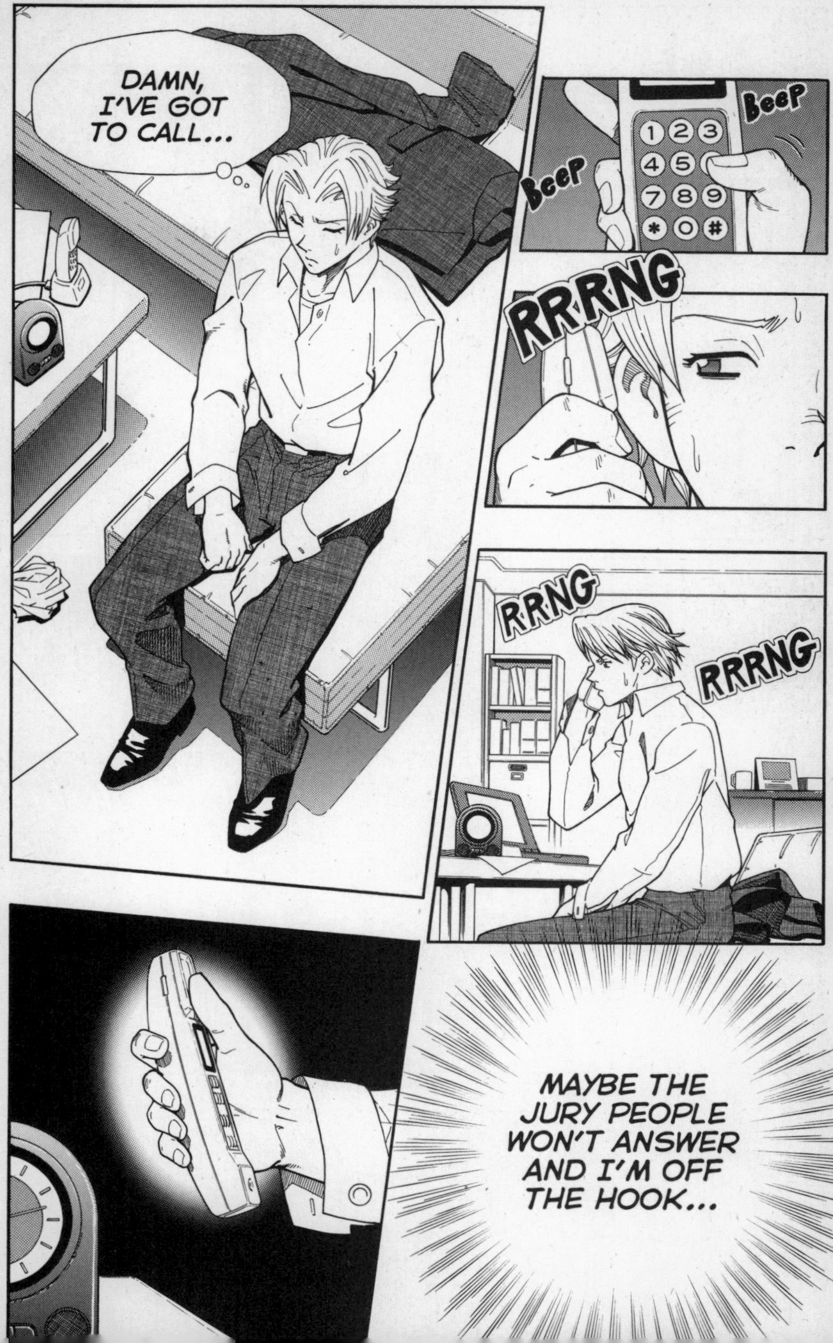
DAMN, I'VE GOT TO CALL...
Beep
Beep
RRRNG
RRNG
RRRNG
MAYBE THE JURY PEOPLE WON'T ANSWER AND I'M OFF THE HOOK...

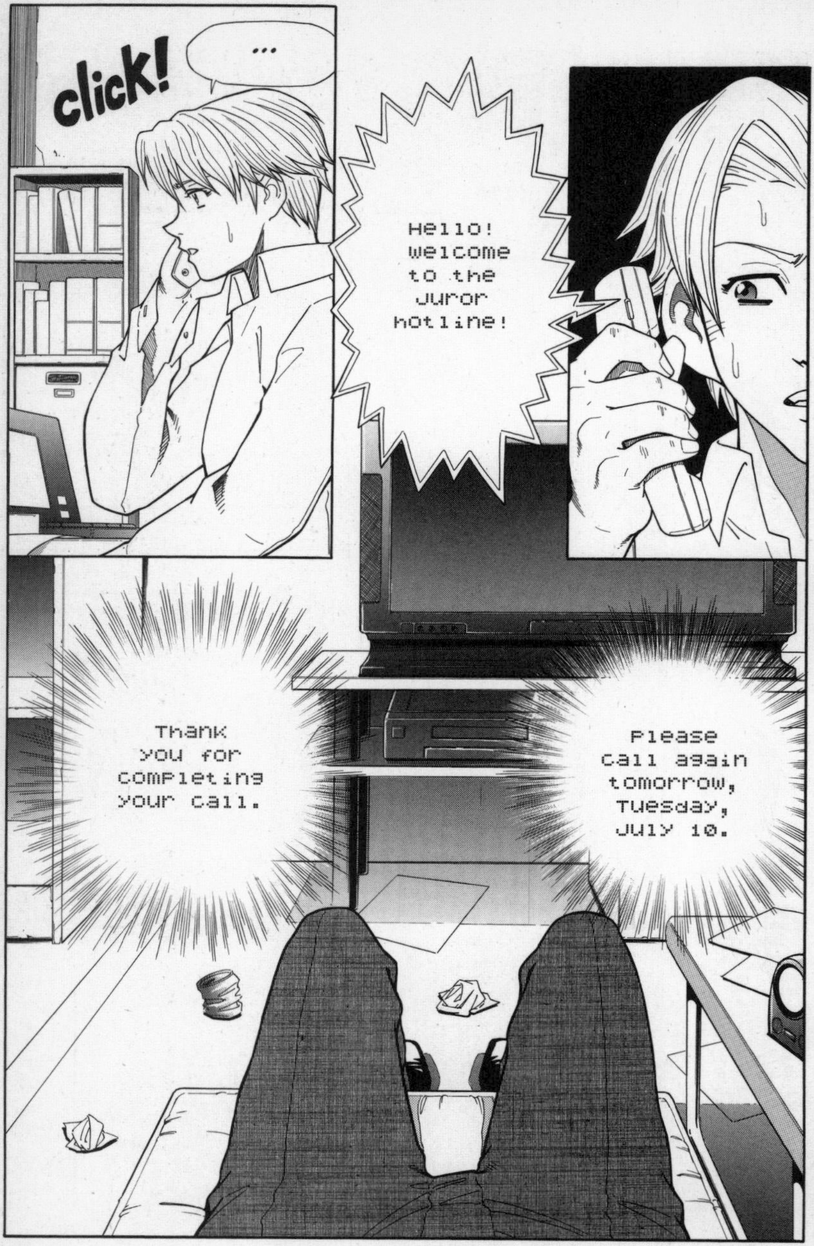
click!
...
Hello! welcome to the juror hotline!
Thank you for completing your call.
Please call again tomorrow, Tuesday, July 10.

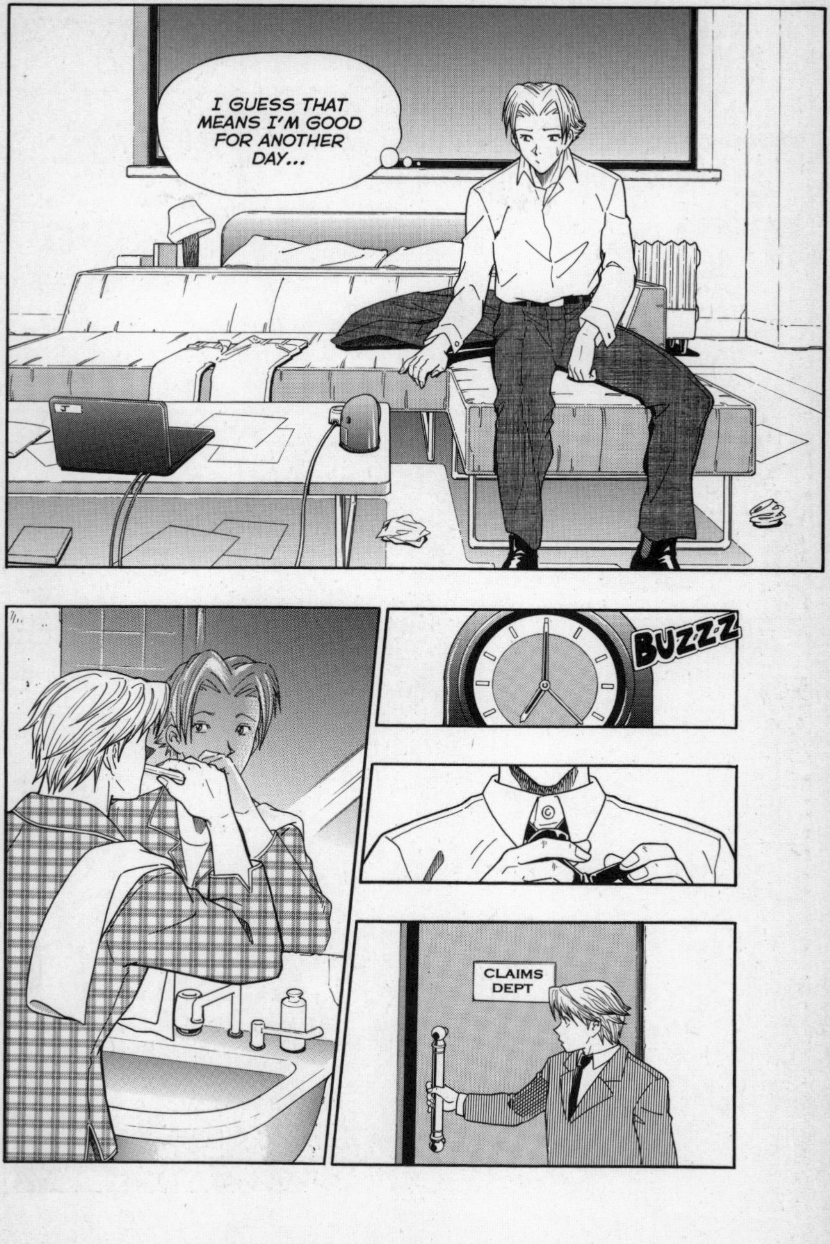
I GUESS THAT MEANS I'M GOOD FOR ANOTHER DAY...
BUZZZ
CLAIMS DEPT

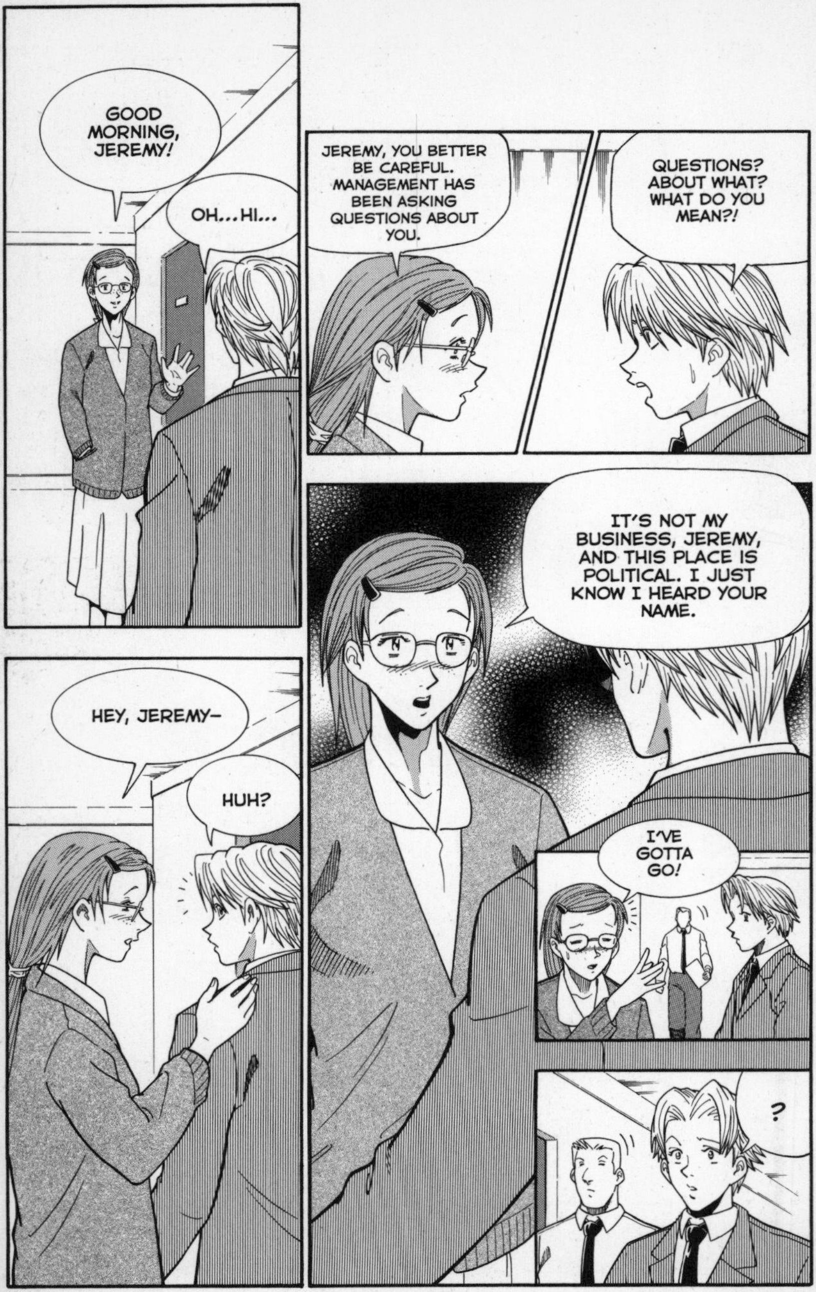
GOOD MORNING, JEREMY!
OH...HI...
JEREMY, YOU BETTER BE CAREFUL. MANAGEMENT HAS BEEN ASKING QUESTIONS ABOUT YOU.
QUESTIONS? ABOUT WHAT? WHAT DO YOU MEAN?!
HEY, JEREMY–
HUH?
IT'S NOT MY BUSINESS, JEREMY, AND THIS PLACE IS POLITICAL. I JUST KNOW I HEARD YOUR NAME.
I'VE GOTTA GO!
?

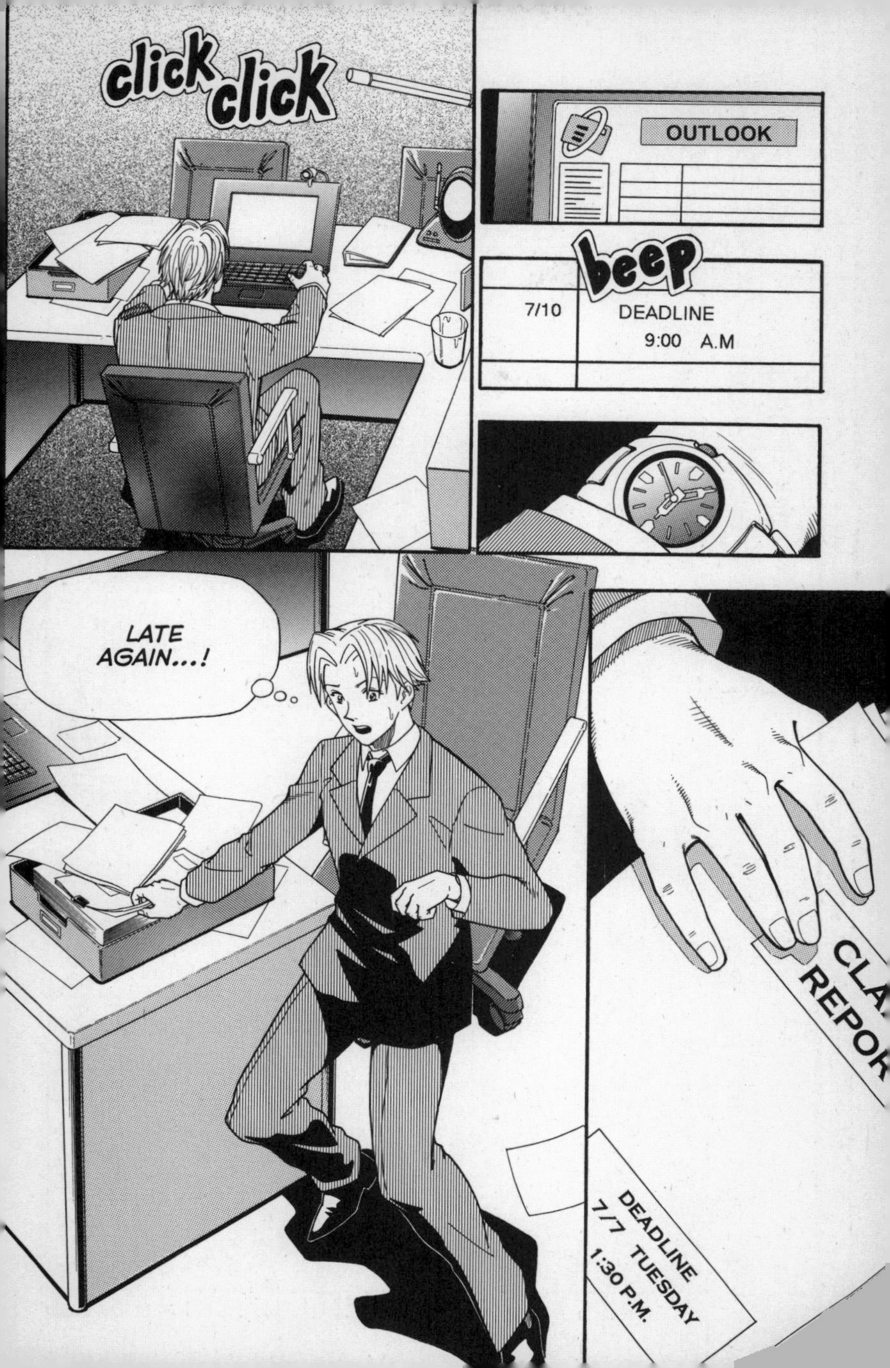
click click
OUTLOOK
beep
7/10
DEADLINE
9:00 A.M
LATE AGAIN...!
CLA
REPOR
DEADLINE
7/7 TUESDAY
1:30 P.M.

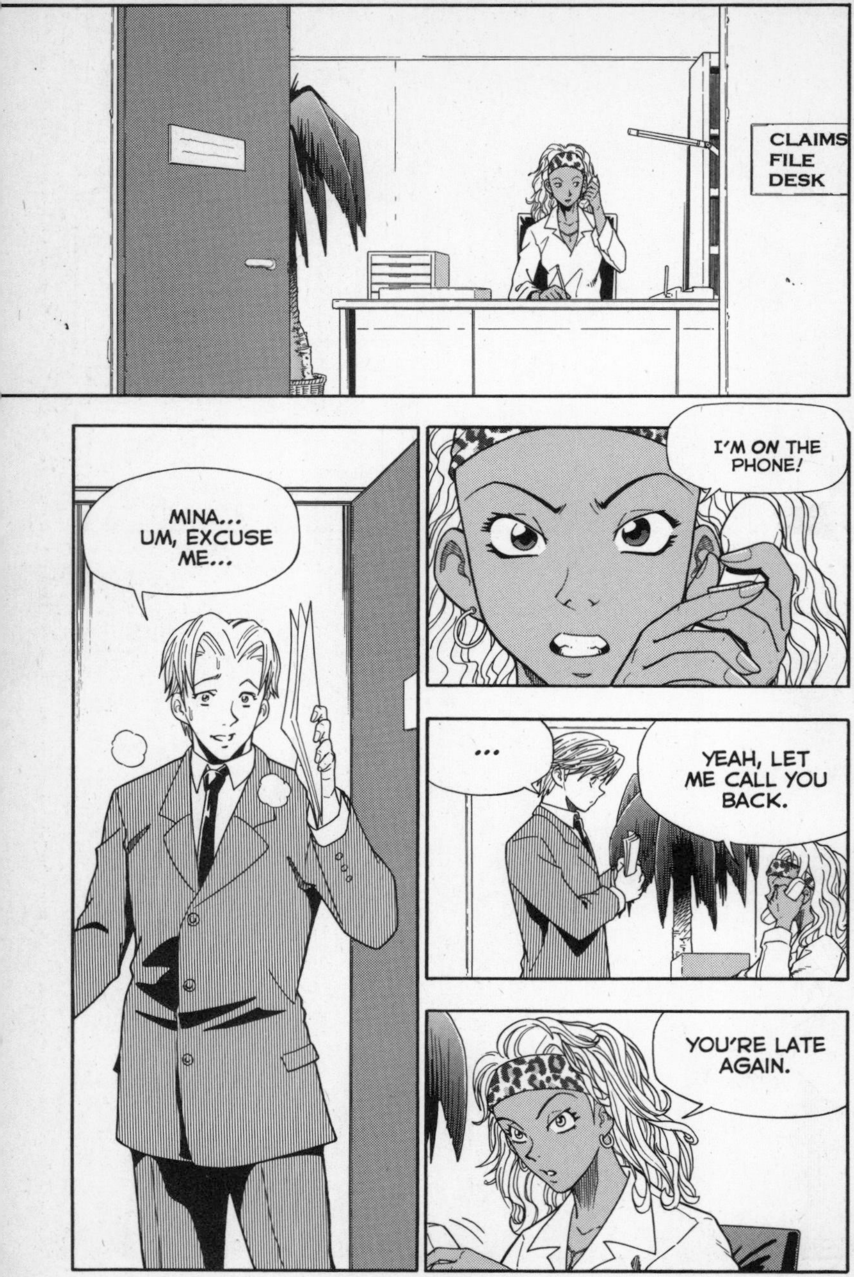
CLAIMS FILE DESK
MINA... UM, EXCUSE ME...
I'M *ON* THE PHONE!
...
YEAH, LET ME CALL YOU BACK.
YOU'RE LATE AGAIN.

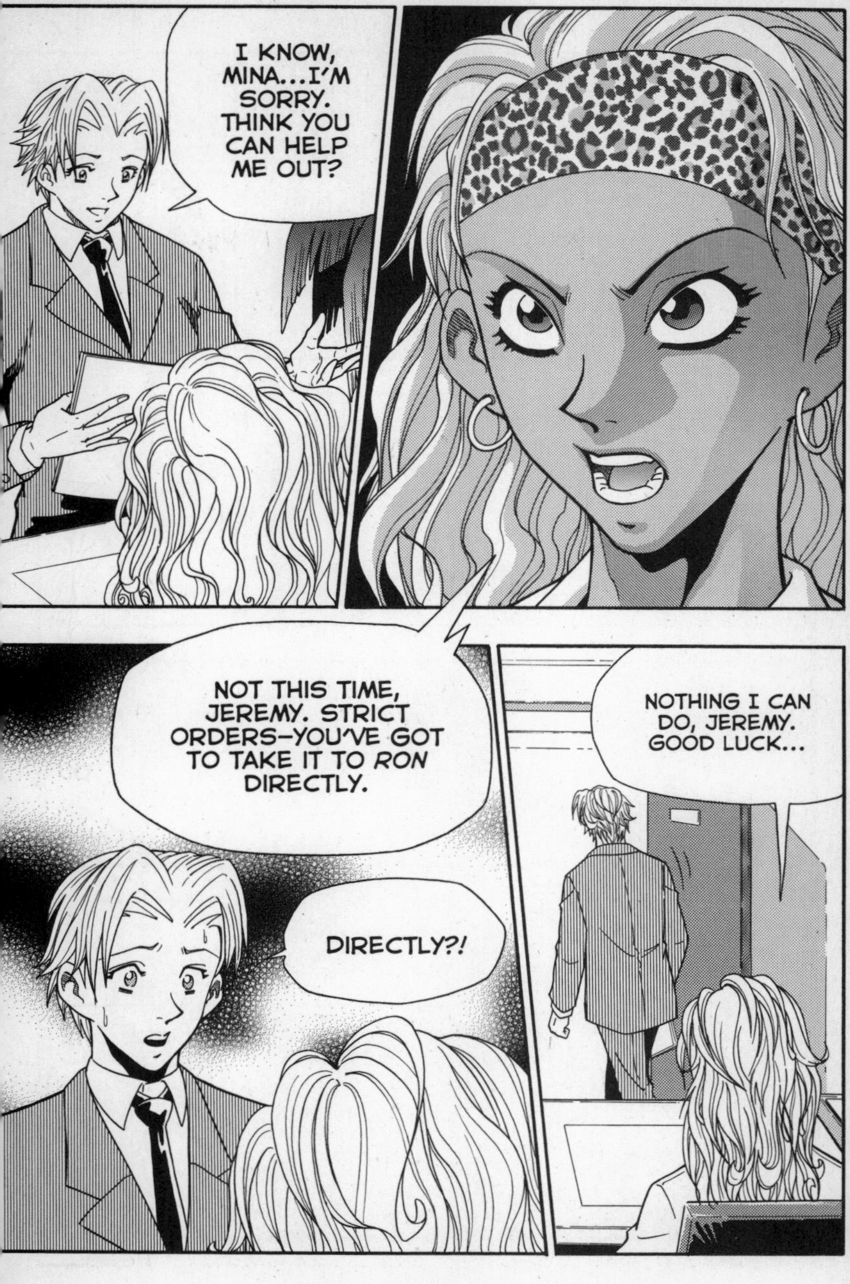
I KNOW, MINA...I'M SORRY. THINK YOU CAN HELP ME OUT?
NOT THIS TIME, JEREMY. STRICT ORDERS–YOU'VE GOT TO TAKE IT TO *RON* DIRECTLY.
DIRECTLY?!
NOTHING I CAN DO, JEREMY. GOOD LUCK...

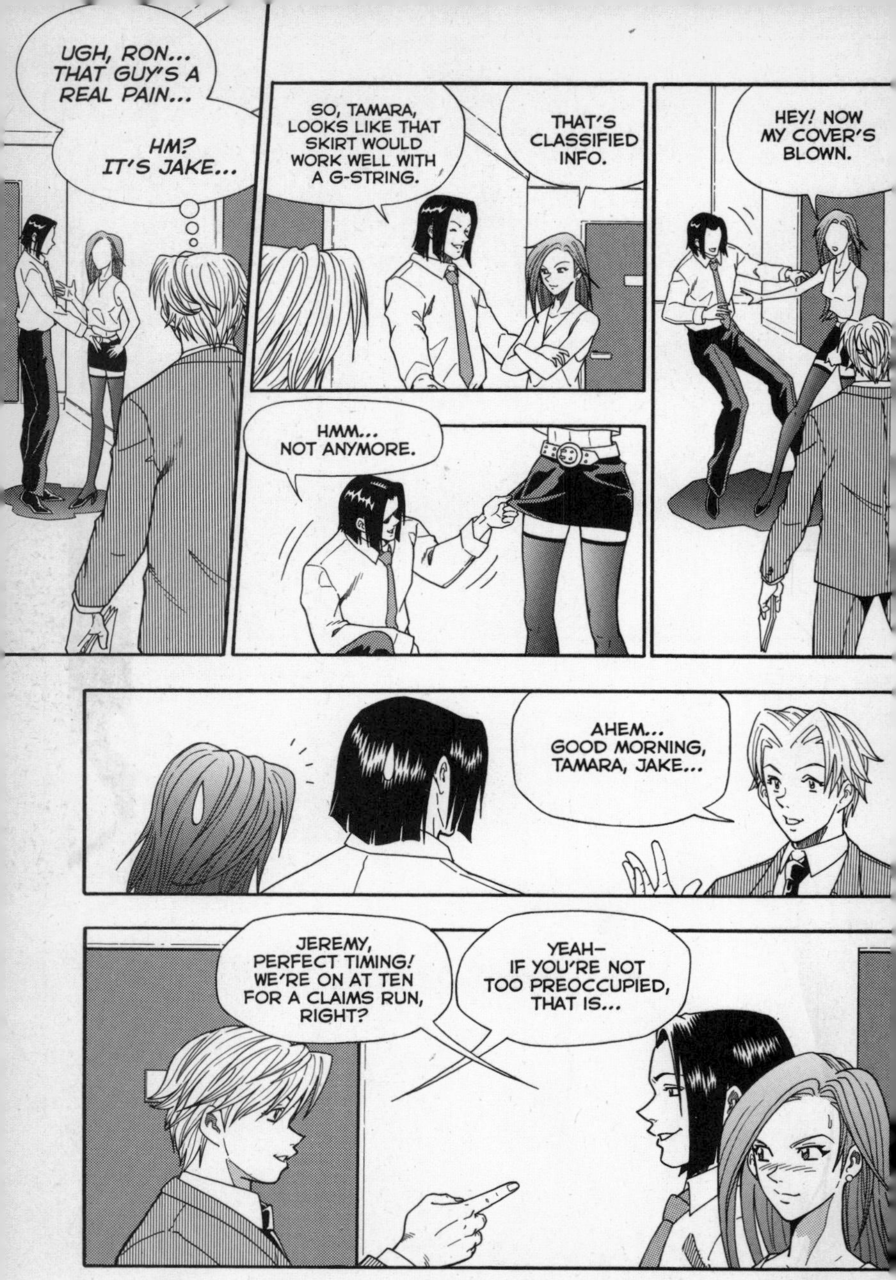
UGH, RON... THAT GUY'S A REAL PAIN...
HM? IT'S JAKE...
SO, TAMARA, LOOKS LIKE THAT SKIRT WOULD WORK WELL WITH A G-STRING.
THAT'S CLASSIFIED INFO.
HMM... NOT ANYMORE.
HEY! NOW MY COVER'S BLOWN.
AHEM... GOOD MORNING, TAMARA, JAKE...
JEREMY, PERFECT TIMING! WE'RE ON AT TEN FOR A CLAIMS RUN, RIGHT?
YEAH— IF YOU'RE NOT TOO PREOCCUPIED, THAT IS...

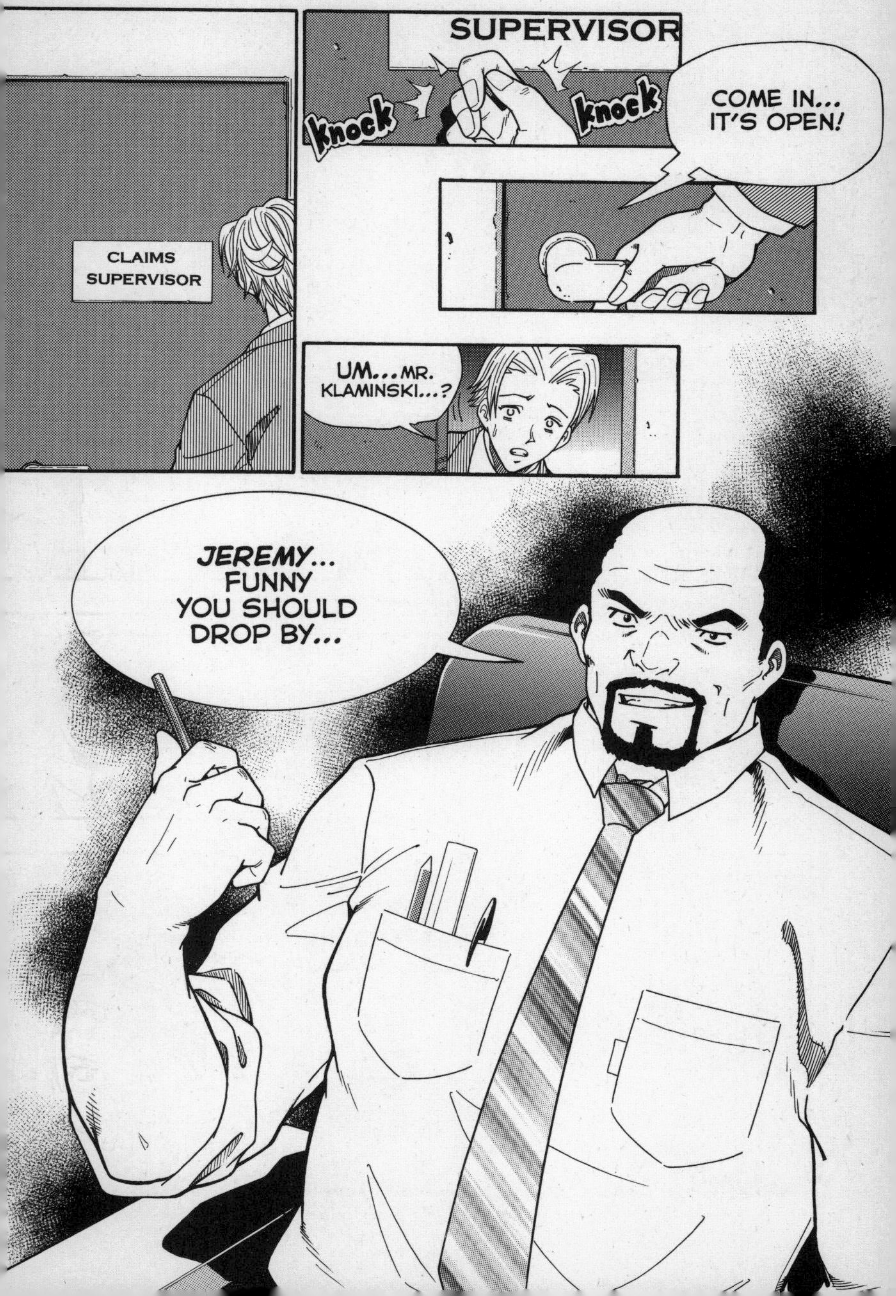
CLAIMS
SUPERVISOR
SUPERVISOR
knock
knock
COME IN... IT'S OPEN!
UM...MR. KLAMINSKI...?
JEREMY... FUNNY YOU SHOULD DROP BY...

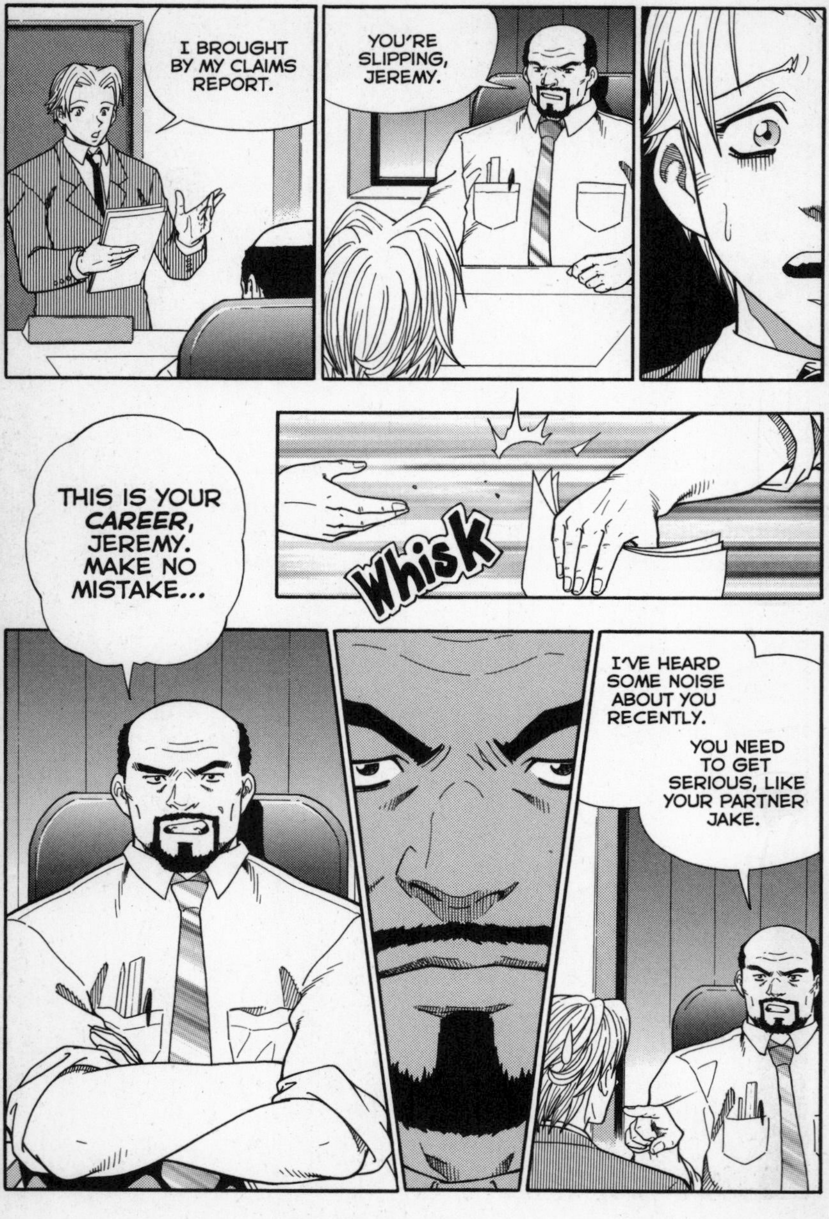
I BROUGHT BY MY CLAIMS REPORT.
YOU'RE SLIPPING, JEREMY.
Whisk
THIS IS YOUR CAREER, JEREMY. MAKE NO MISTAKE...
I'VE HEARD SOME NOISE ABOUT YOU RECENTLY.
YOU NEED TO GET SERIOUS, LIKE YOUR PARTNER JAKE.

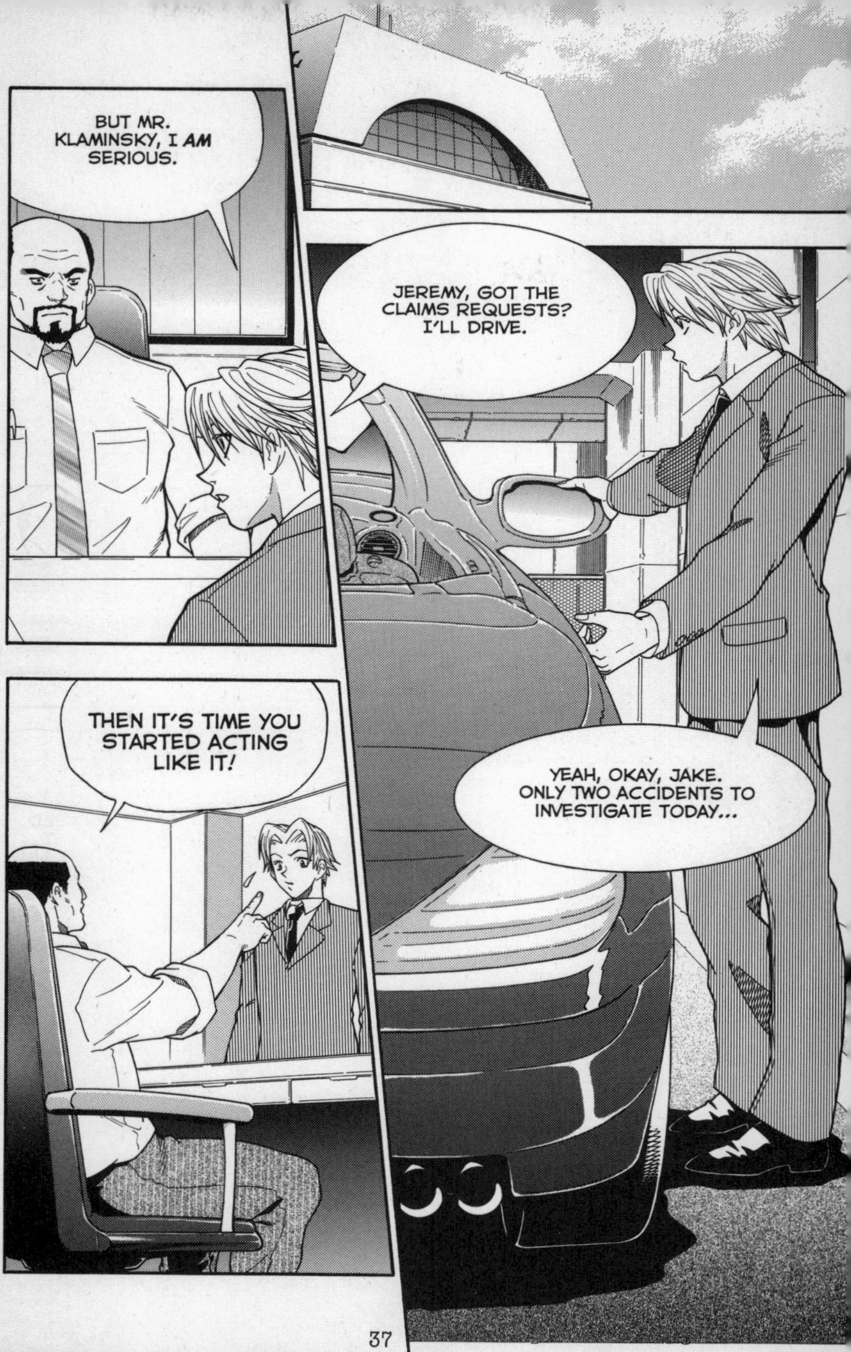
BUT MR. KLAMINSKY, I *AM* SERIOUS.
THEN IT'S TIME YOU STARTED ACTING LIKE IT!
JEREMY, GOT THE CLAIMS REQUESTS? I'LL DRIVE.
YEAH, OKAY, JAKE. ONLY TWO ACCIDENTS TO INVESTIGATE TODAY...

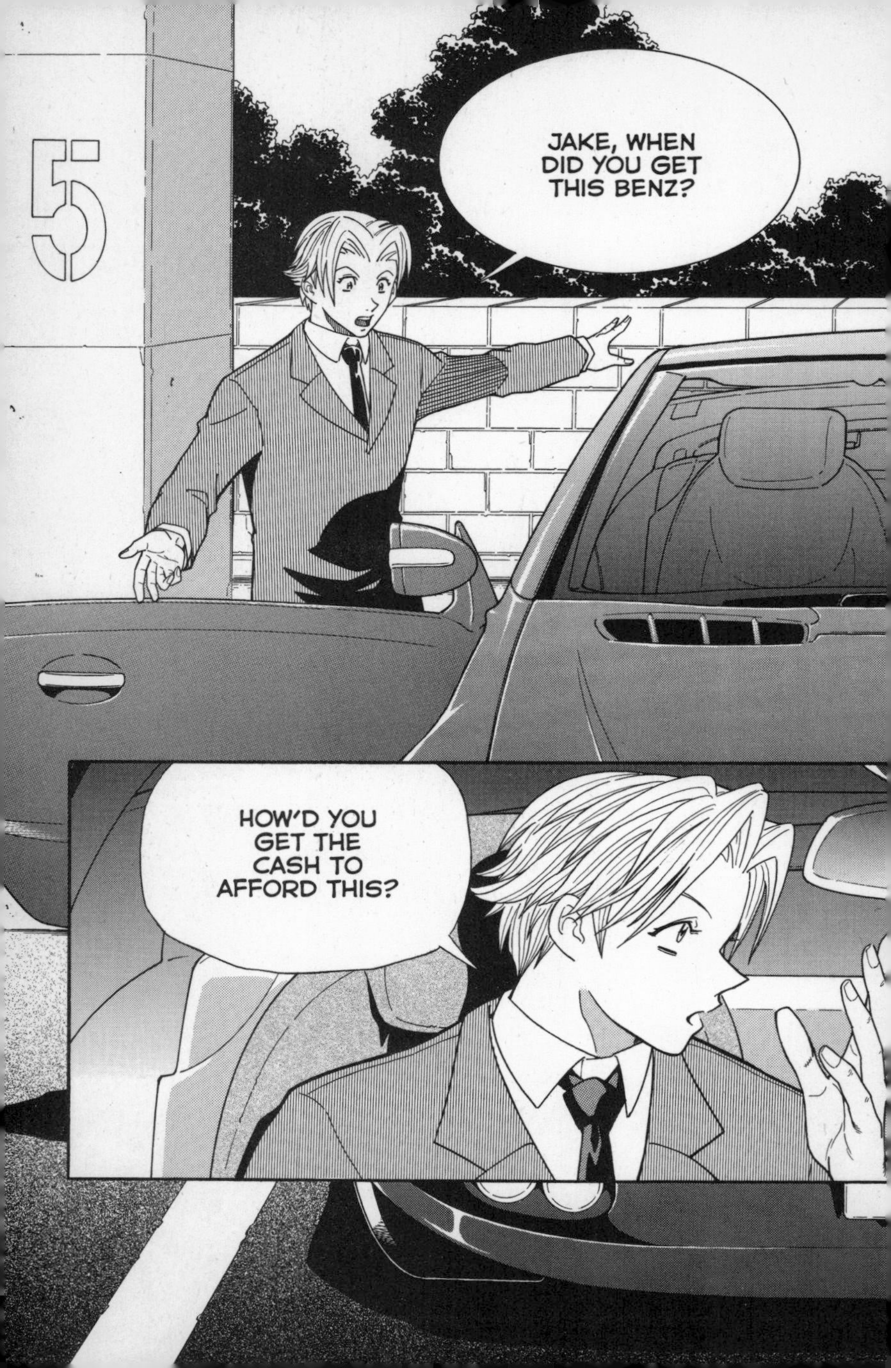
5
JAKE, WHEN DID YOU GET THIS BENZ?
HOW'D YOU GET THE CASH TO AFFORD THIS?

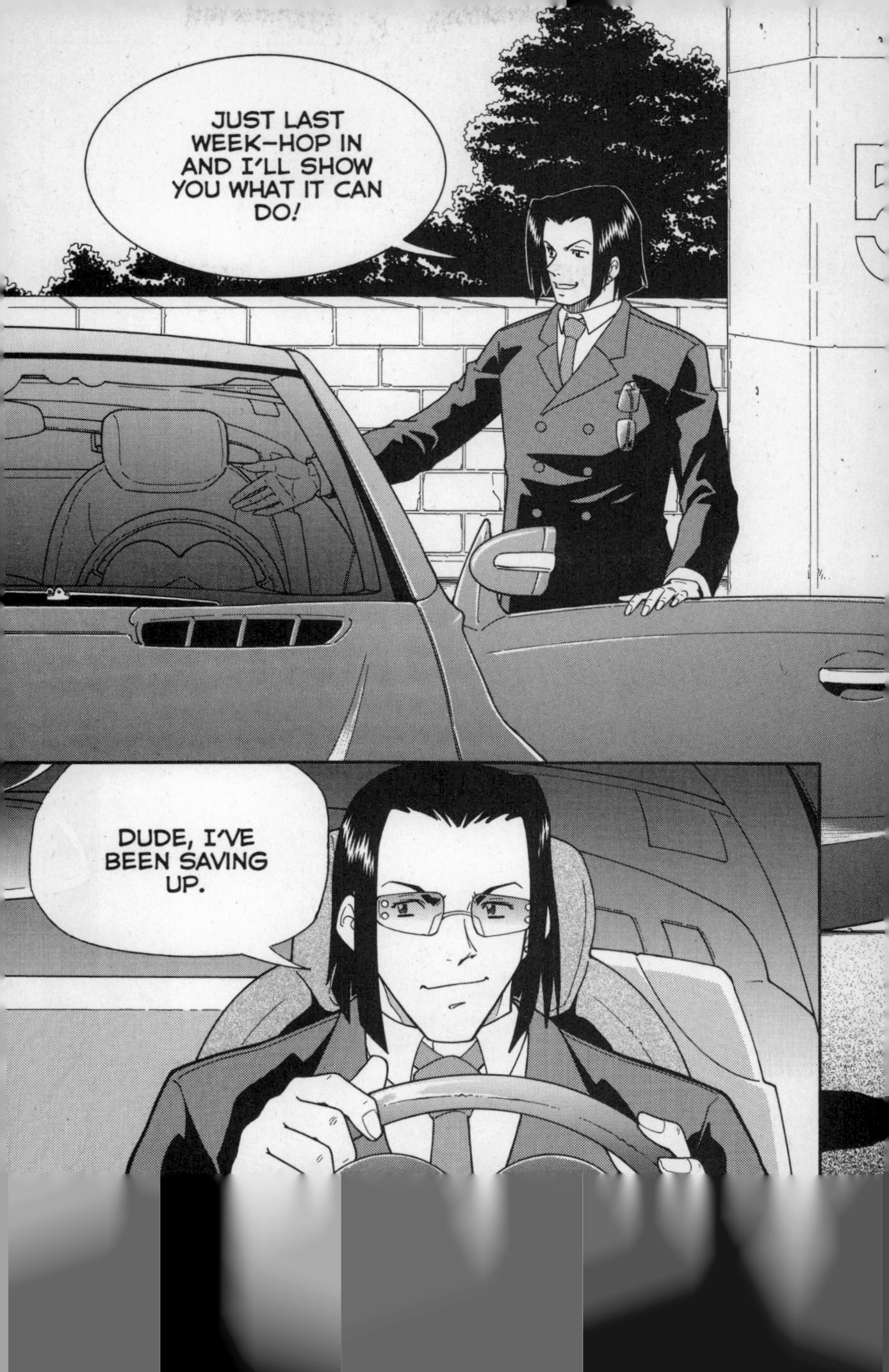
JUST LAST WEEK—HOP IN AND I'LL SHOW YOU WHAT IT CAN DO!
DUDE, I'VE BEEN SAVING UP.

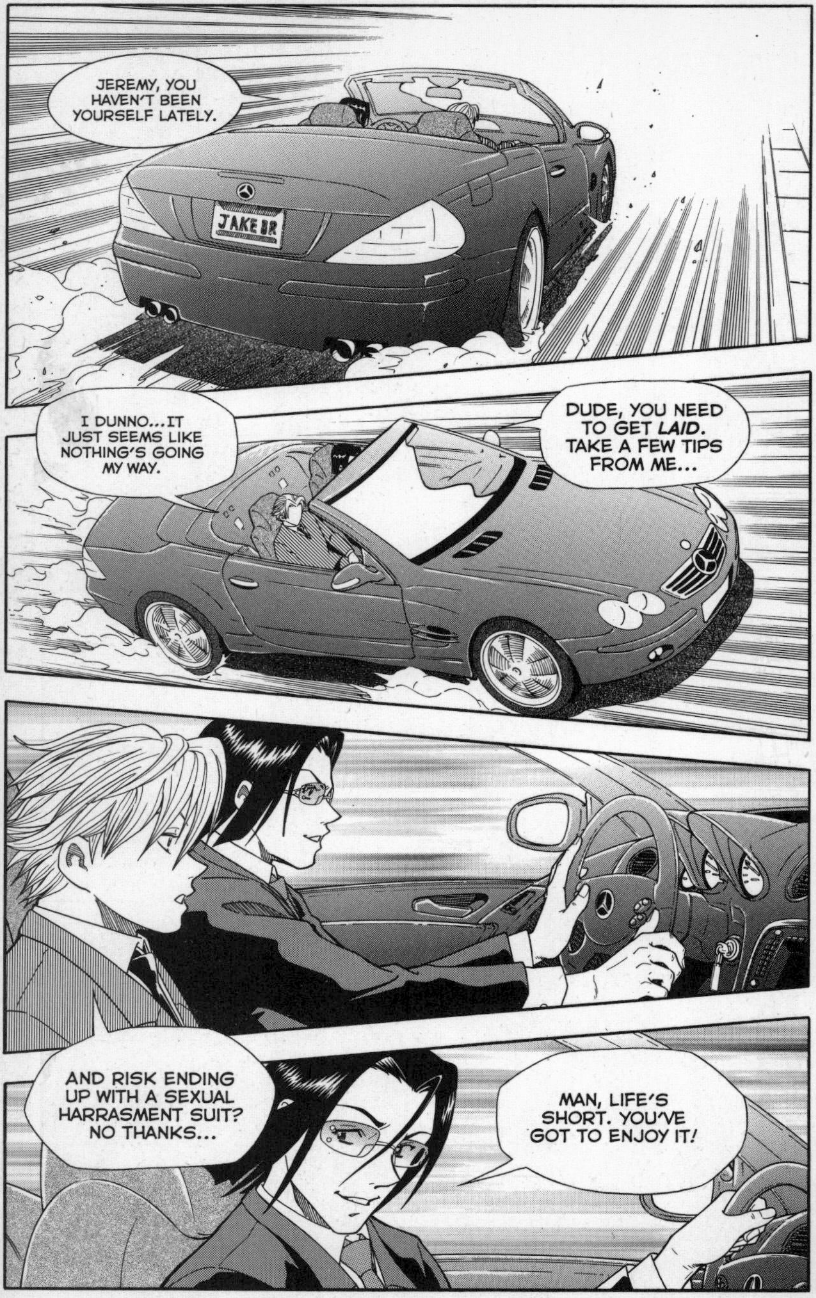
JEREMY, YOU HAVEN'T BEEN YOURSELF LATELY.
JAKE 8R
I DUNNO...IT JUST SEEMS LIKE NOTHING'S GOING MY WAY.
DUDE, YOU NEED TO GET *LAID*. TAKE A FEW TIPS FROM ME...
AND RISK ENDING UP WITH A SEXUAL HARRASMENT SUIT? NO THANKS...
MAN, LIFE'S SHORT. YOU'VE GOT TO ENJOY IT!

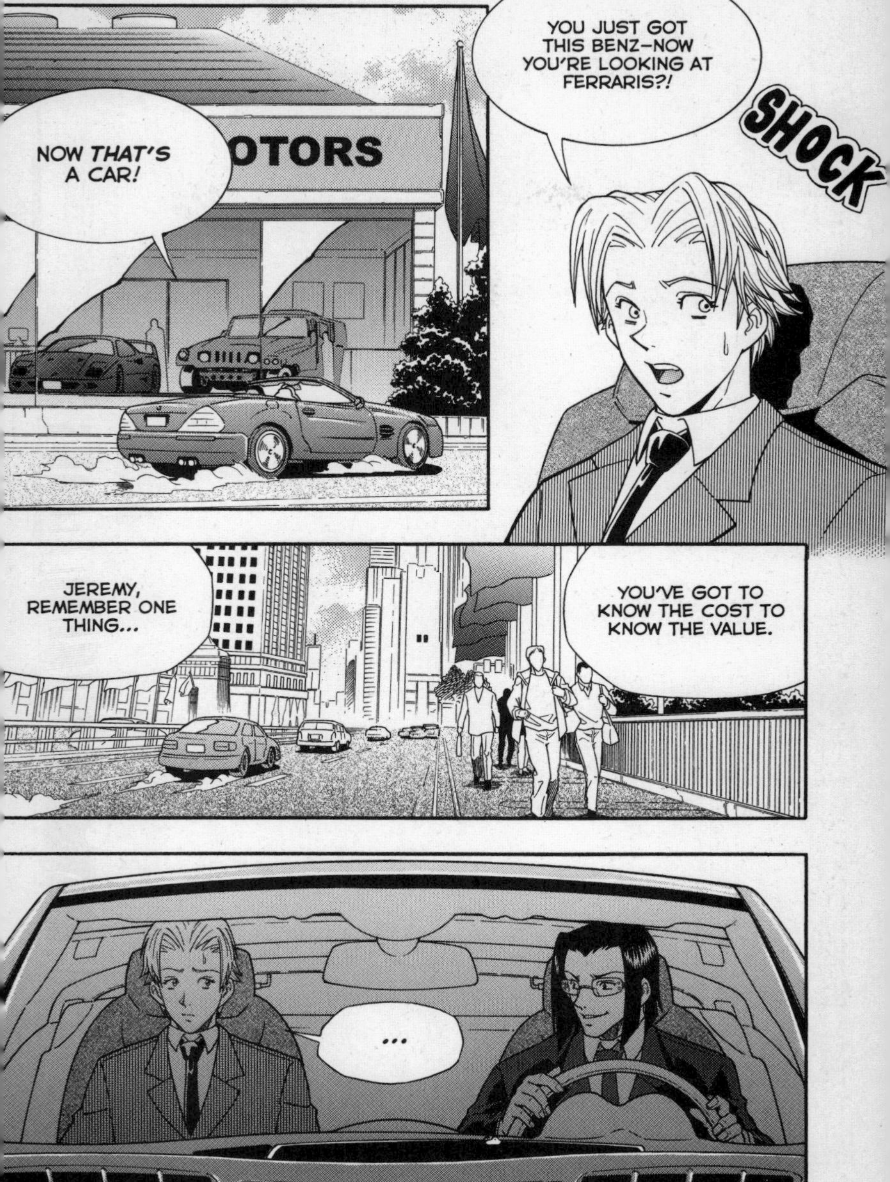
NOW THAT'S A CAR!
OTORS
YOU JUST GOT THIS BENZ–NOW YOU'RE LOOKING AT FERRARIS?!
SHOCK
JEREMY, REMEMBER ONE THING...
YOU'VE GOT TO KNOW THE COST TO KNOW THE VALUE.
...

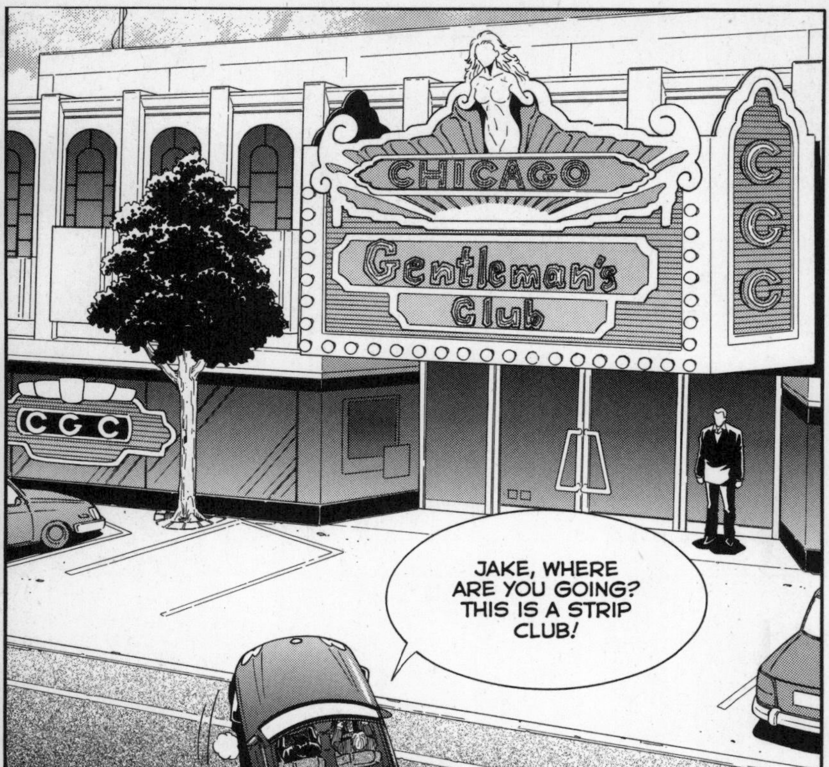
CHICAGO
Gentleman's
Club
CGC
CGC
JAKE, WHERE ARE YOU GOING? THIS IS A STRIP CLUB!

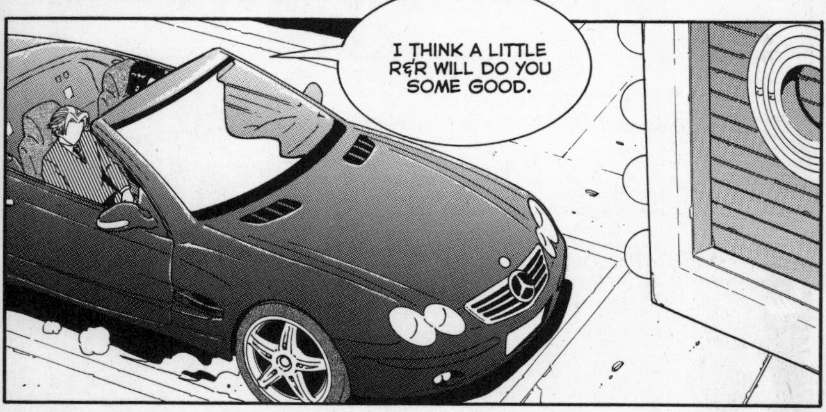
I THINK A LITTLE R&R WILL DO YOU SOME GOOD.

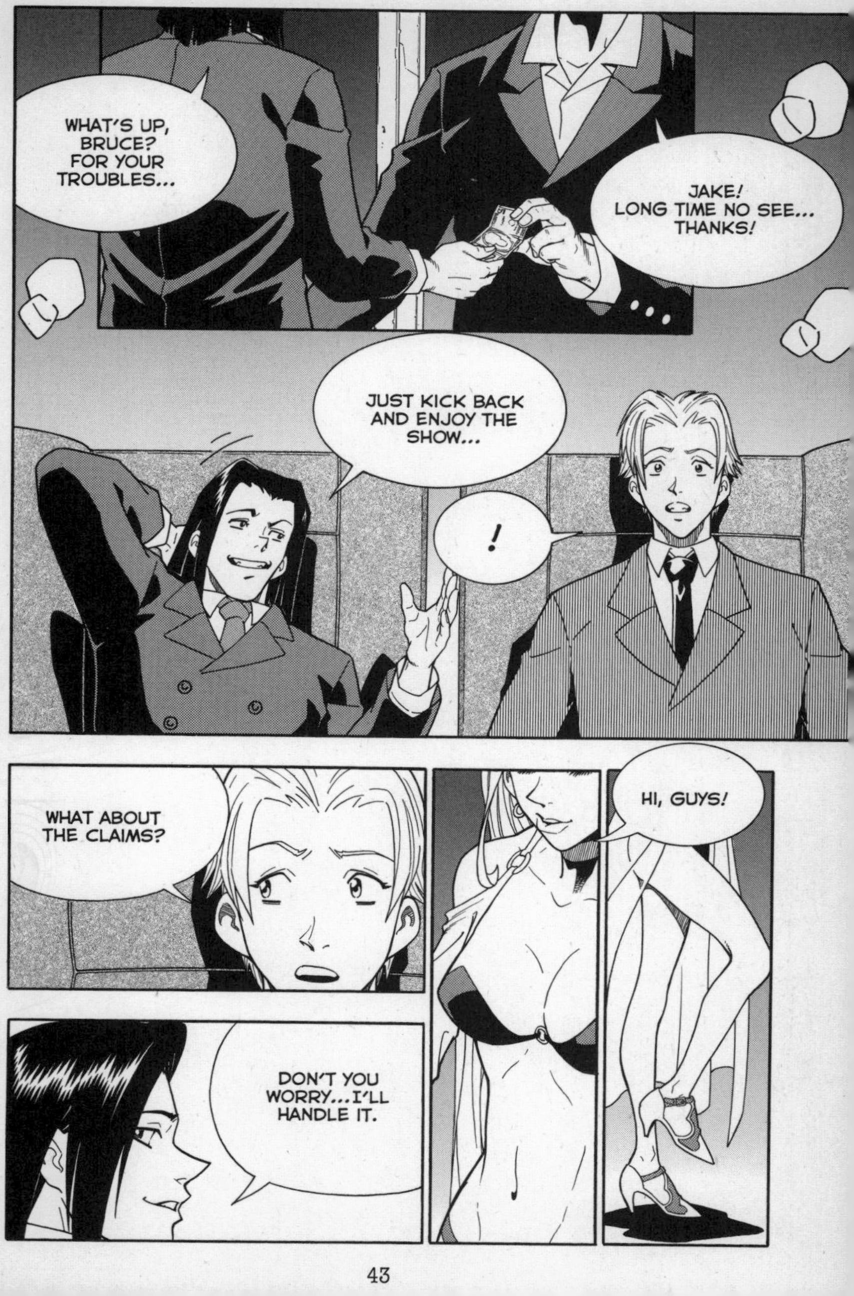
WHAT'S UP, BRUCE? FOR YOUR TROUBLES...
JAKE! LONG TIME NO SEE... THANKS!
JUST KICK BACK AND ENJOY THE SHOW...
!
WHAT ABOUT THE CLAIMS?
DON'T YOU WORRY...I'LL HANDLE IT.
HI, GUYS!

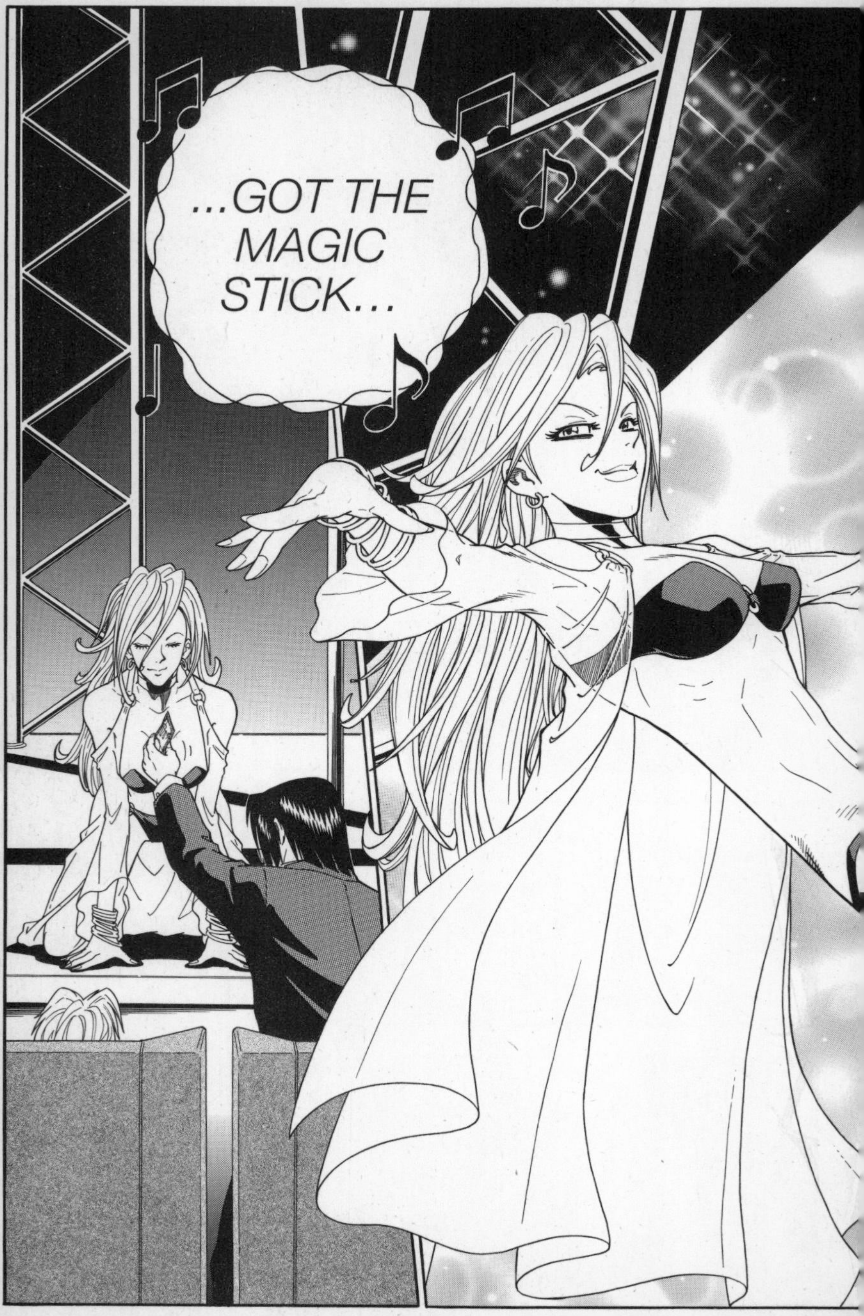
...GOT THE MAGIC STICK...

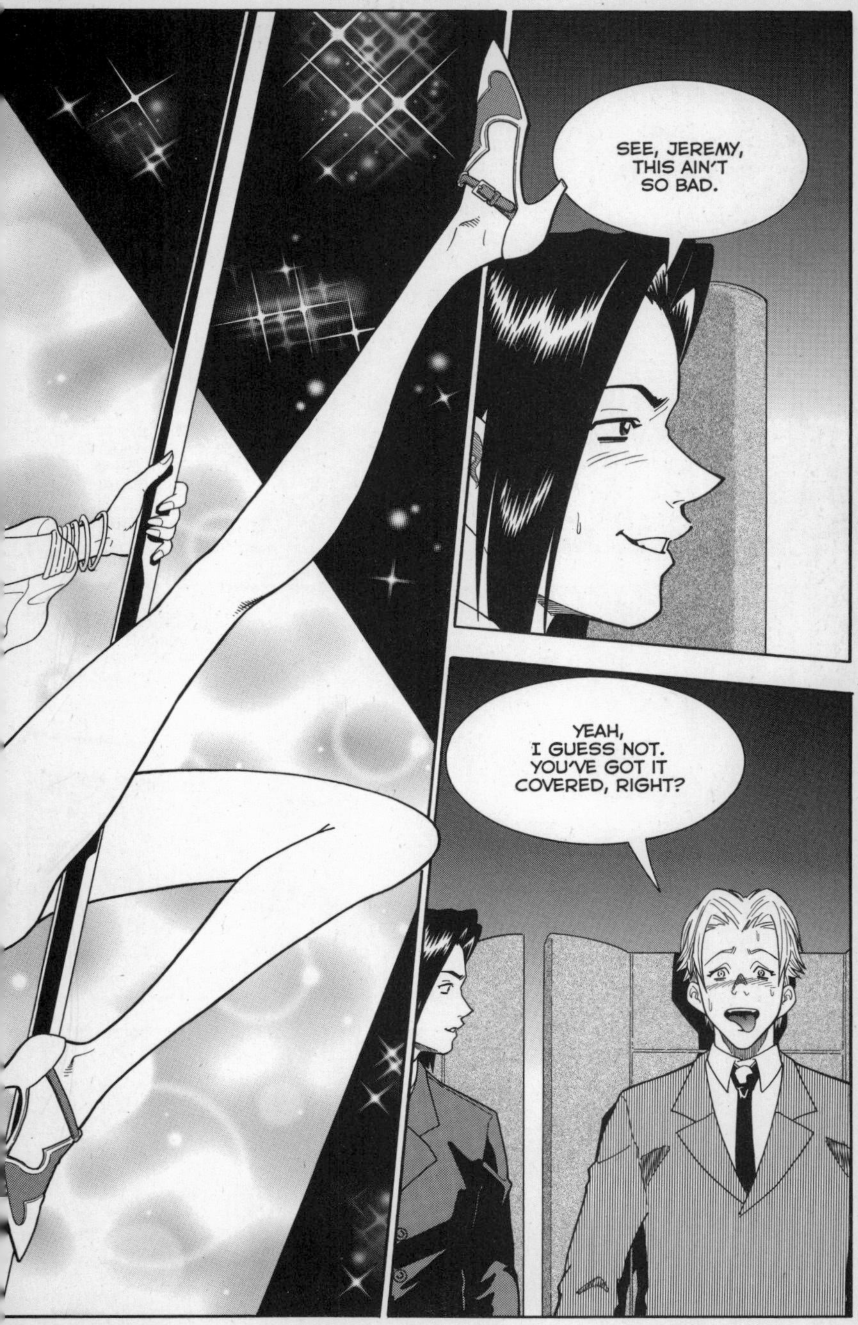
SEE, JEREMY, THIS AIN'T SO BAD.
YEAH, I GUESS NOT. YOU'VE GOT IT COVERED, RIGHT?

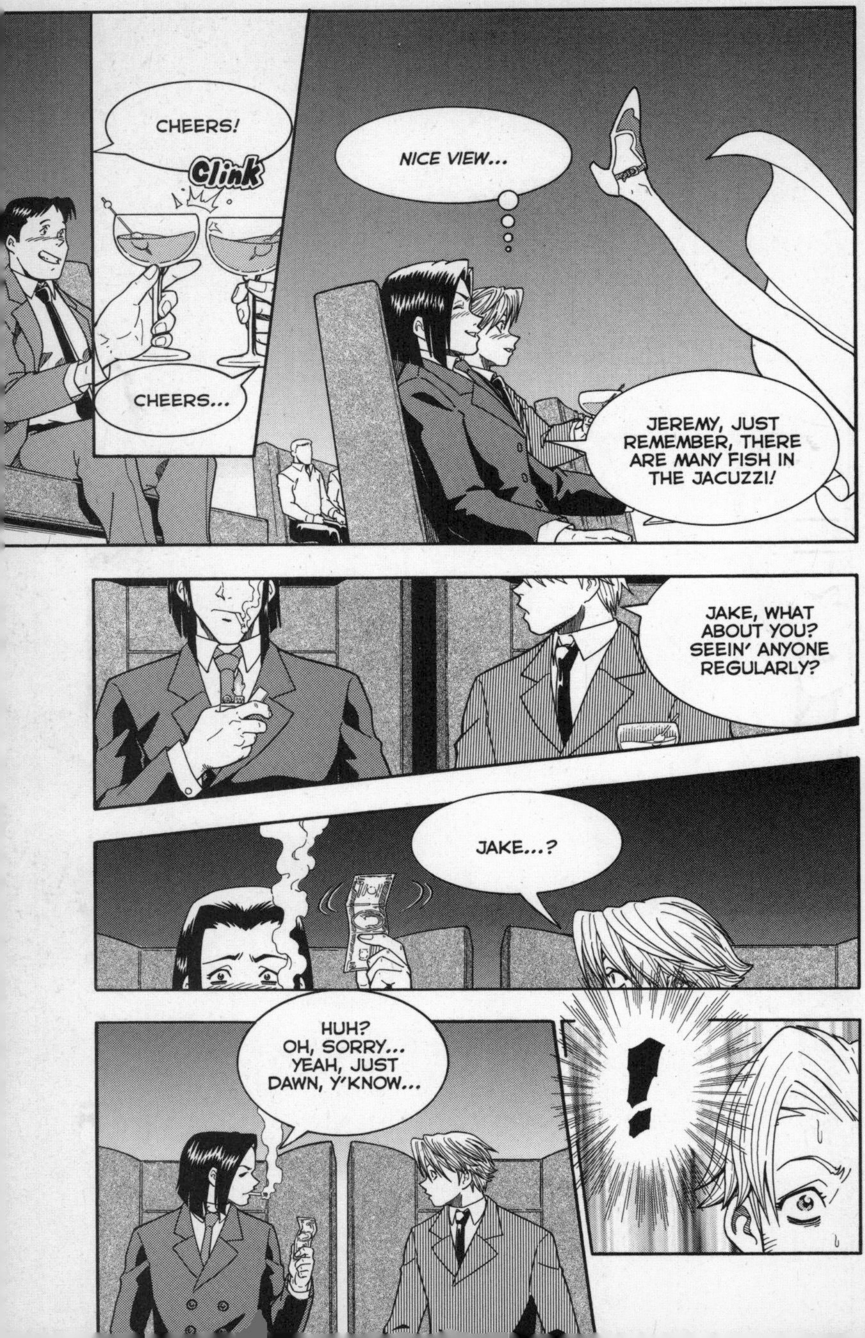
CHEERS!
Clink
CHEERS...
NICE VIEW...
JEREMY, JUST REMEMBER, THERE ARE MANY FISH IN THE JACUZZI!
JAKE, WHAT ABOUT YOU? SEEIN' ANYONE REGULARLY?
JAKE...?
HUH? OH, SORRY... YEAH, JUST DAWN, Y'KNOW...
!

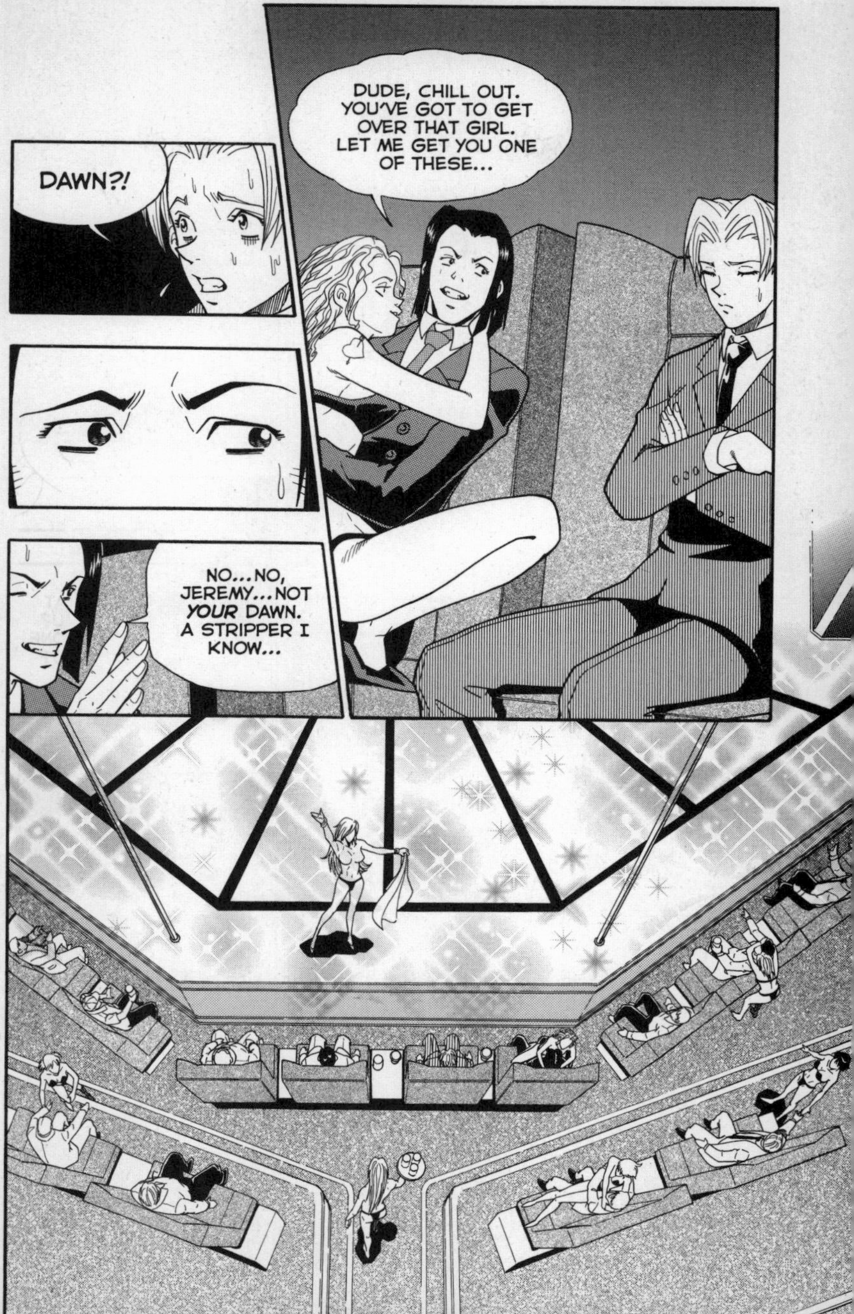
DAWN?!
DUDE, CHILL OUT. YOU'VE GOT TO GET OVER THAT GIRL. LET ME GET YOU ONE OF THESE...
NO...NO, JEREMY...NOT *YOUR* DAWN. A STRIPPER I KNOW...

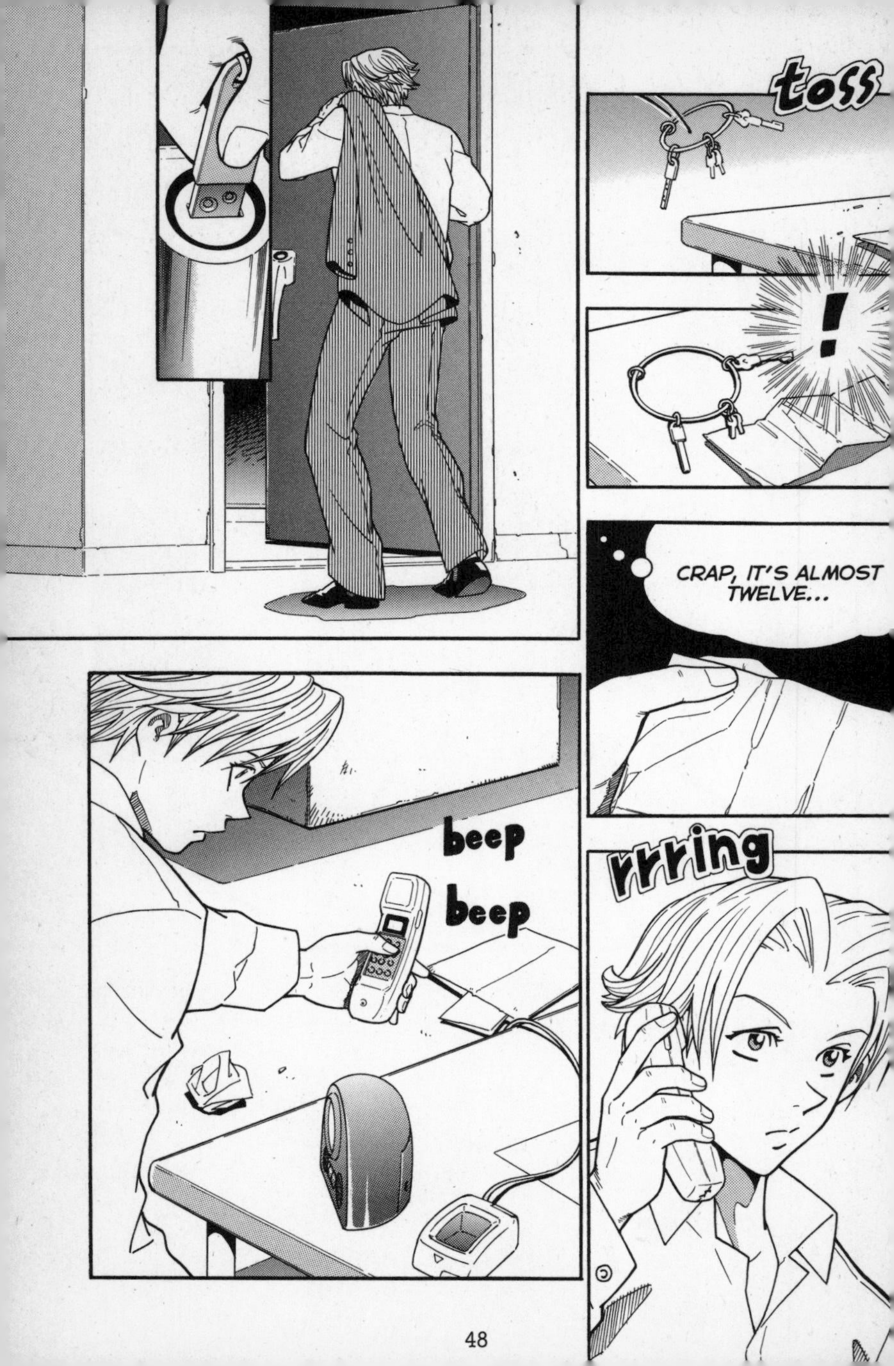
toss
!
CRAP, IT'S ALMOST TWELVE...
beep
beep
rrring

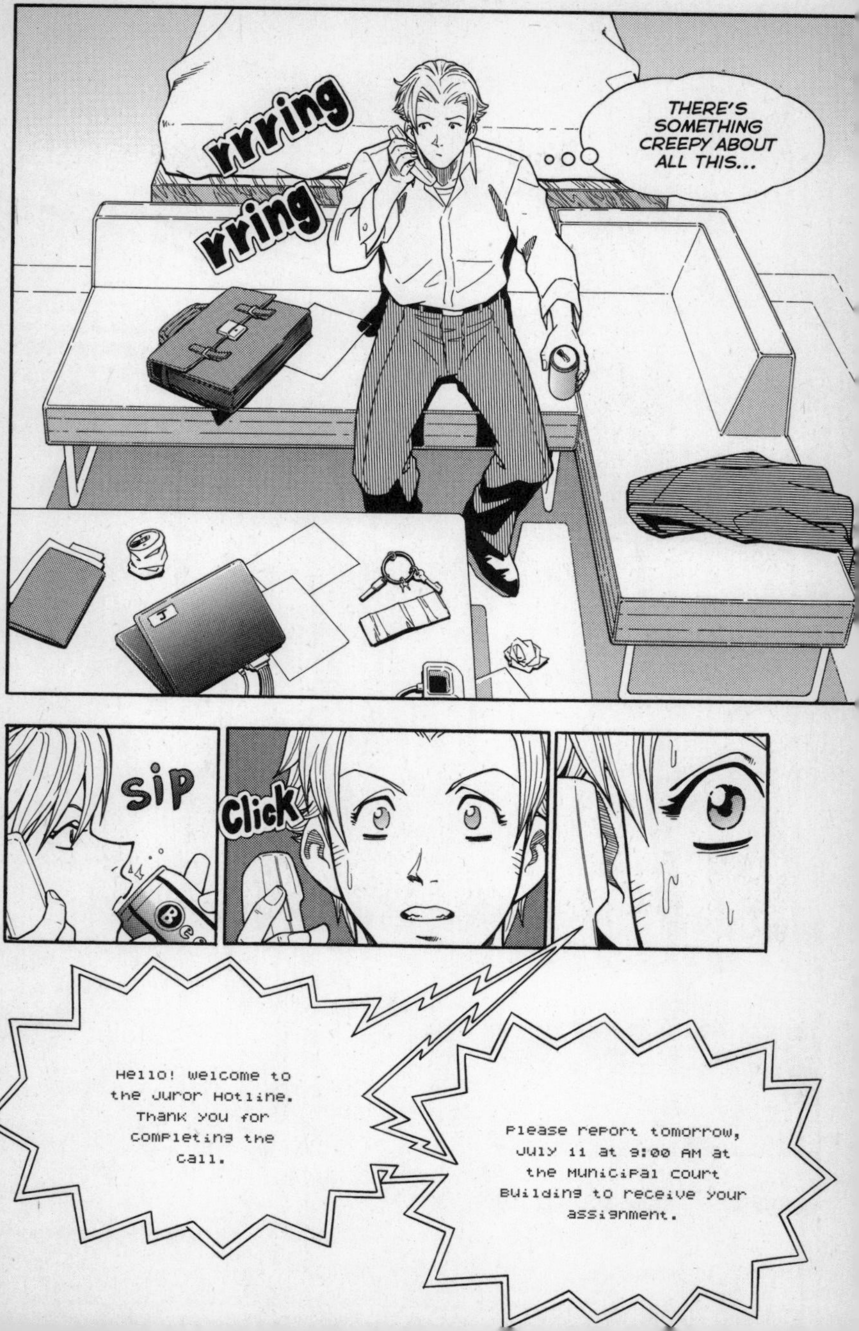
rrring
rring
THERE'S SOMETHING CREEPY ABOUT ALL THIS...
sip
Click
Hello! Welcome to the Juror Hotline. Thank you for completing the call.
Please report tomorrow, July 11 at 9:00 AM at the Municipal Court Building to receive your assignment.

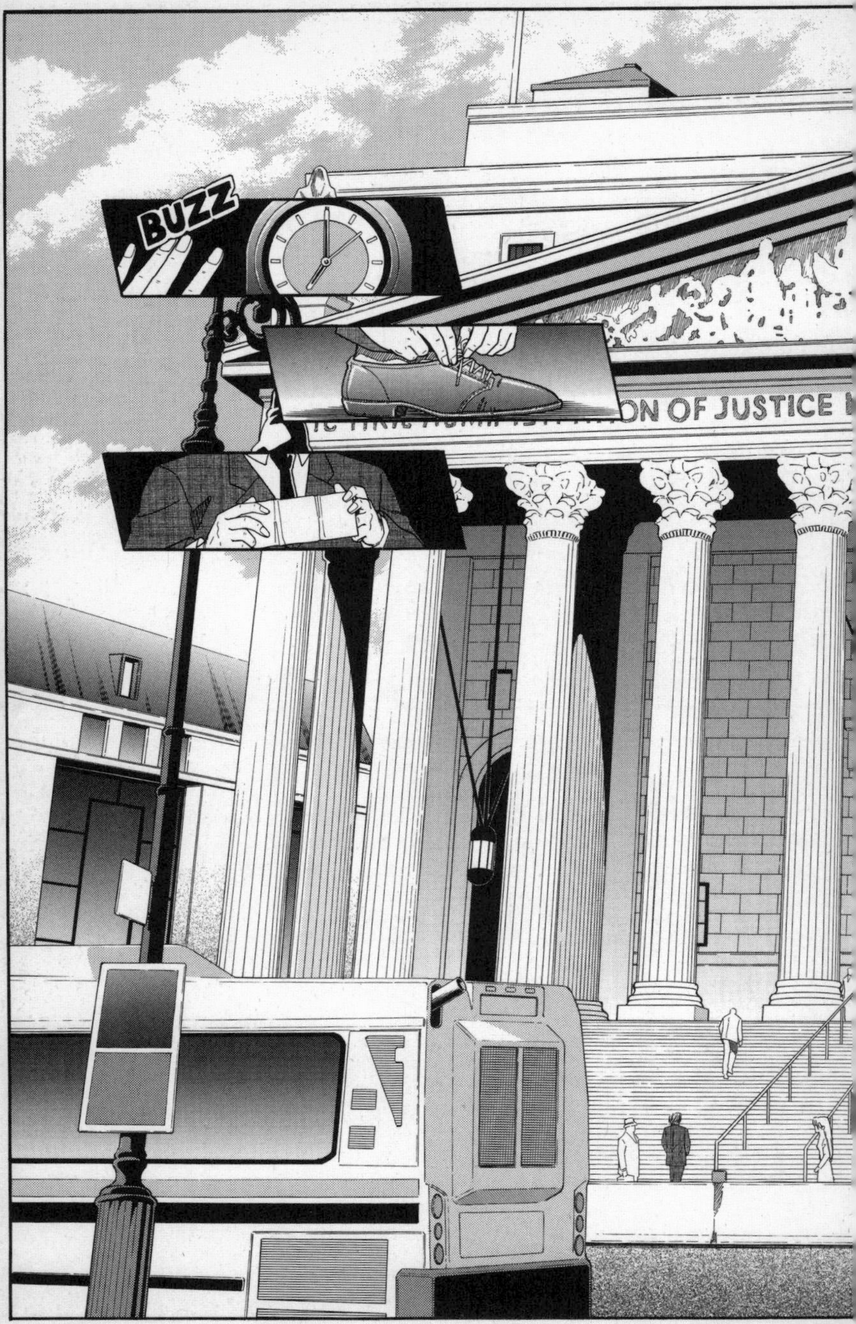
BUZZ
ON OF JUSTICE

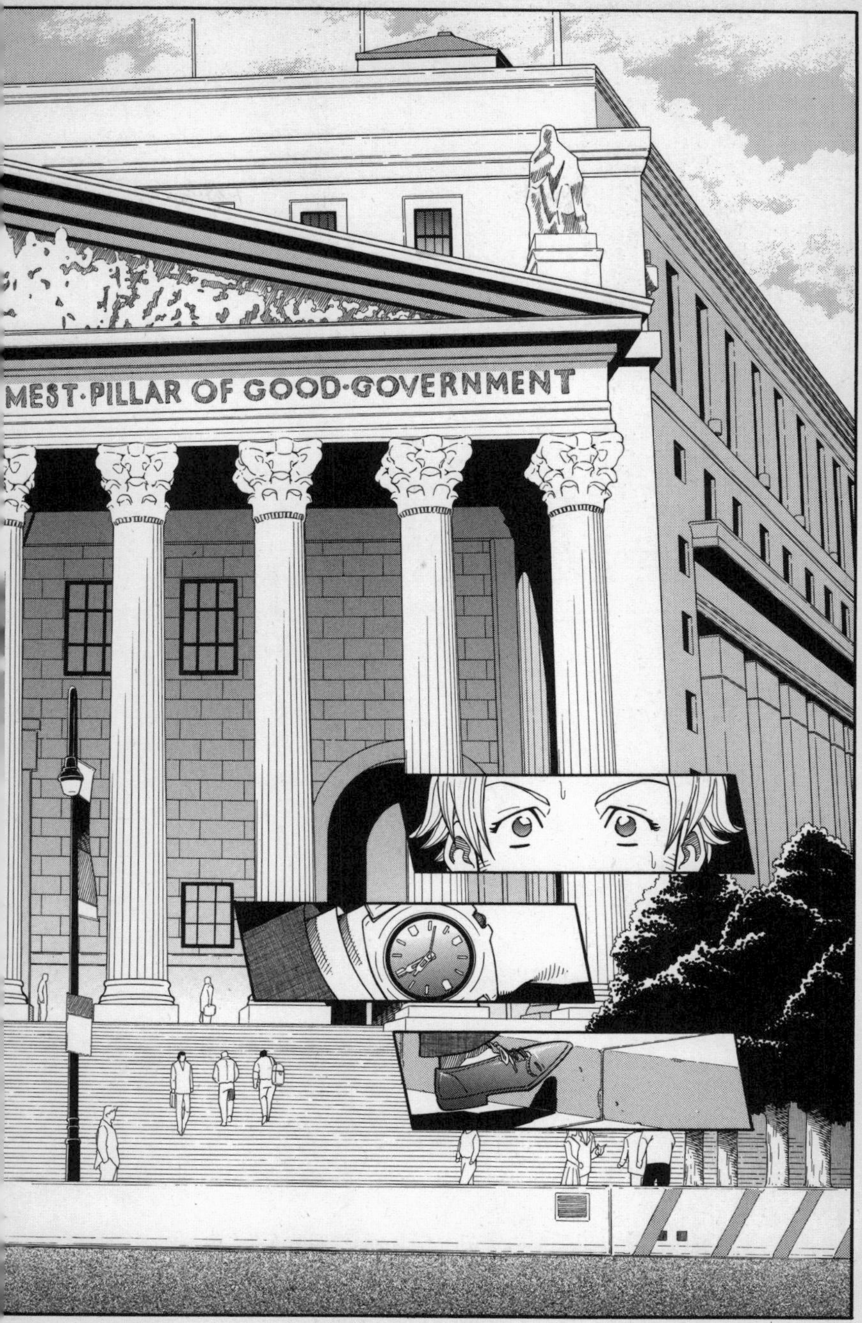
MEST·PILLAR OF GOOD·GOVERNMENT

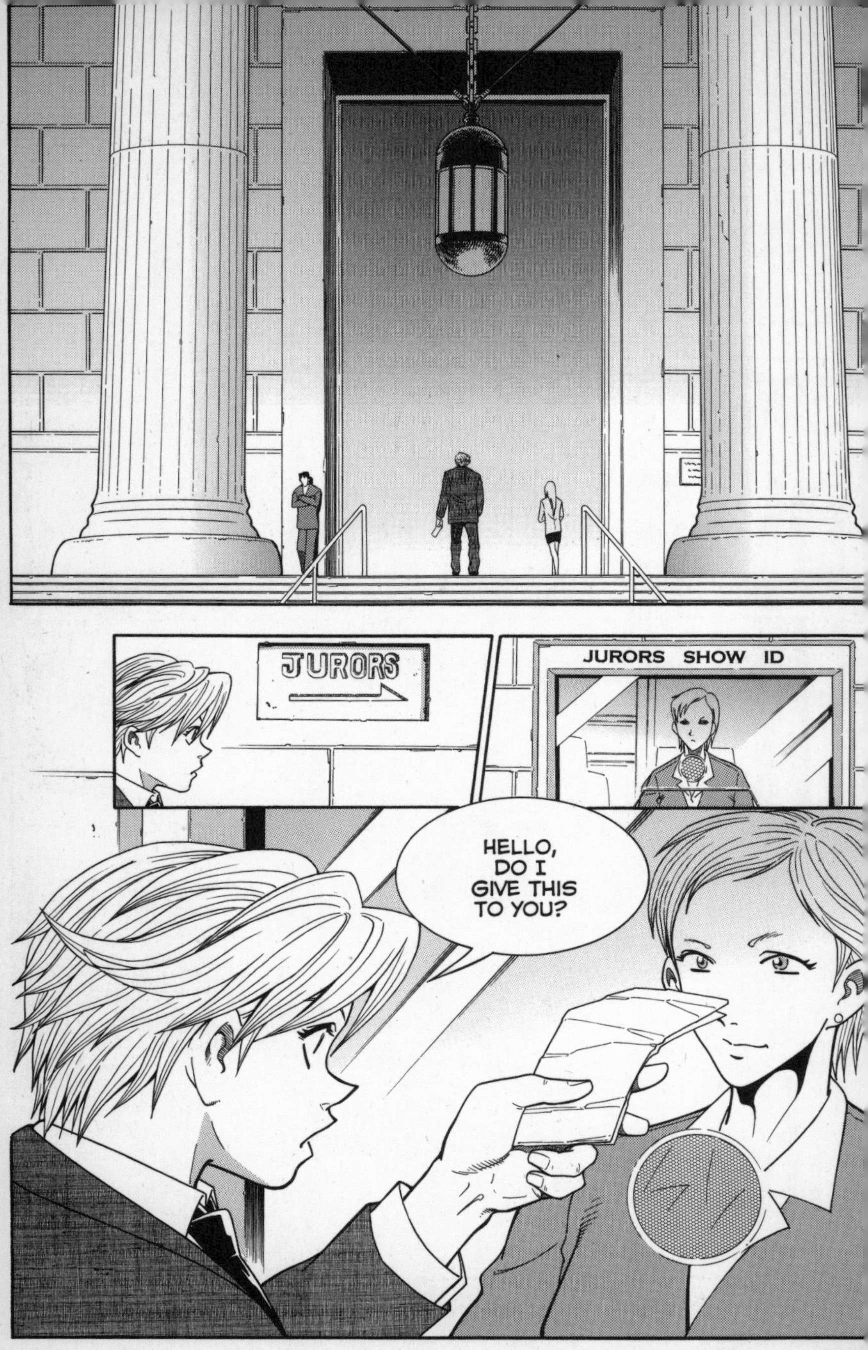
JURORS
JURORS SHOW ID
HELLO, DO I GIVE THIS TO YOU?

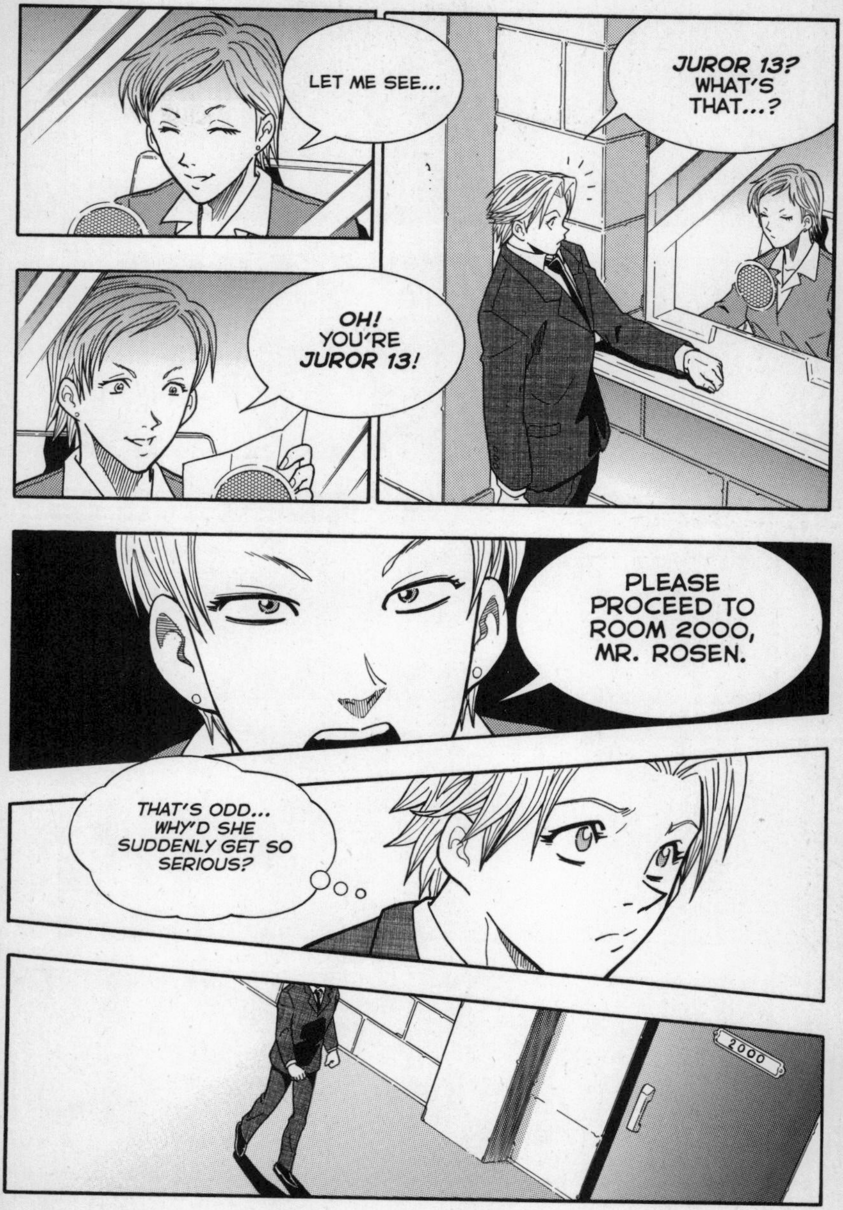
LET ME SEE...
OH! YOU'RE JUROR 13!
JUROR 13? WHAT'S THAT...?
PLEASE PROCEED TO ROOM 2000, MR. ROSEN.
THAT'S ODD... WHY'D SHE SUDDENLY GET SO SERIOUS?
2000

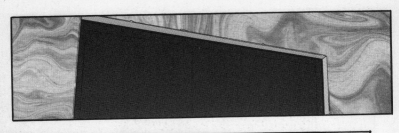

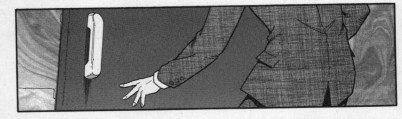

JuRor 13™

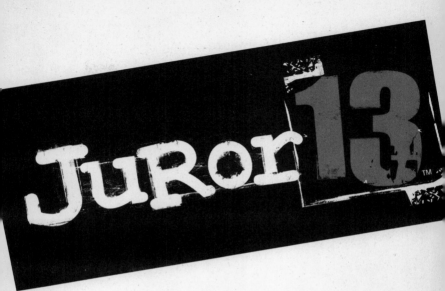

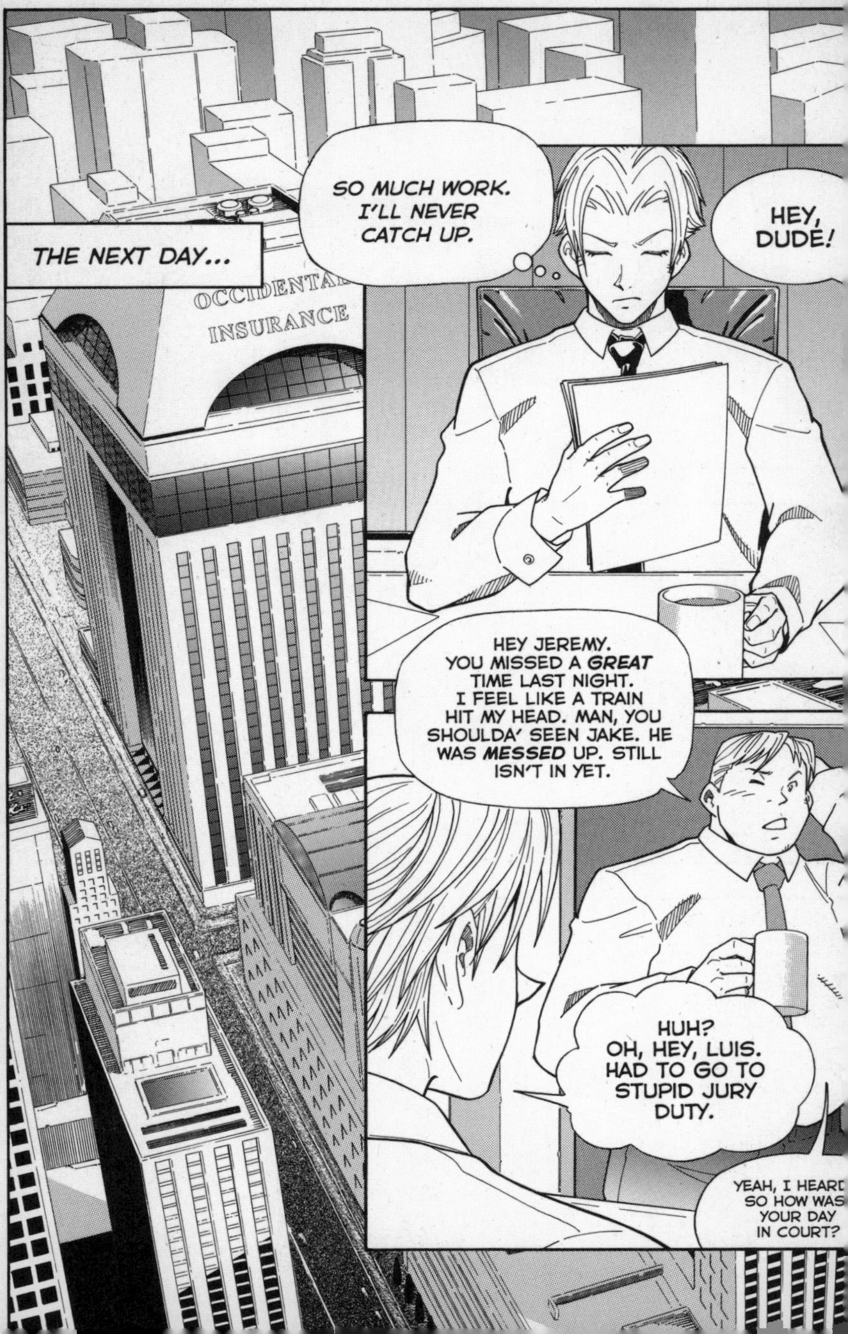
THE NEXT DAY...
OCCIDENTAL
INSURANCE
SO MUCH WORK. I'LL NEVER CATCH UP.
HEY, DUDE!
HEY JEREMY. YOU MISSED A *GREAT* TIME LAST NIGHT. I FEEL LIKE A TRAIN HIT MY HEAD. MAN, YOU SHOULDA' SEEN JAKE. HE WAS *MESSED* UP. STILL ISN'T IN YET.
HUH? OH, HEY, LUIS. HAD TO GO TO STUPID JURY DUTY.
YEAH, I HEARD SO HOW WAS YOUR DAY IN COURT?

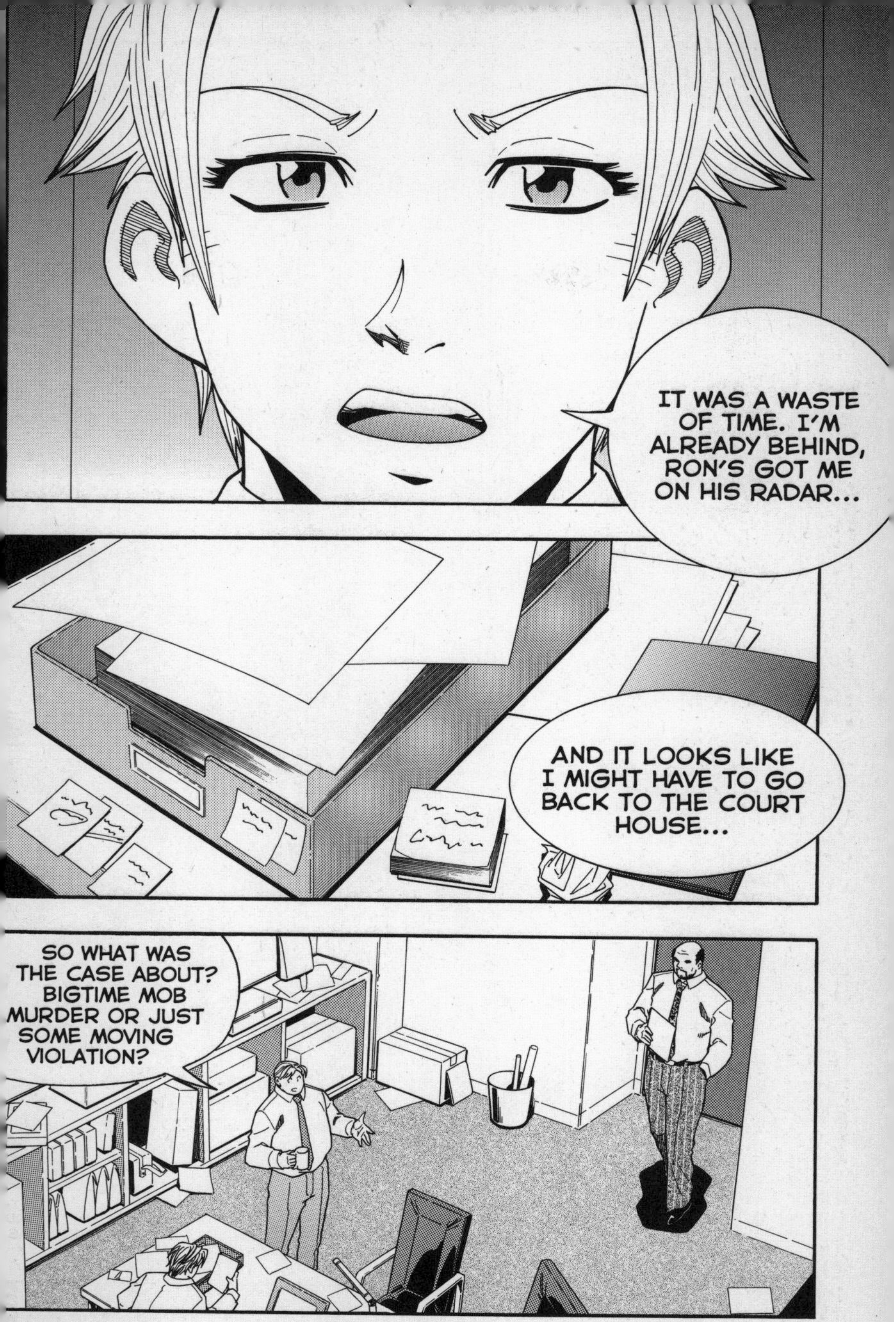
IT WAS A WASTE OF TIME. I'M ALREADY BEHIND, RON'S GOT ME ON HIS RADAR...
AND IT LOOKS LIKE I MIGHT HAVE TO GO BACK TO THE COURT HOUSE...
SO WHAT WAS THE CASE ABOUT? BIGTIME MOB MURDER OR JUST SOME MOVING VIOLATION?

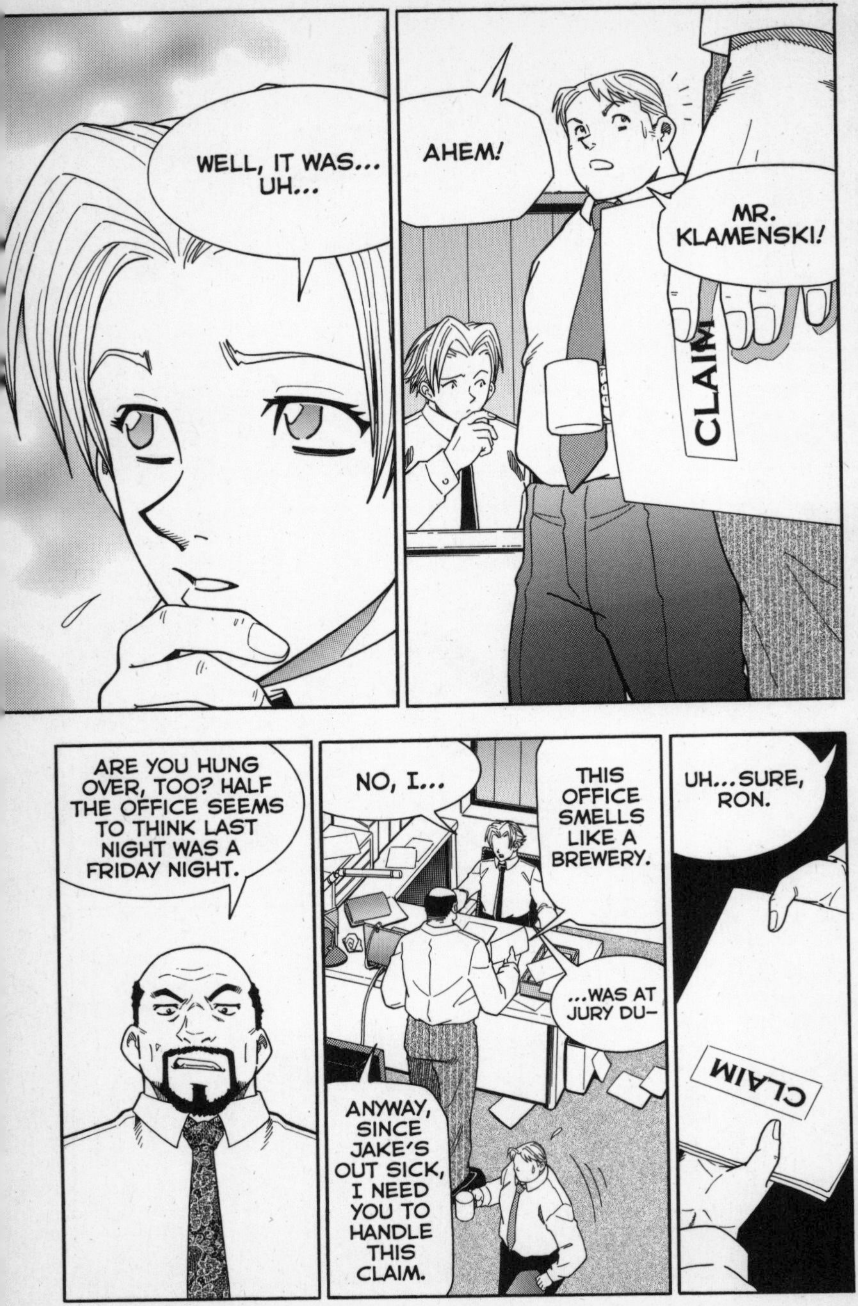
WELL, IT WAS... UH...
AHEM!
MR. KLAMENSKI!
CLAIM
ARE YOU HUNG OVER, TOO? HALF THE OFFICE SEEMS TO THINK LAST NIGHT WAS A FRIDAY NIGHT.
NO, I...
THIS OFFICE SMELLS LIKE A BREWERY.
...WAS AT JURY DU–
ANYWAY, SINCE JAKE'S OUT SICK, I NEED YOU TO HANDLE THIS CLAIM.
UH...SURE, RON.
CLAIM

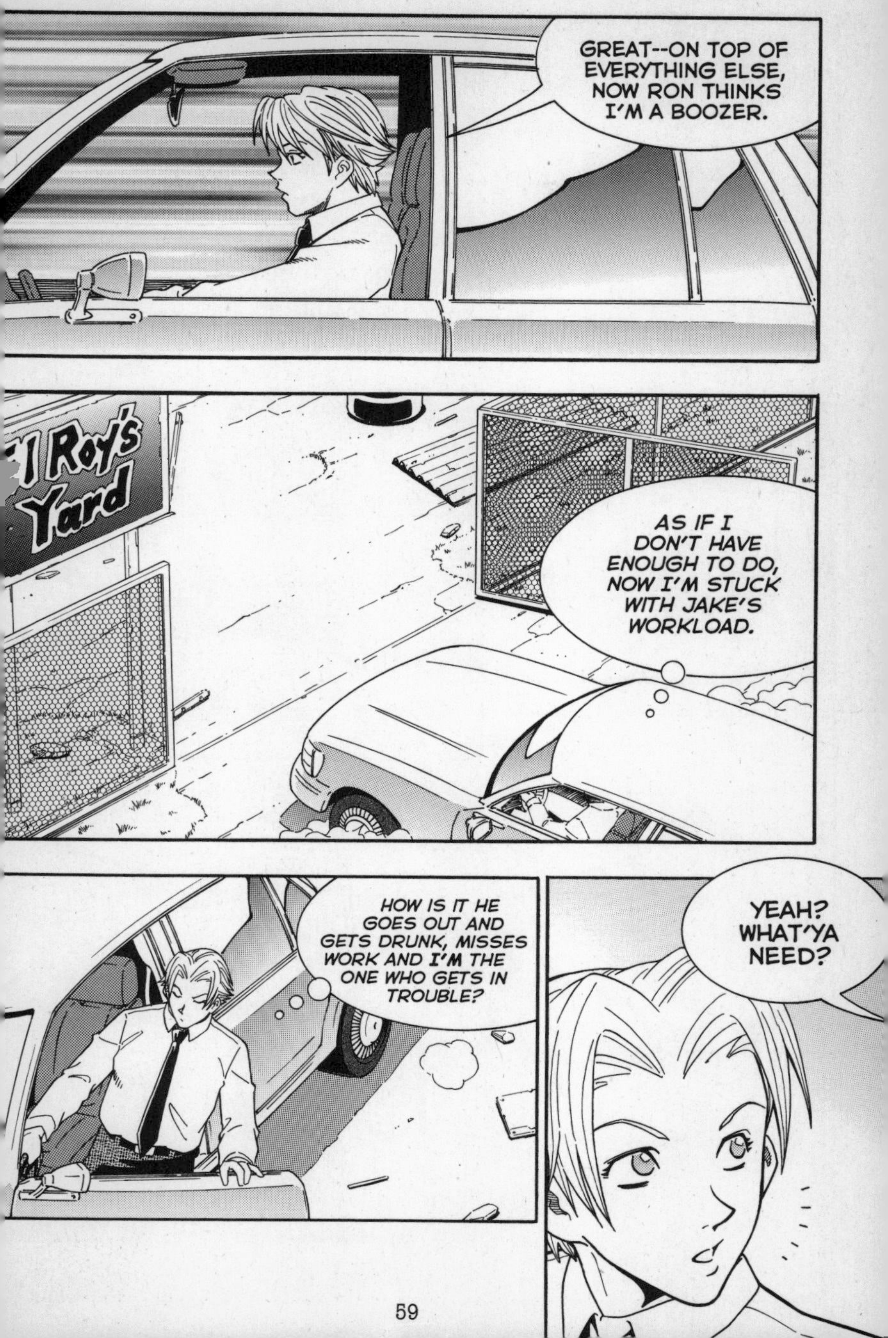
GREAT--ON TOP OF EVERYTHING ELSE, NOW RON THINKS I'M A BOOZER.
Roy's Yard
AS IF I DON'T HAVE ENOUGH TO DO, NOW I'M STUCK WITH JAKE'S WORKLOAD.
HOW IS IT HE GOES OUT AND GETS DRUNK, MISSES WORK AND I'M THE ONE WHO GETS IN TROUBLE?
YEAH? WHAT'YA NEED?

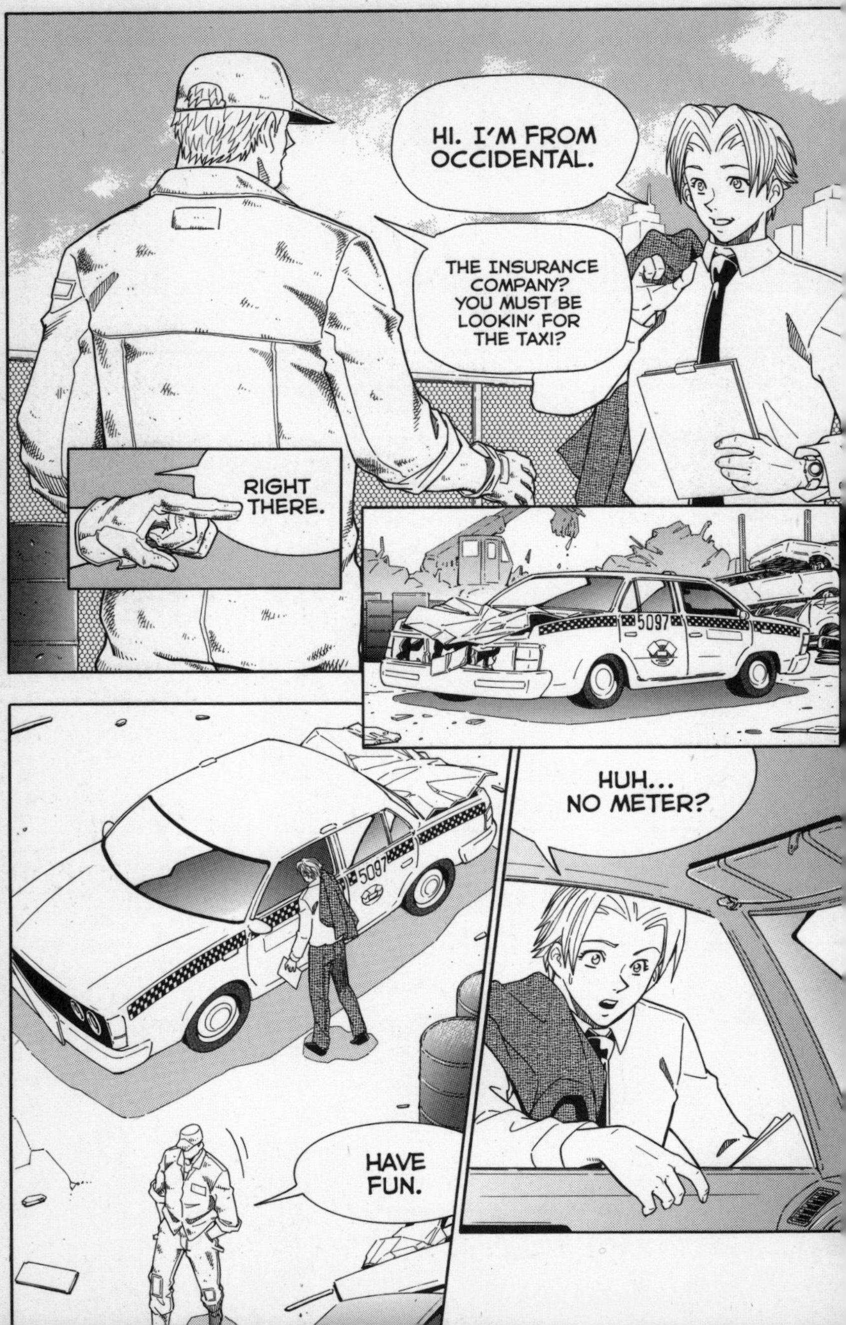
HI. I'M FROM OCCIDENTAL.
THE INSURANCE COMPANY? YOU MUST BE LOOKIN' FOR THE TAXI?
RIGHT THERE.
5097
5097
HUH... NO METER?
HAVE FUN.

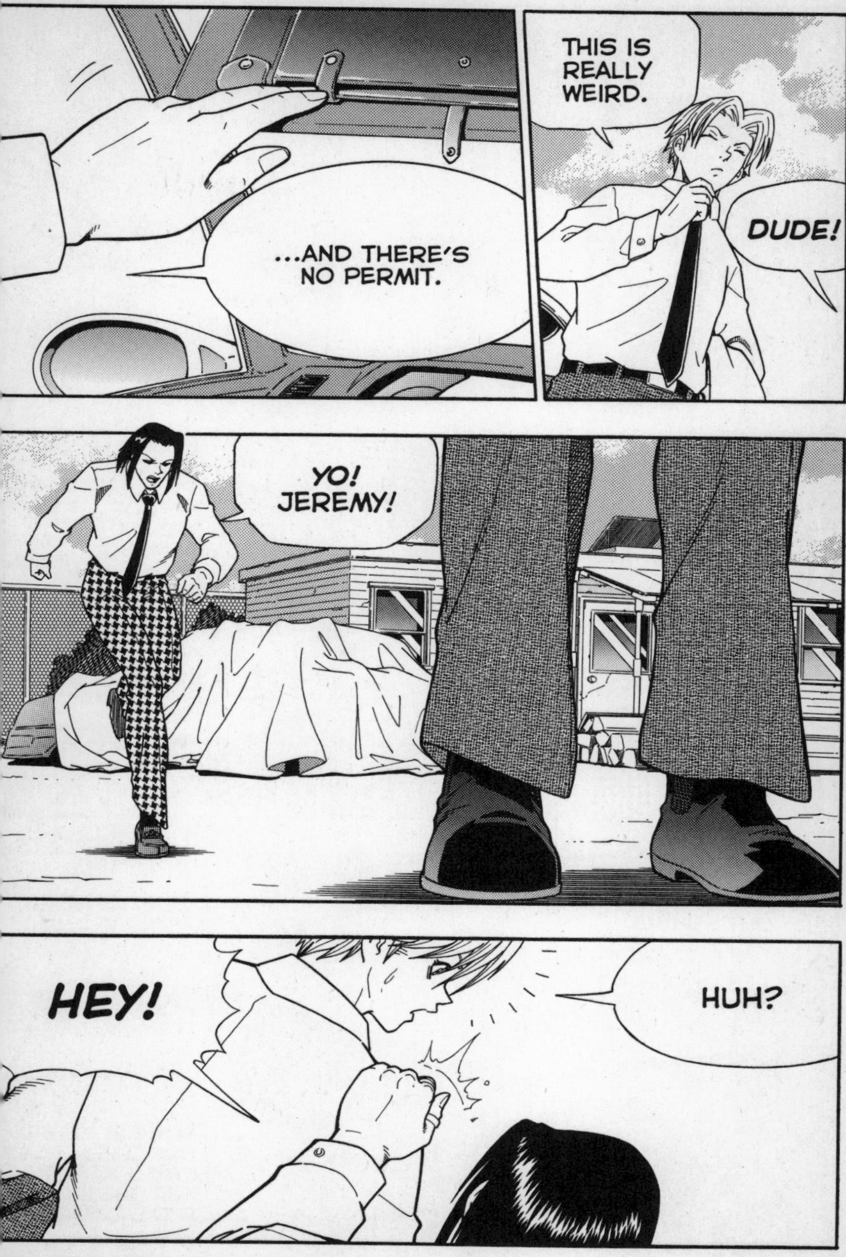
...AND THERE'S NO PERMIT.
THIS IS REALLY WEIRD.
DUDE!
YO! JEREMY!
HEY!
HUH?

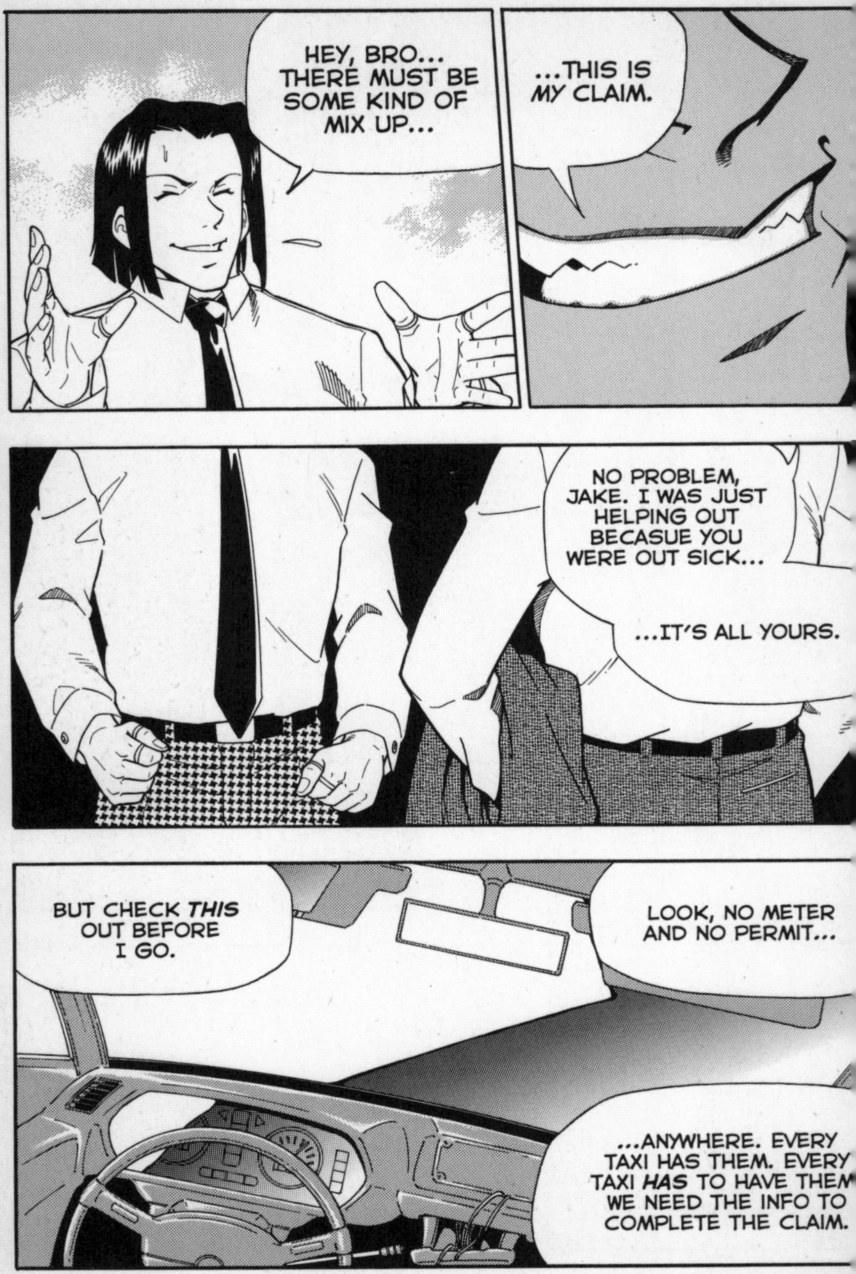
HEY, BRO... THERE MUST BE SOME KIND OF MIX UP...
...THIS IS *MY* CLAIM.
NO PROBLEM, JAKE. I WAS JUST HELPING OUT BECASUE YOU WERE OUT SICK...
...IT'S ALL YOURS.
BUT CHECK *THIS* OUT BEFORE I GO.
LOOK, NO METER AND NO PERMIT...
...ANYWHERE. EVERY TAXI HAS THEM. EVERY TAXI *HAS* TO HAVE THEM. WE NEED THE INFO TO COMPLETE THE CLAIM.

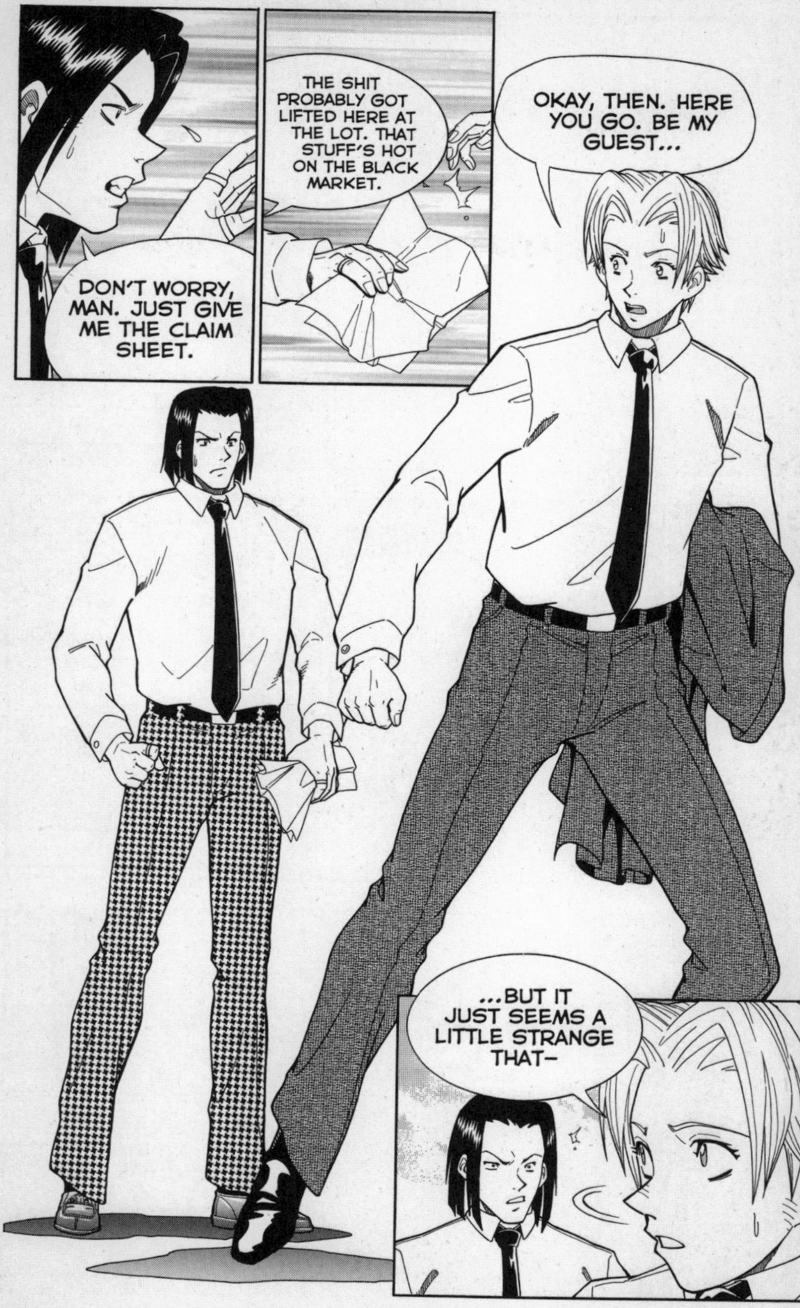
DON'T WORRY, MAN. JUST GIVE ME THE CLAIM SHEET.
THE SHIT PROBABLY GOT LIFTED HERE AT THE LOT. THAT STUFF'S HOT ON THE BLACK MARKET.
OKAY, THEN. HERE YOU GO. BE MY GUEST...
...BUT IT JUST SEEMS A LITTLE STRANGE THAT–

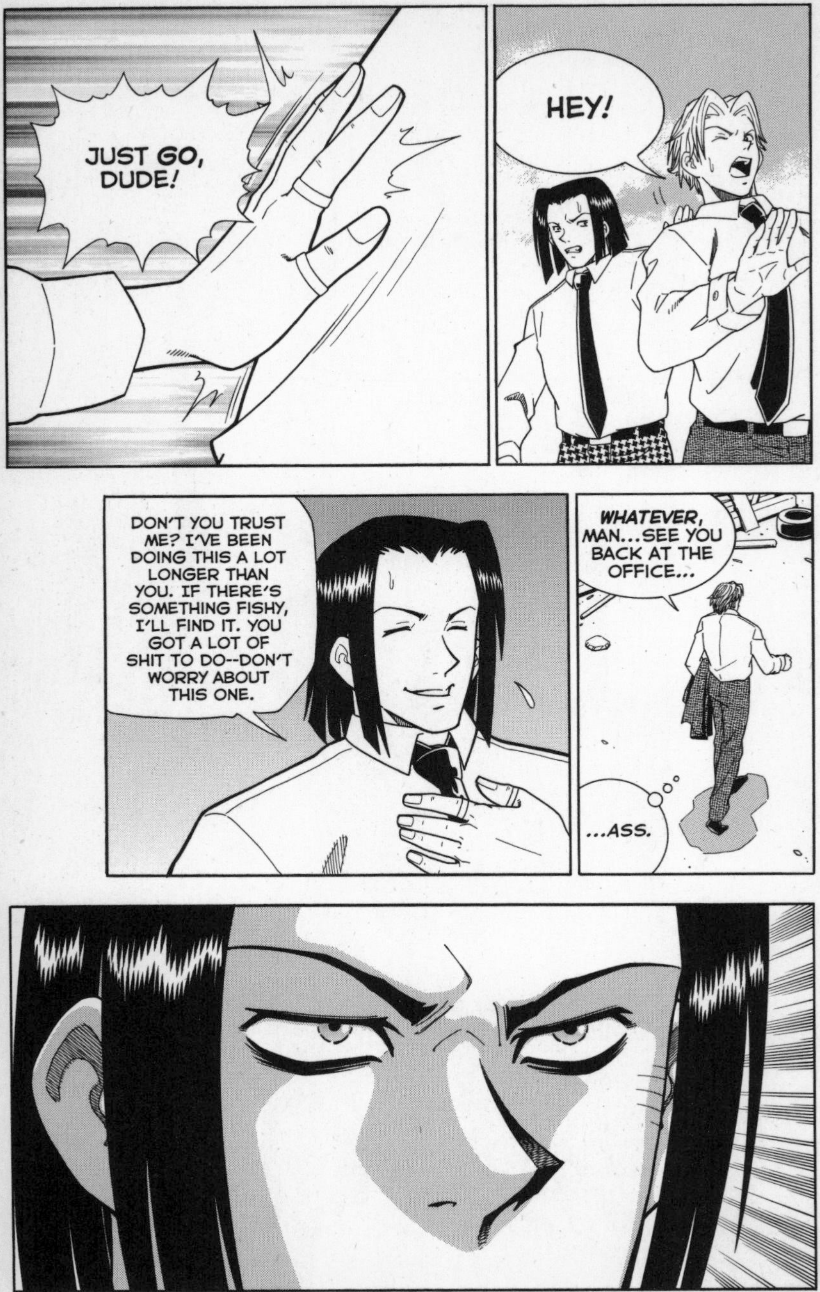
JUST GO, DUDE!
HEY!
DON'T YOU TRUST ME? I'VE BEEN DOING THIS A LOT LONGER THAN YOU. IF THERE'S SOMETHING FISHY, I'LL FIND IT. YOU GOT A LOT OF SHIT TO DO--DON'T WORRY ABOUT THIS ONE.
WHATEVER, MAN...SEE YOU BACK AT THE OFFICE...
...ASS.

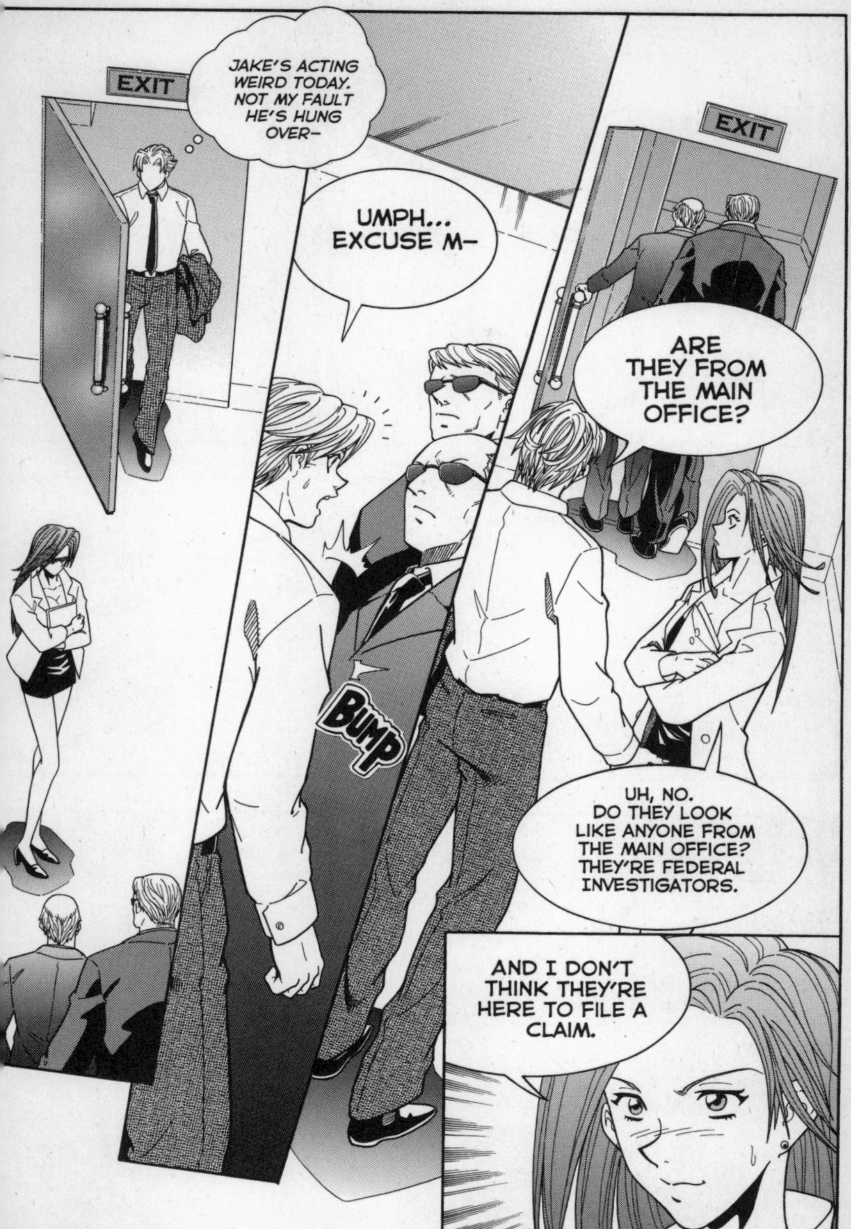
JAKE'S ACTING WEIRD TODAY. NOT MY FAULT HE'S HUNG OVER–
EXIT
UMPH... EXCUSE M–
BUMP
EXIT
ARE THEY FROM THE MAIN OFFICE?
UH, NO. DO THEY LOOK LIKE ANYONE FROM THE MAIN OFFICE? THEY'RE FEDERAL INVESTIGATORS.
AND I DON'T THINK THEY'RE HERE TO FILE A CLAIM.

OH, I'M GLAD YOU'RE HERE.

Y-YOU ARE?

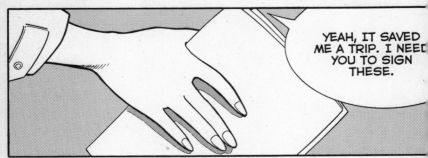

YEAH, IT SAVED ME A TRIP. I NEED YOU TO SIGN THESE.

OH...

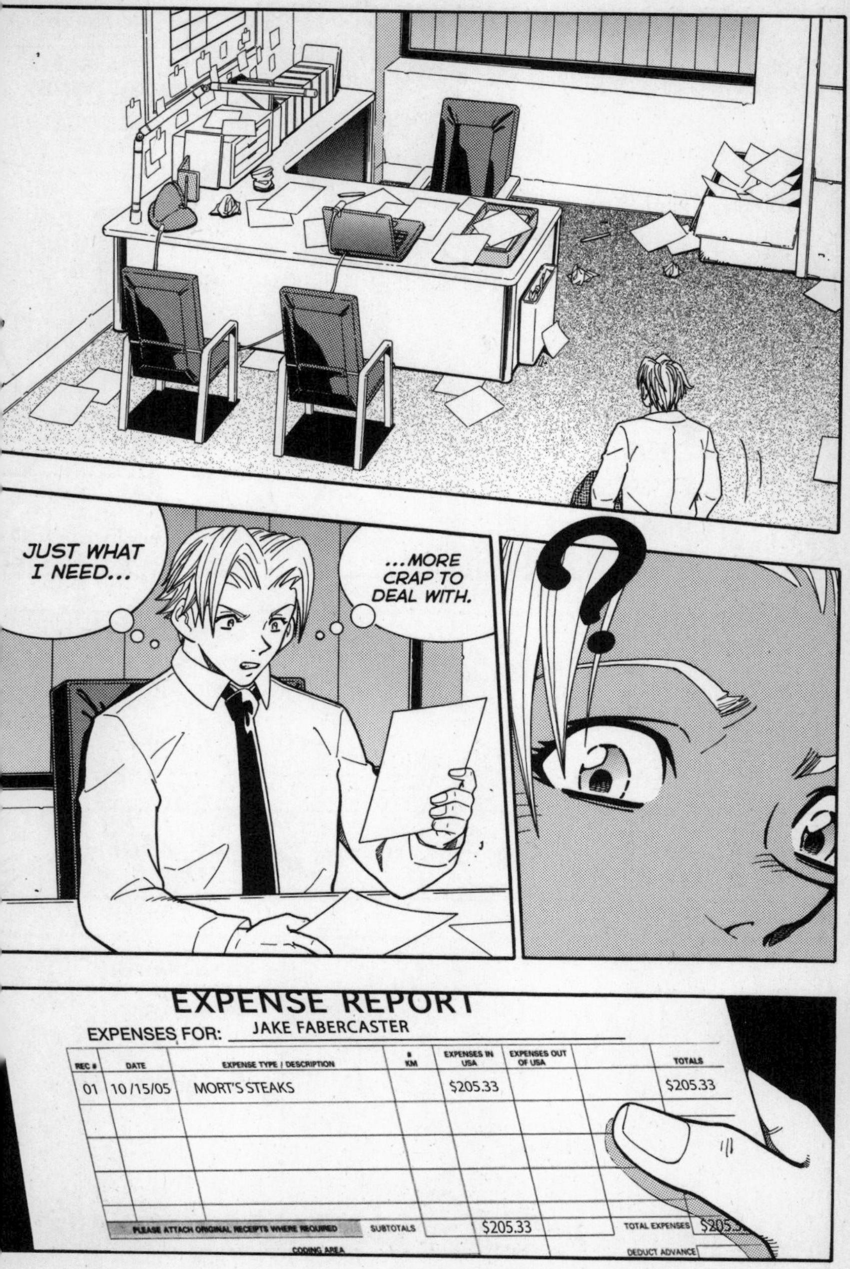

JUST WHAT I NEED...
...MORE CRAP TO DEAL WITH.
EXPENSE REPORT
EXPENSES FOR: JAKE FABERCASTER
REC #
DATE
EXPENSE TYPE / DESCRIPTION
# KM
EXPENSES IN USA
EXPENSES OUT OF USA
TOTALS
01 10/15/05 MORT'S STEAKS $205.33 $205.33
PLEASE ATTACH ORIGINAL RECEIPTS WHERE REQUIRED
SUBTOTALS $205.33
TOTAL EXPENSES
CODING AREA
DEDUCT ADVANCE

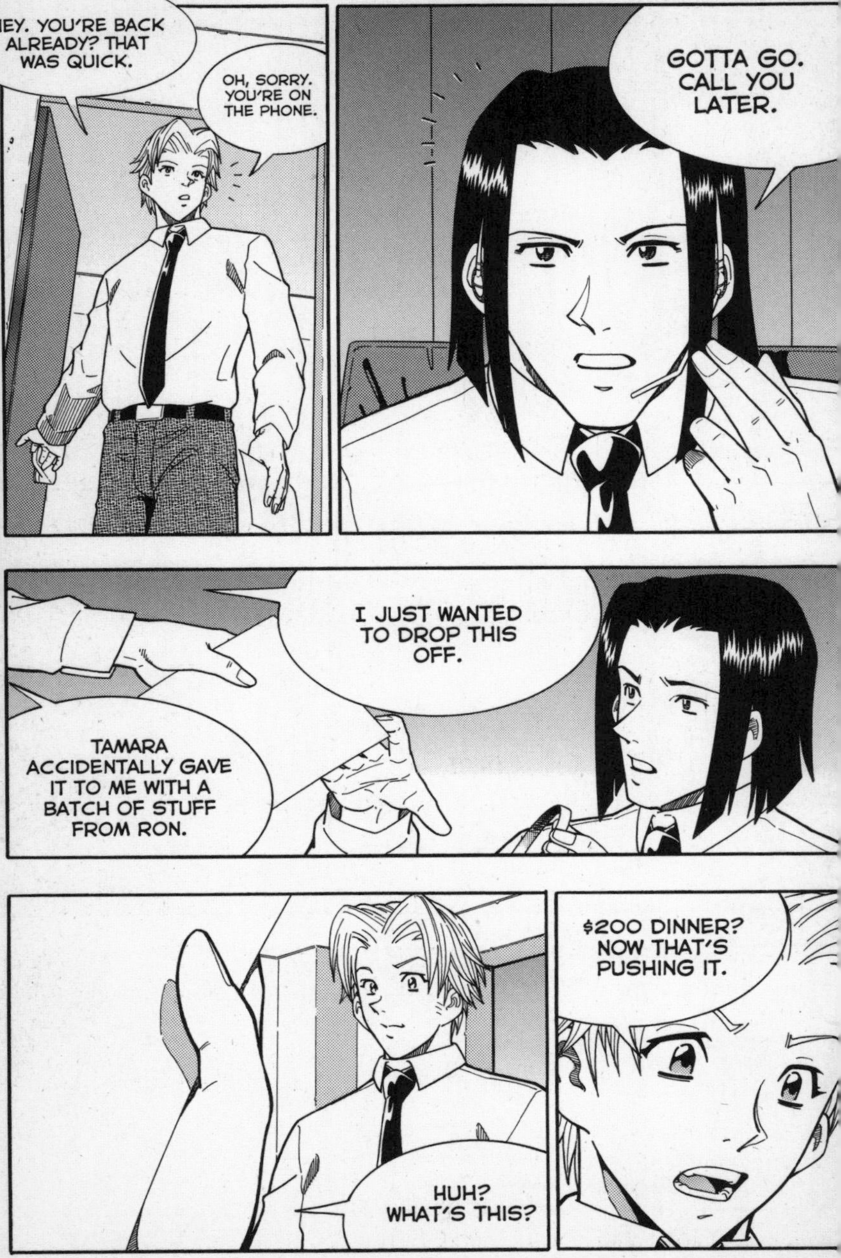
HEY. YOU'RE BACK ALREADY? THAT WAS QUICK.
OH, SORRY. YOU'RE ON THE PHONE.
GOTTA GO. CALL YOU LATER.
I JUST WANTED TO DROP THIS OFF.
TAMARA ACCIDENTALLY GAVE IT TO ME WITH A BATCH OF STUFF FROM RON.
HUH? WHAT'S THIS?
$200 DINNER? NOW THAT'S PUSHING IT.

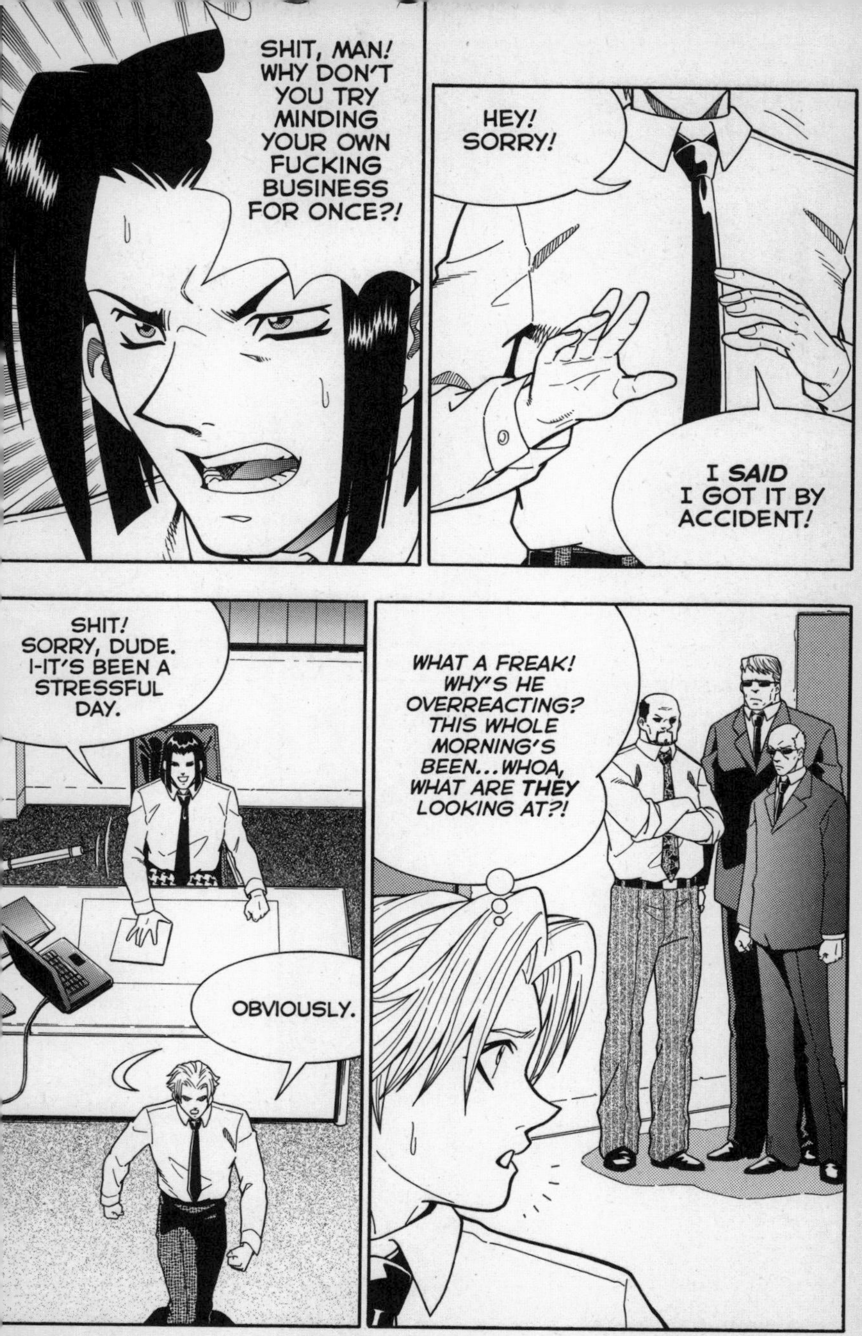
SHIT, MAN! WHY DON'T YOU TRY MINDING YOUR OWN FUCKING BUSINESS FOR ONCE?!
HEY! SORRY!
I *SAID* I GOT IT BY ACCIDENT!
SHIT! SORRY, DUDE. I-IT'S BEEN A STRESSFUL DAY.
OBVIOUSLY.
*WHAT A FREAK! WHY'S HE OVERREACTING? THIS WHOLE MORNING'S BEEN...WHOA, WHAT ARE* **THEY** *LOOKING AT?!*

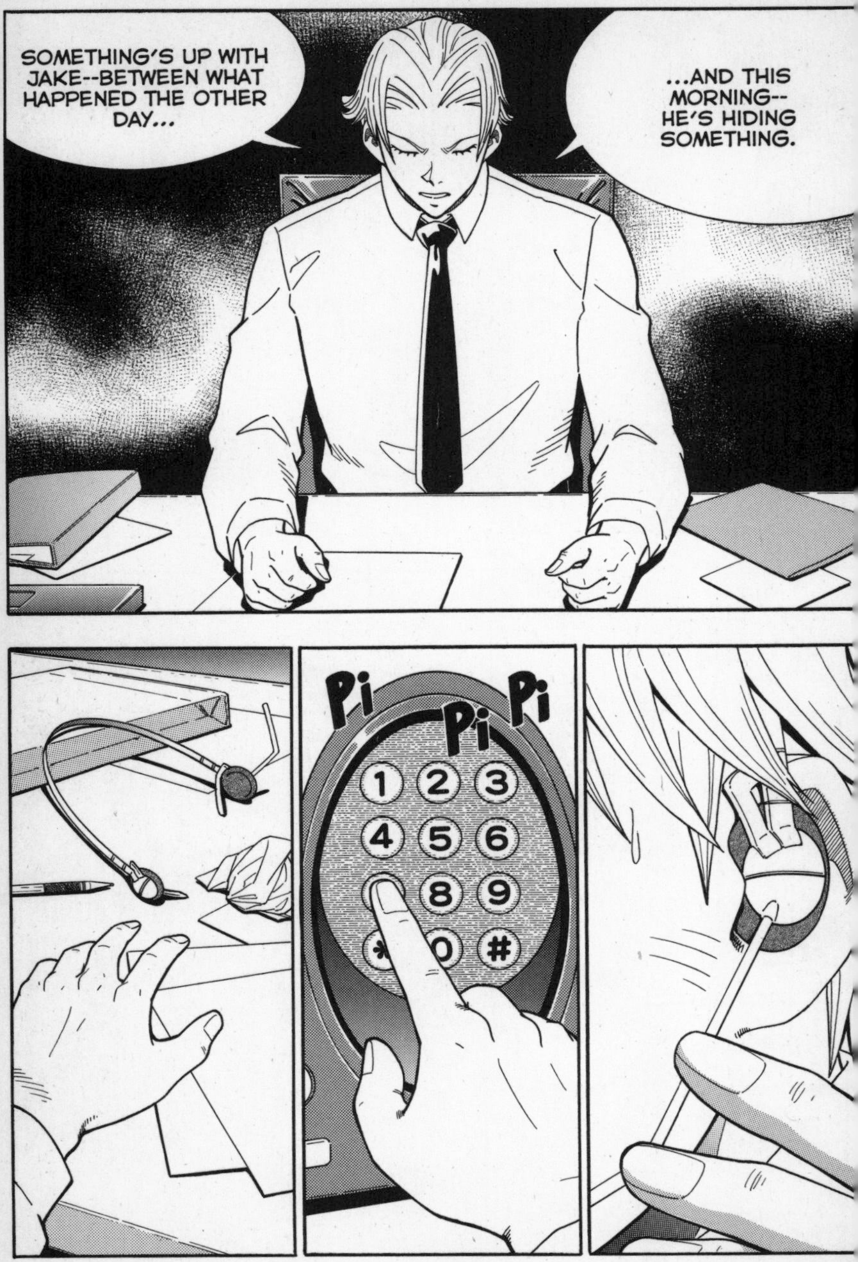
SOMETHING'S UP WITH JAKE--BETWEEN WHAT HAPPENED THE OTHER DAY...
...AND THIS MORNING--HE'S HIDING SOMETHING.
Pi Pi Pi
1 2 3
4 5 6
8 9
* 0 #

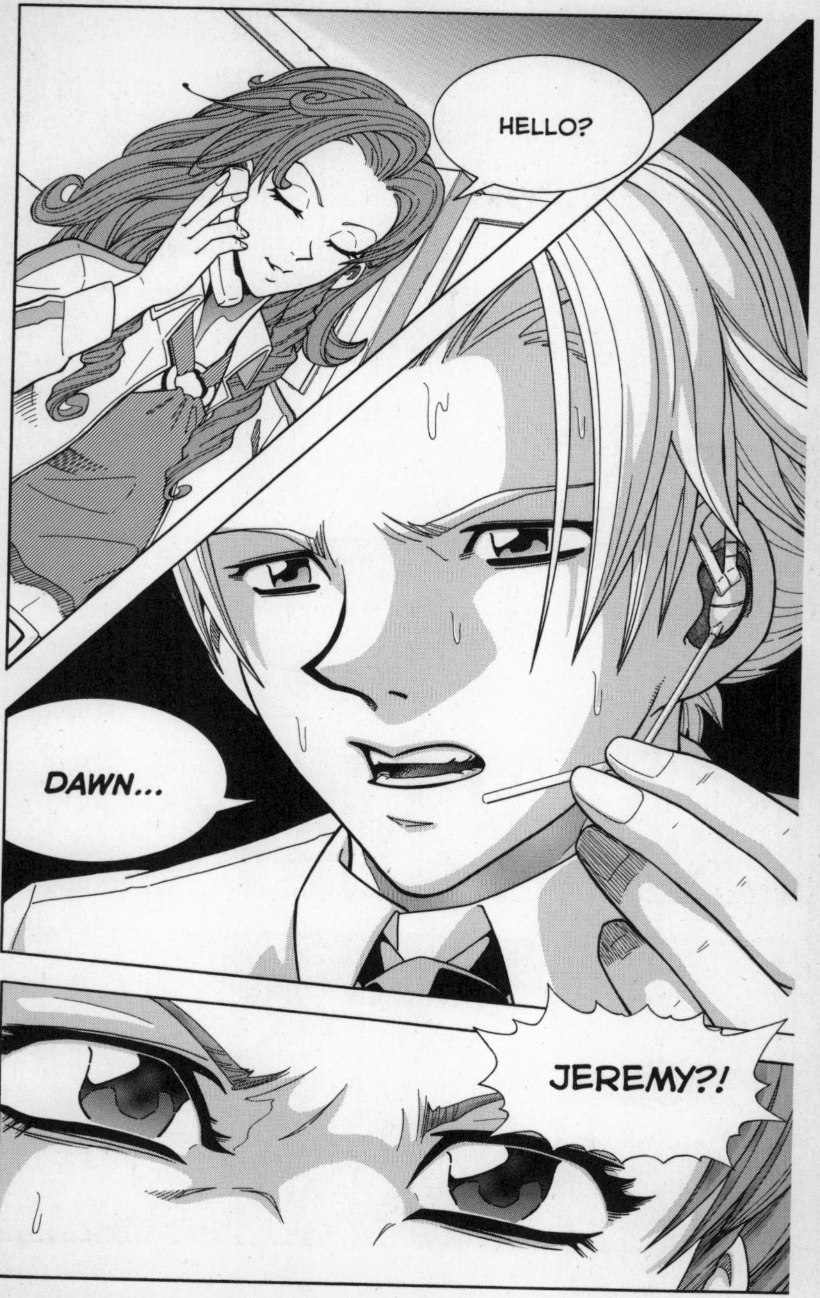
HELLO?
DAWN...
JEREMY?!

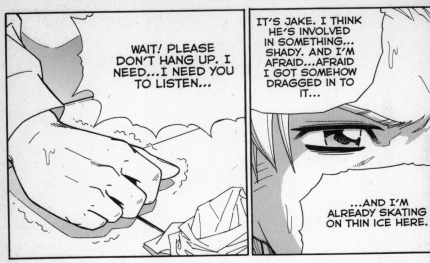

WAIT! PLEASE DON'T HANG UP. I NEED...I NEED YOU TO LISTEN...

IT'S JAKE. I THINK HE'S INVOLVED IN SOMETHING... SHADY. AND I'M AFRAID...AFRAID I GOT SOMEHOW DRAGGED IN TO IT...

...AND I'M ALREADY SKATING ON THIN ICE HERE.

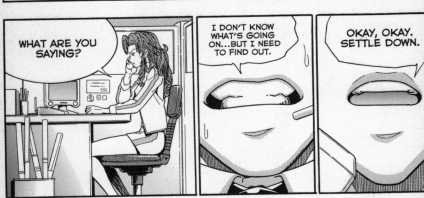

WHAT ARE YOU SAYING?

I DON'T KNOW WHAT'S GOING ON...BUT I NEED TO FIND OUT.

OKAY, OKAY. SETTLE DOWN.

LOOK, LET'S MEET AFTER WORK. WE CAN TALK ABOUT IT THEN, OKAY?

O-OKAY.

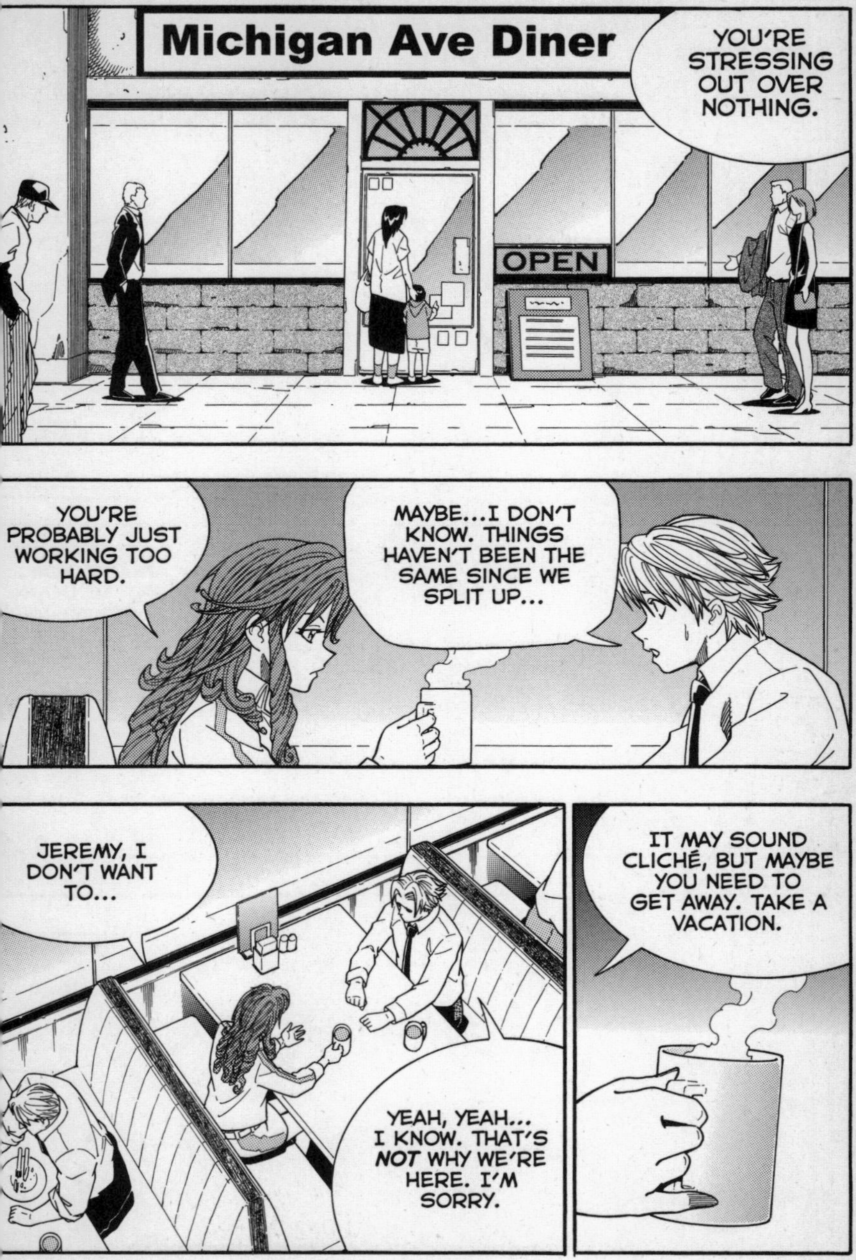
Michigan Ave Diner
YOU'RE STRESSING OUT OVER NOTHING.
OPEN
MAYBE...I DON'T KNOW. THINGS HAVEN'T BEEN THE SAME SINCE WE SPLIT UP...
YOU'RE PROBABLY JUST WORKING TOO HARD.
IT MAY SOUND CLICHÉ, BUT MAYBE YOU NEED TO GET AWAY. TAKE A VACATION.
JEREMY, I DON'T WANT TO...
YEAH, YEAH... I KNOW. THAT'S *NOT* WHY WE'RE HERE. I'M SORRY.

YOU MUST THINK I'M CRAZY.

HEY, HEY... THAT'S NOT TRUE.

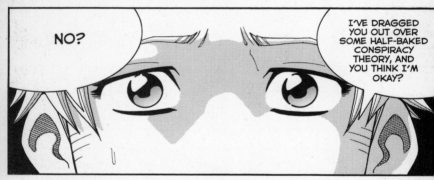

NO?

I'VE DRAGGED YOU OUT OVER SOME HALF-BAKED CONSPIRACY THEORY, AND YOU THINK I'M OKAY?

LOOK, YOU'RE JUST GOING THROUGH A HARD TIME, IS ALL.

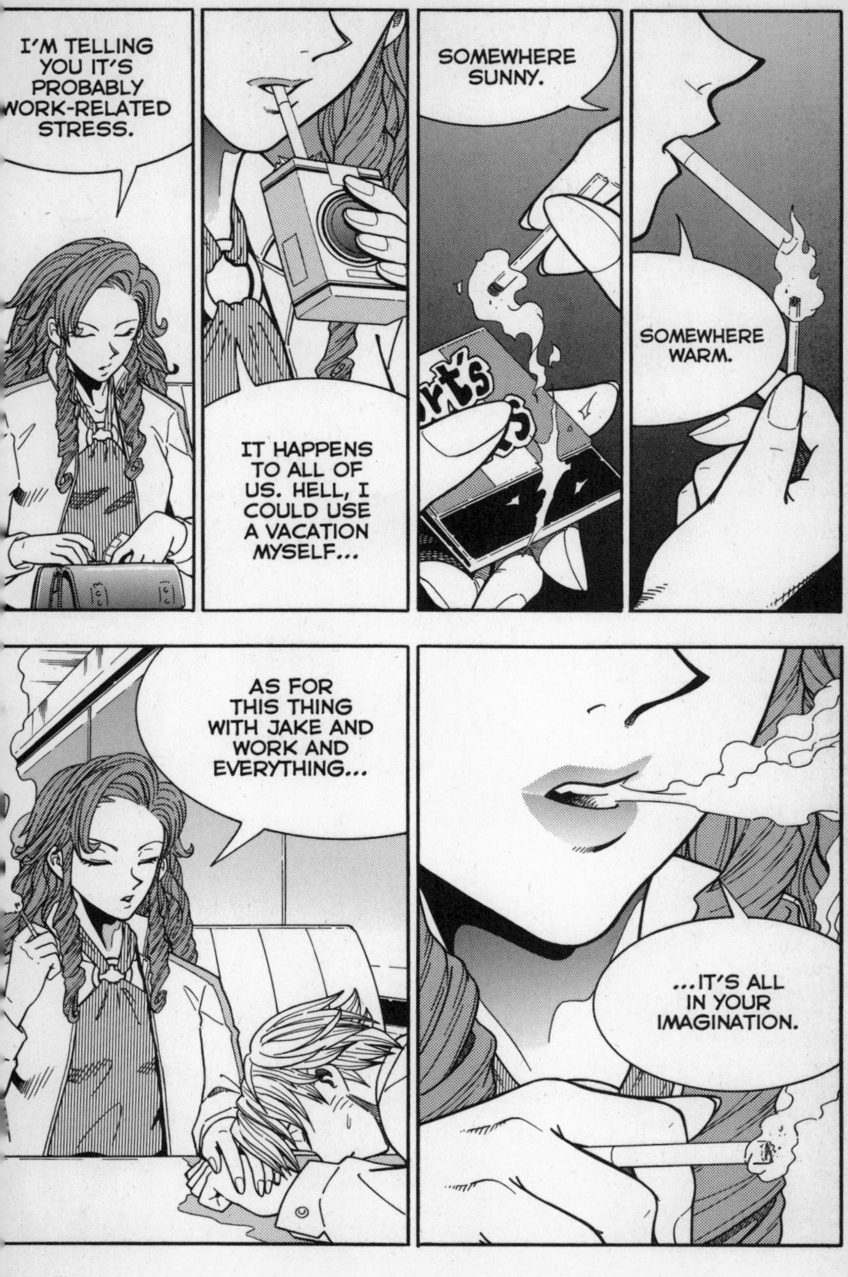
I'M TELLING YOU IT'S PROBABLY WORK-RELATED STRESS.
IT HAPPENS TO ALL OF US. HELL, I COULD USE A VACATION MYSELF...
SOMEWHERE SUNNY.
SOMEWHERE WARM.
AS FOR THIS THING WITH JAKE AND WORK AND EVERYTHING...
...IT'S ALL IN YOUR IMAGINATION.

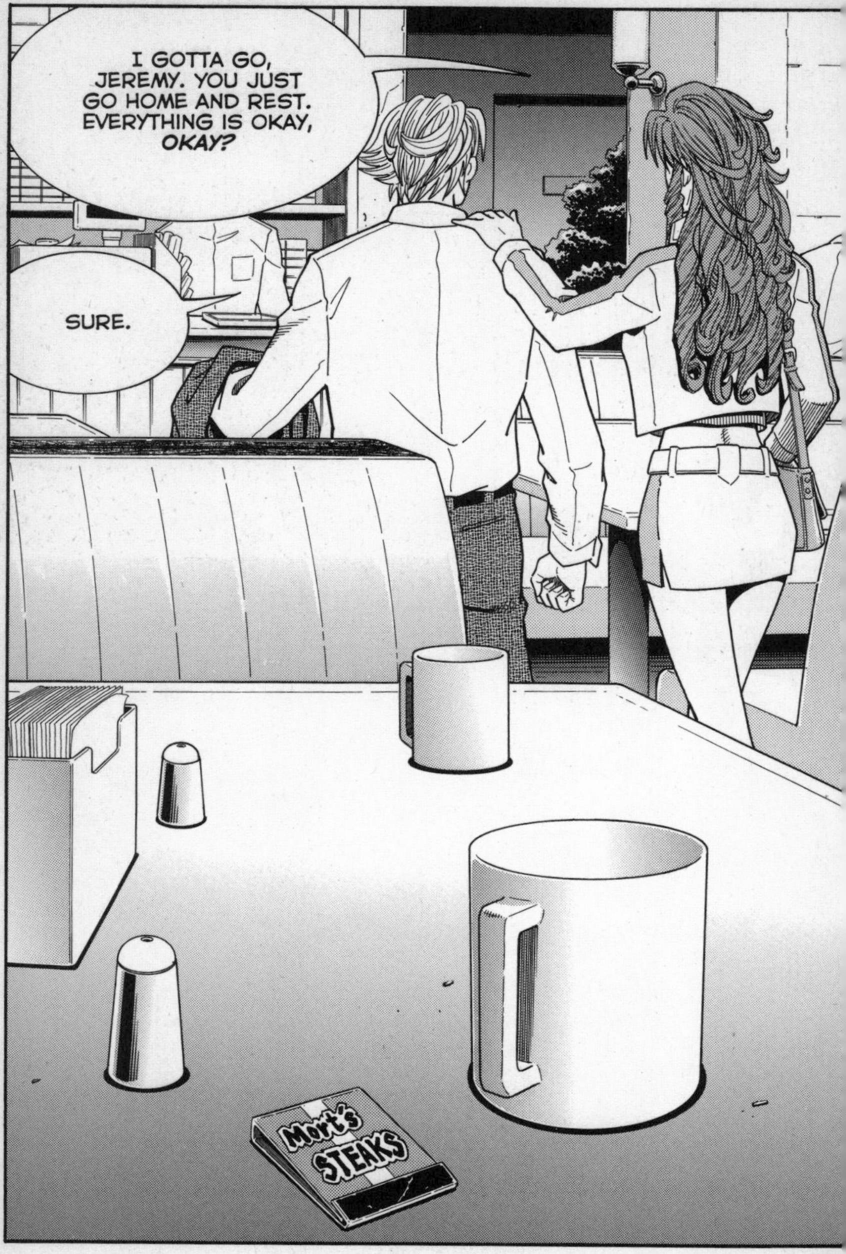
I GOTTA GO, JEREMY. YOU JUST GO HOME AND REST. EVERYTHING IS OKAY, *OKAY?*
SURE.
Mort's STEAKS

JuRor 13™

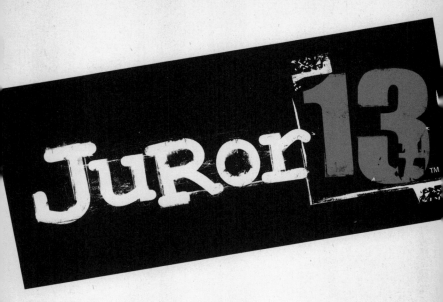

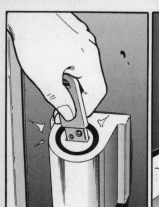

CLICK

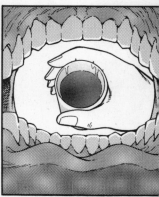

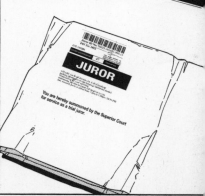

JUROR

You are hereby summoned by the Superior Court
for service as a trial juror.

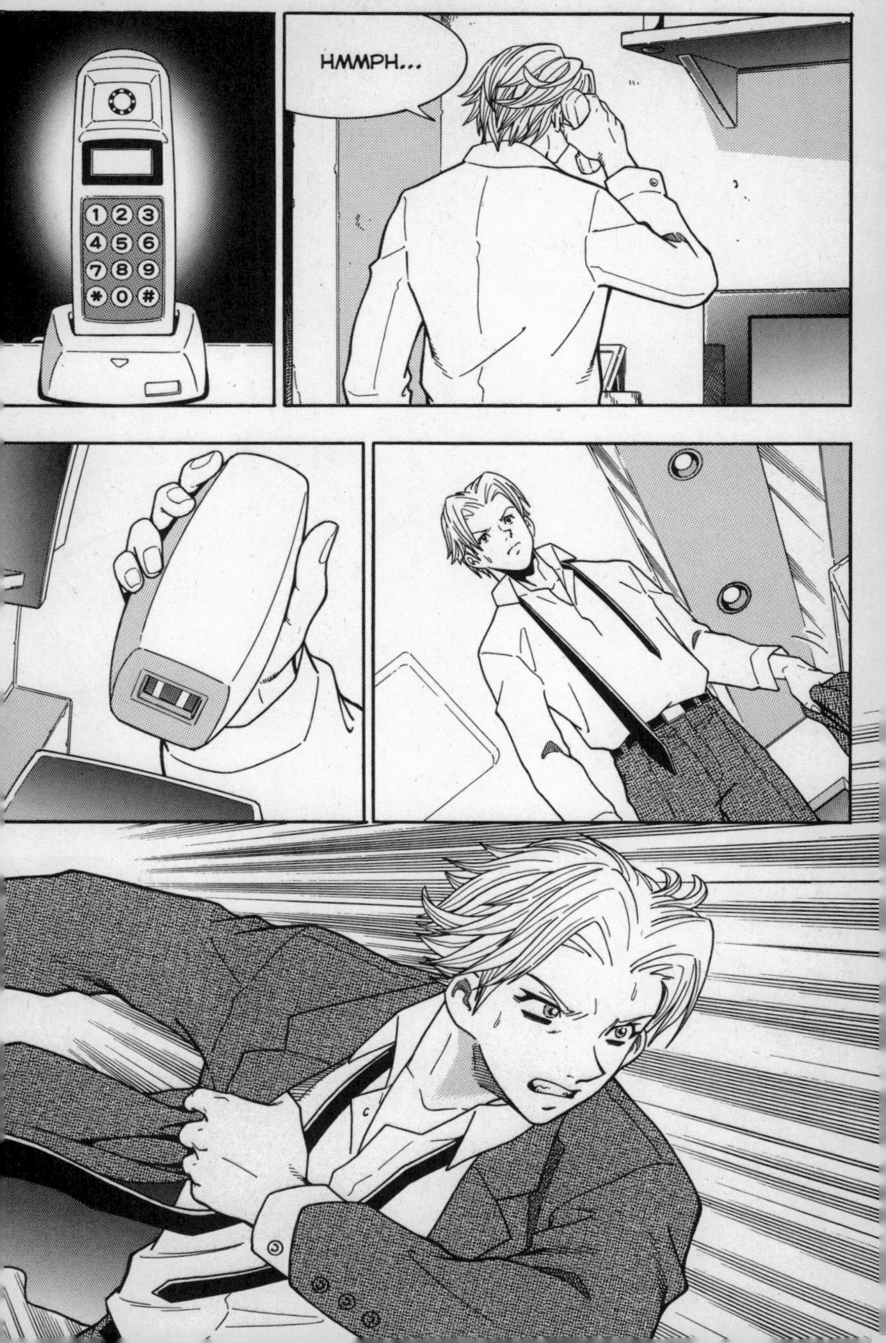
HMMPH...

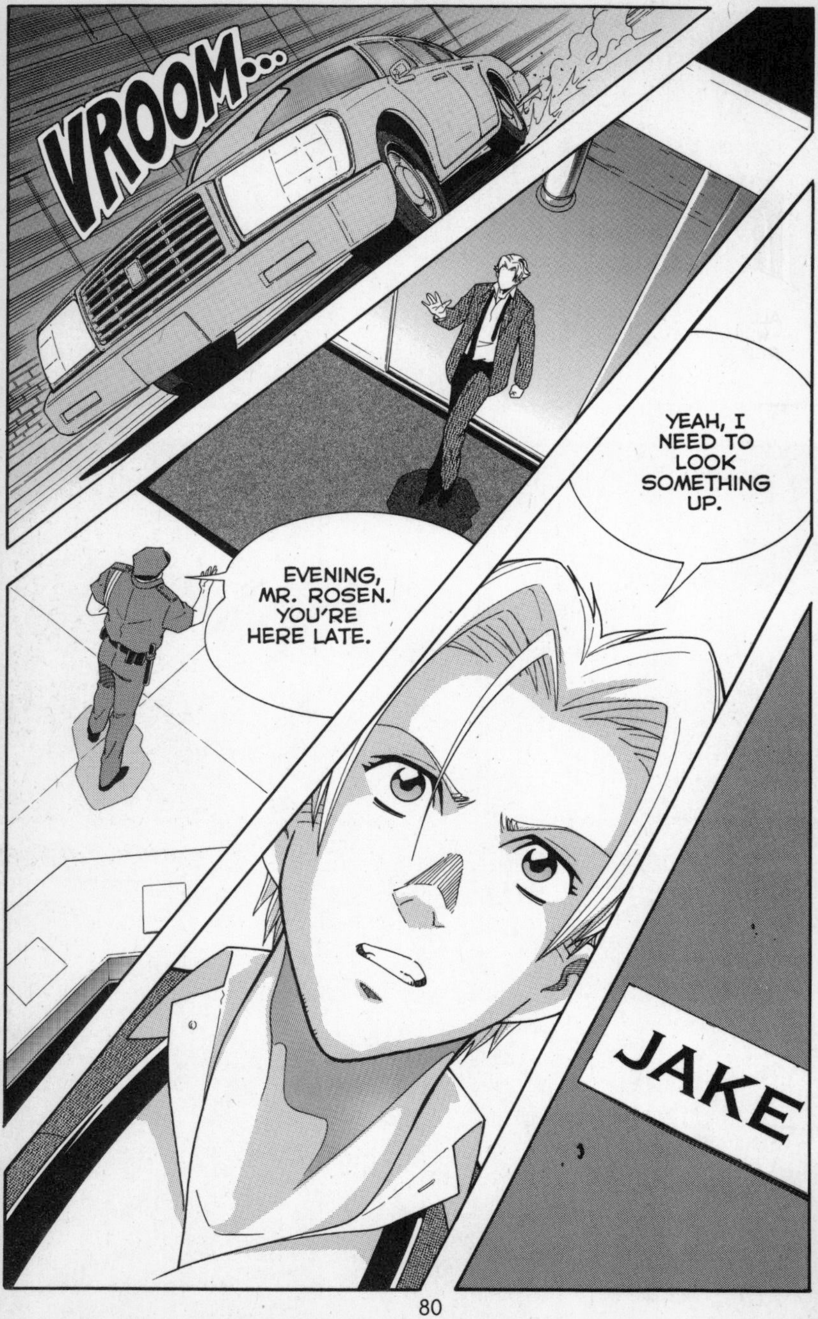
VROOM...
YEAH, I NEED TO LOOK SOMETHING UP.
EVENING, MR. ROSEN. YOU'RE HERE LATE.
JAKE

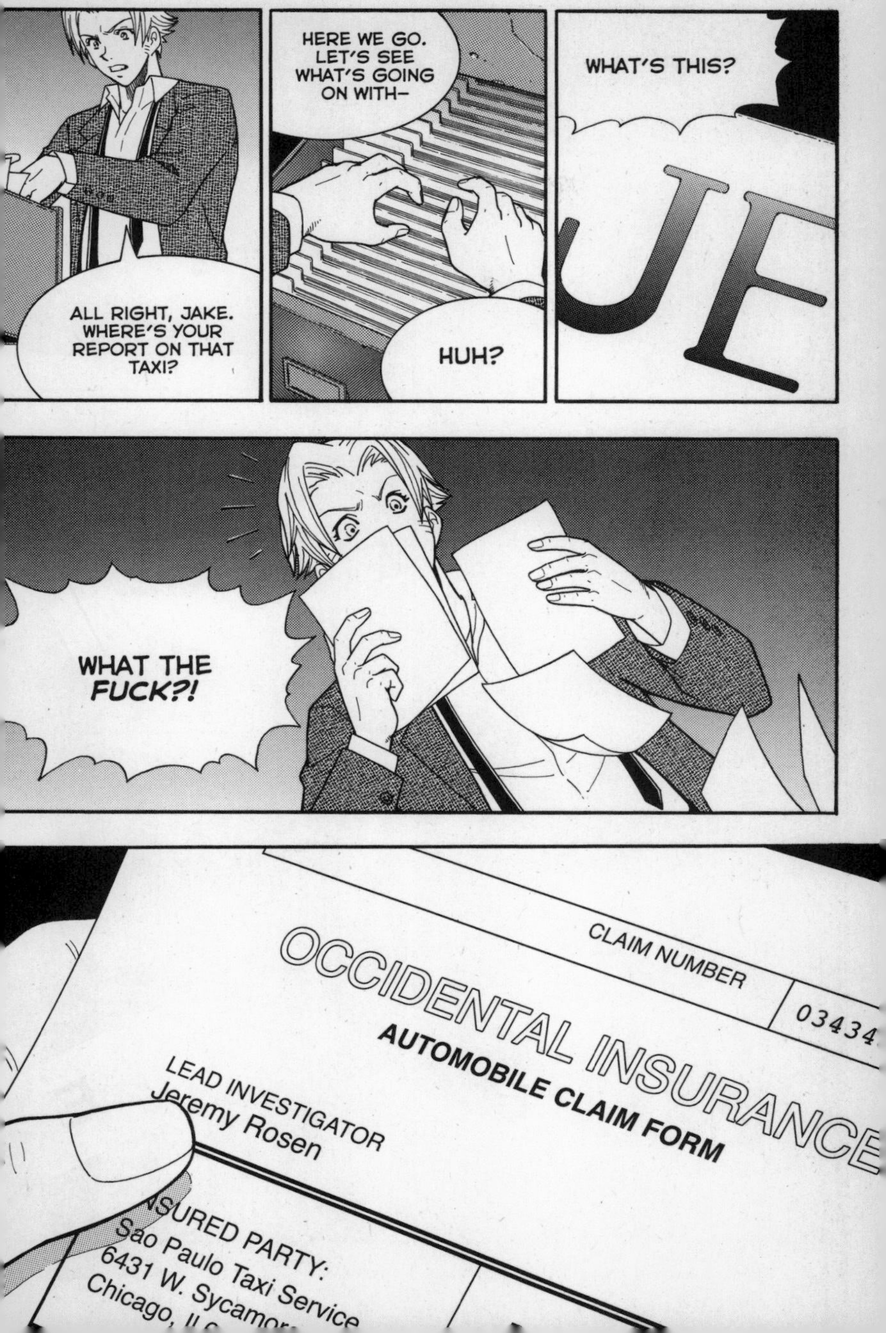
ALL RIGHT, JAKE. WHERE'S YOUR REPORT ON THAT TAXI?
HERE WE GO. LET'S SEE WHAT'S GOING ON WITH–
HUH?
WHAT'S THIS?
JE
WHAT THE *FUCK?!*
OCCIDENTAL INSURANCE
CLAIM NUMBER
03434
AUTOMOBILE CLAIM FORM
LEAD INVESTIGATOR
Jeremy Rosen
SURED PARTY:
Sao Paulo Taxi Service
6431 W. Sycamor
Chicago, IL

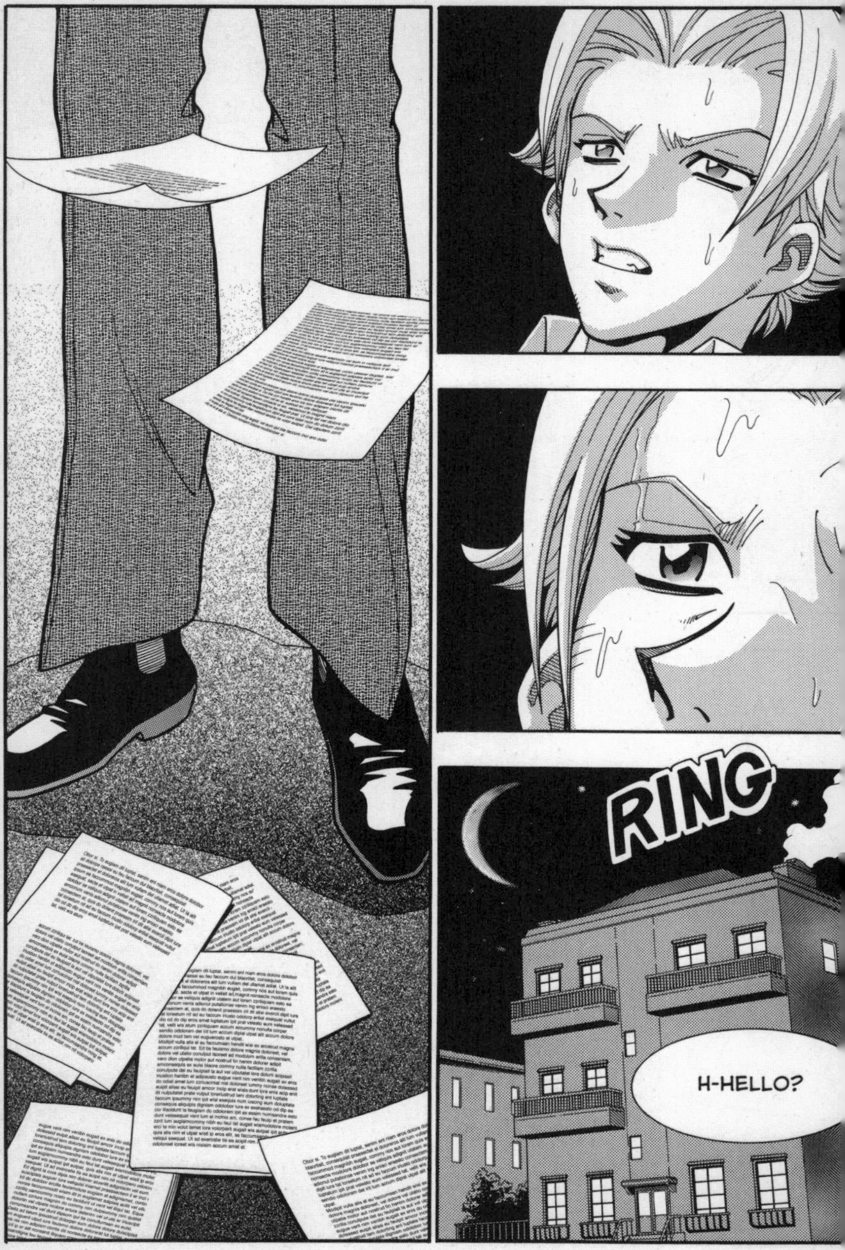
RING
H-HELLO?

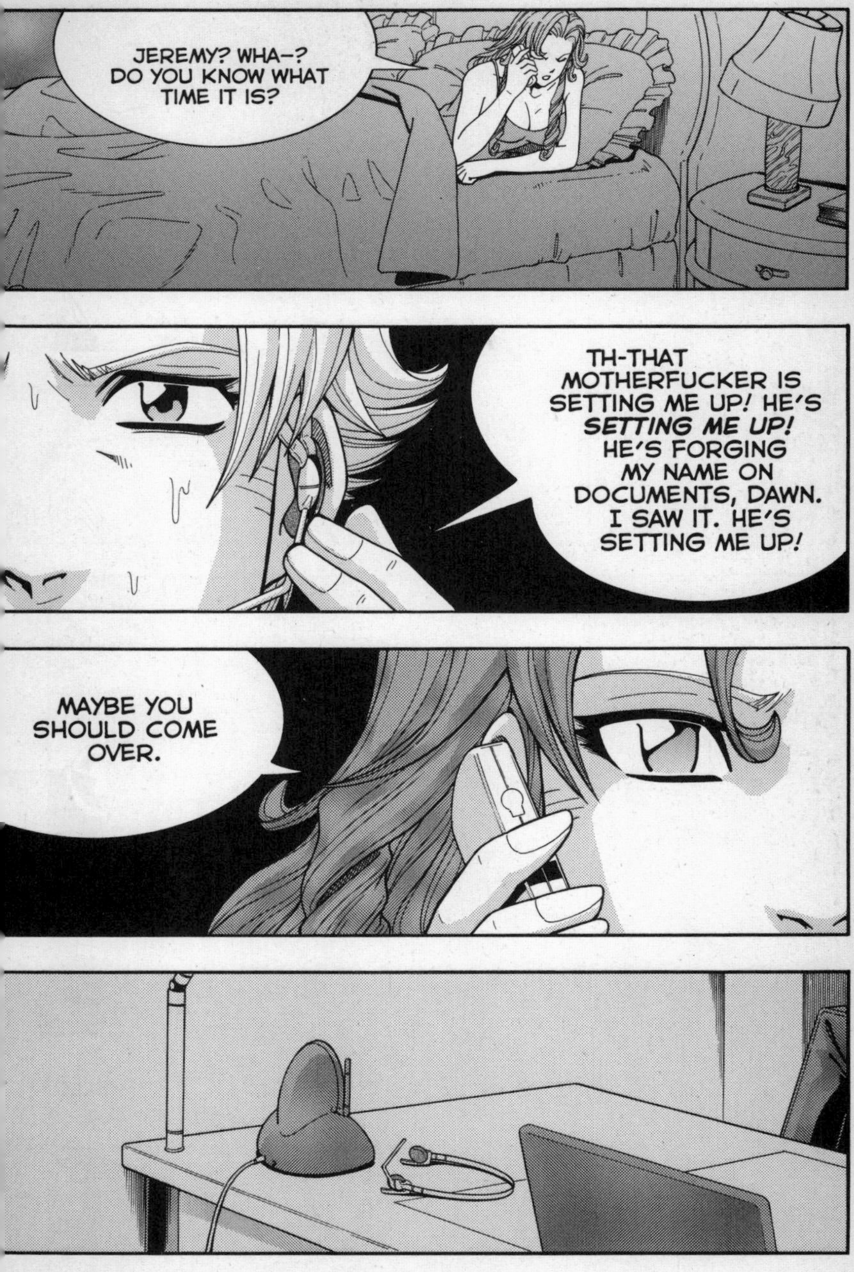
JEREMY? WHA-? DO YOU KNOW WHAT TIME IT IS?
TH-THAT MOTHERFUCKER IS SETTING ME UP! HE'S *SETTING ME UP!* HE'S FORGING MY NAME ON DOCUMENTS, DAWN. I SAW IT. HE'S SETTING ME UP!
MAYBE YOU SHOULD COME OVER.

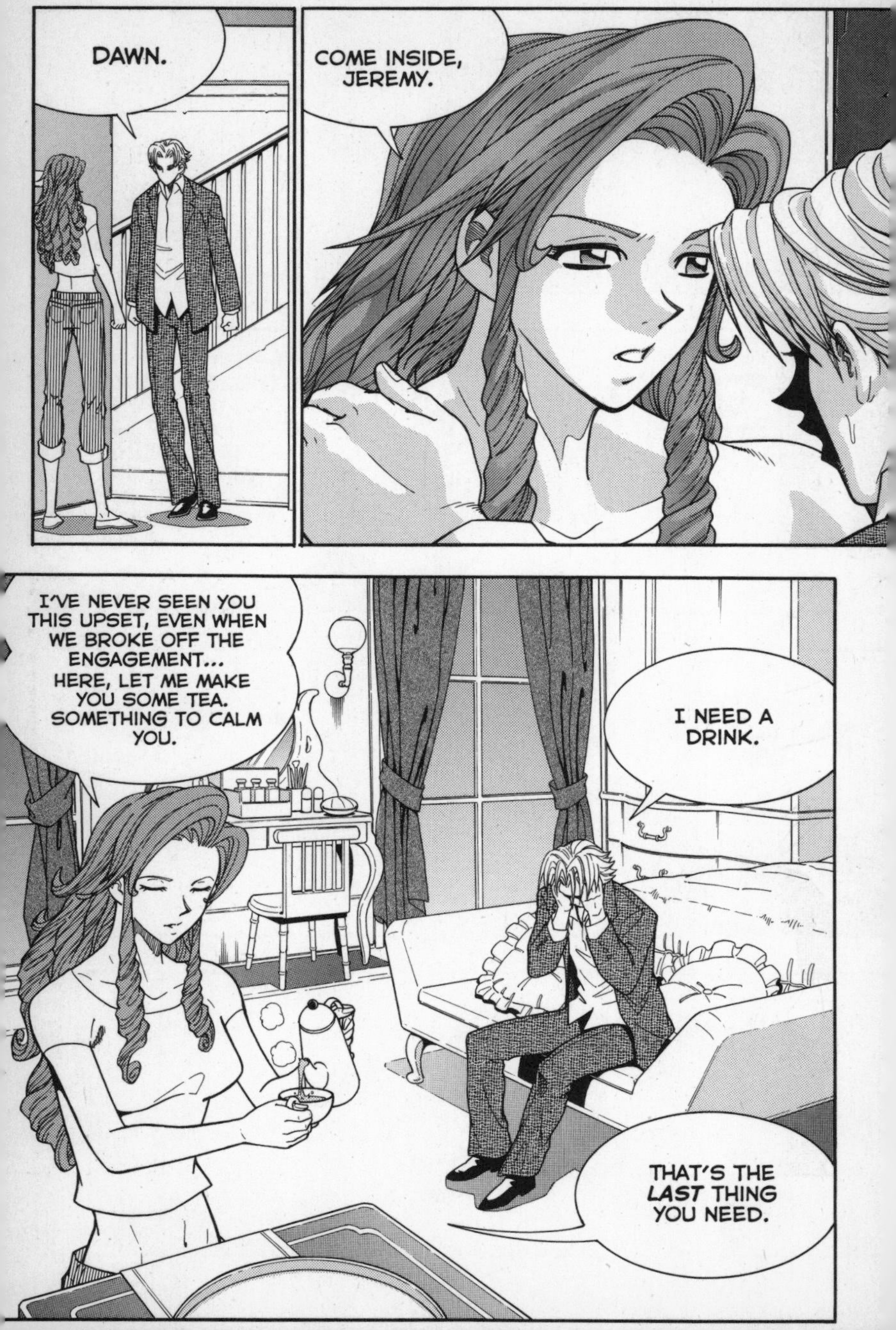
DAWN.
COME INSIDE, JEREMY.
I'VE NEVER SEEN YOU THIS UPSET, EVEN WHEN WE BROKE OFF THE ENGAGEMENT... HERE, LET ME MAKE YOU SOME TEA. SOMETHING TO CALM YOU.
I NEED A DRINK.
THAT'S THE *LAST* THING YOU NEED.

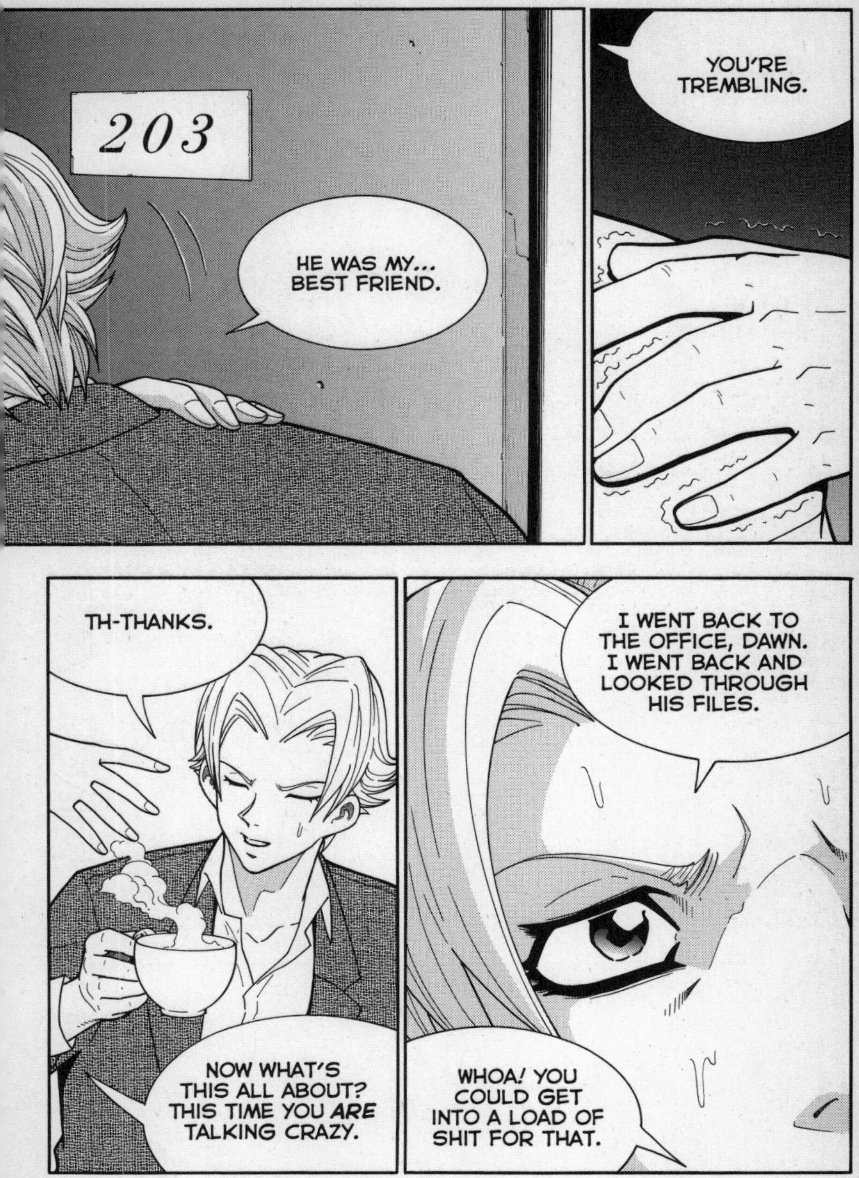
203
HE WAS MY... BEST FRIEND.
YOU'RE TREMBLING.
TH-THANKS.
NOW WHAT'S THIS ALL ABOUT? THIS TIME YOU *ARE* TALKING CRAZY.
I WENT BACK TO THE OFFICE, DAWN. I WENT BACK AND LOOKED THROUGH HIS FILES.
WHOA! YOU COULD GET INTO A LOAD OF SHIT FOR THAT.

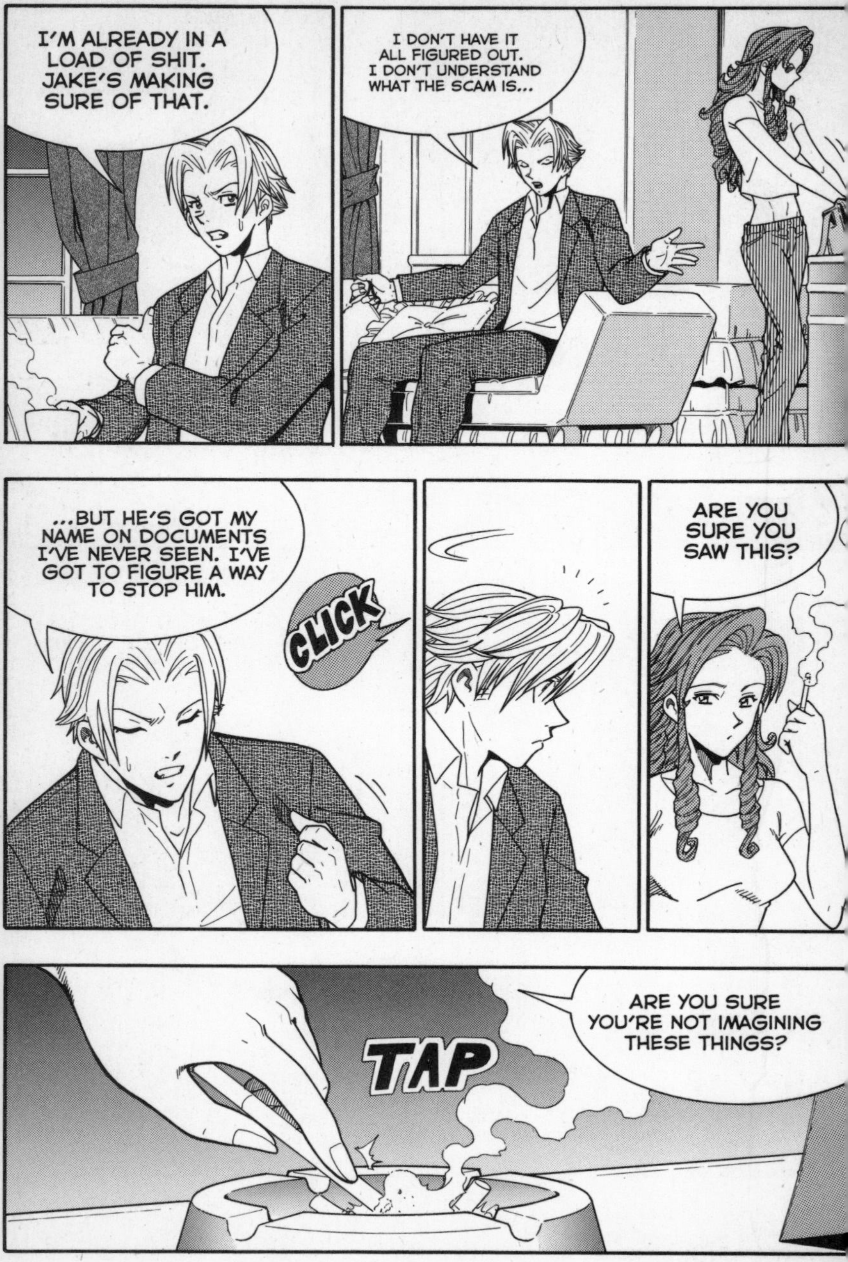
I'M ALREADY IN A LOAD OF SHIT. JAKE'S MAKING SURE OF THAT.
I DON'T HAVE IT ALL FIGURED OUT. I DON'T UNDERSTAND WHAT THE SCAM IS...
...BUT HE'S GOT MY NAME ON DOCUMENTS I'VE NEVER SEEN. I'VE GOT TO FIGURE A WAY TO STOP HIM.
CLICK
ARE YOU SURE YOU SAW THIS?
TAP
ARE YOU SURE YOU'RE NOT IMAGINING THESE THINGS?

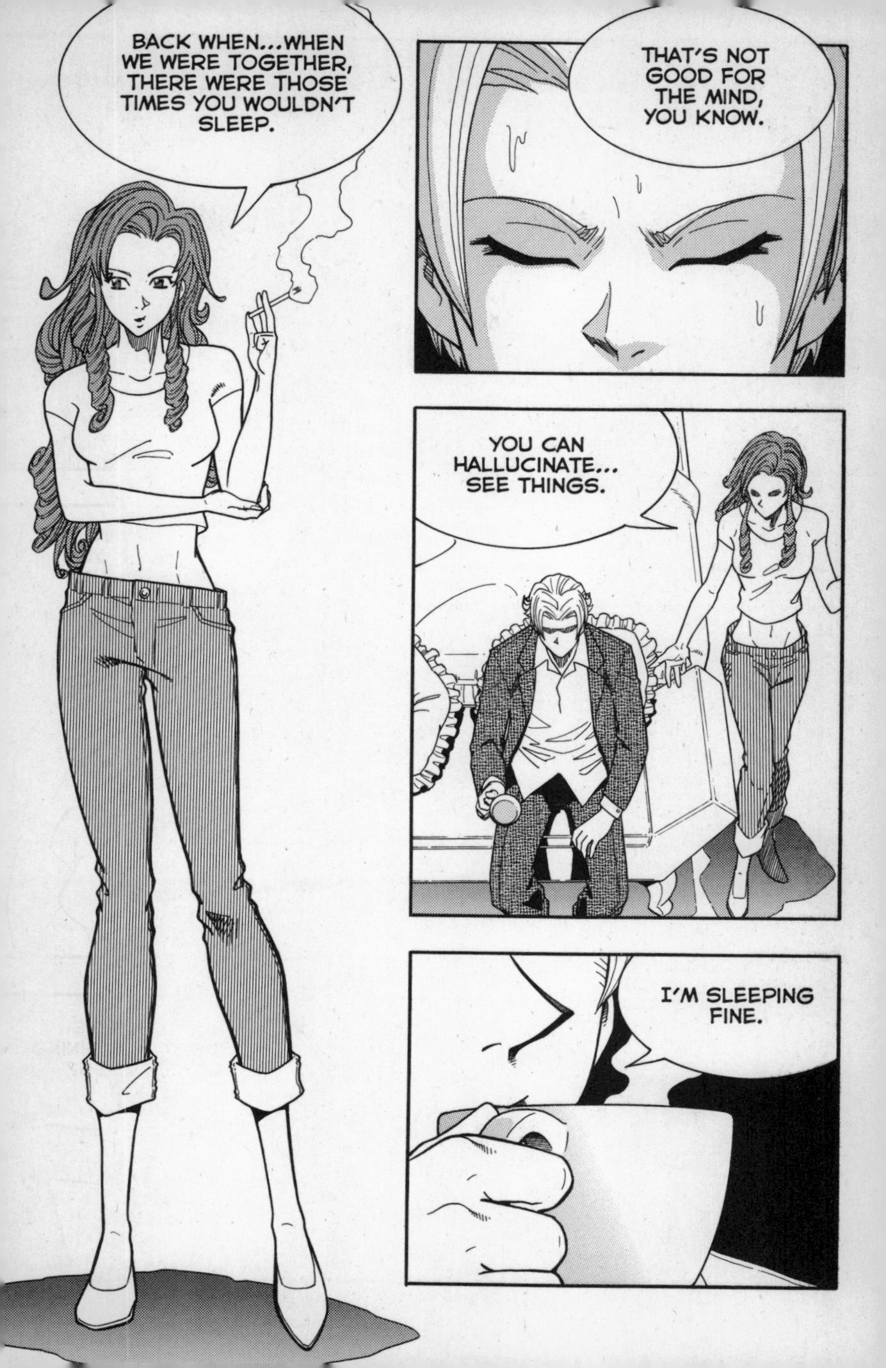
BACK WHEN...WHEN WE WERE TOGETHER, THERE WERE THOSE TIMES YOU WOULDN'T SLEEP.
THAT'S NOT GOOD FOR THE MIND, YOU KNOW.
YOU CAN HALLUCINATE... SEE THINGS.
I'M SLEEPING FINE.

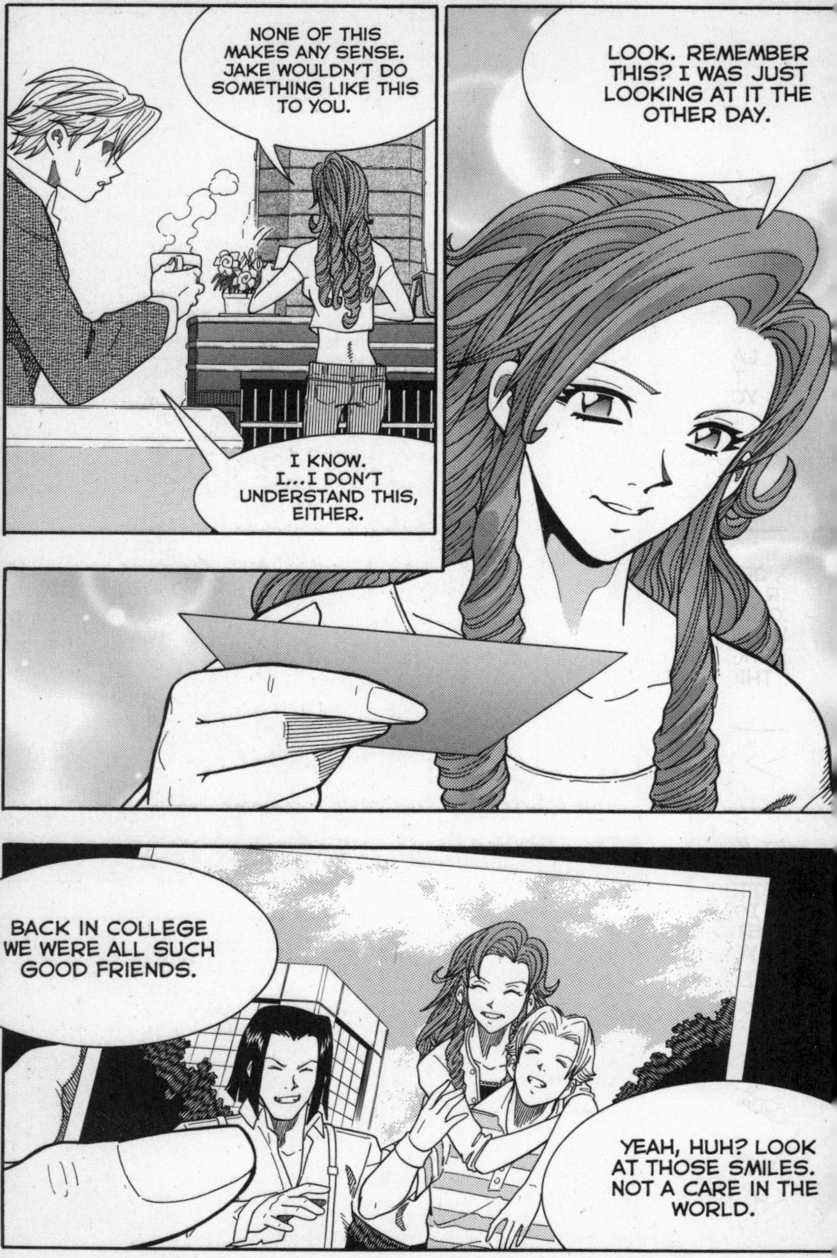
NONE OF THIS MAKES ANY SENSE. JAKE WOULDN'T DO SOMETHING LIKE THIS TO YOU.
I KNOW. I...I DON'T UNDERSTAND THIS, EITHER.
LOOK. REMEMBER THIS? I WAS JUST LOOKING AT IT THE OTHER DAY.
BACK IN COLLEGE WE WERE ALL SUCH GOOD FRIENDS.
YEAH, HUH? LOOK AT THOSE SMILES. NOT A CARE IN THE WORLD.

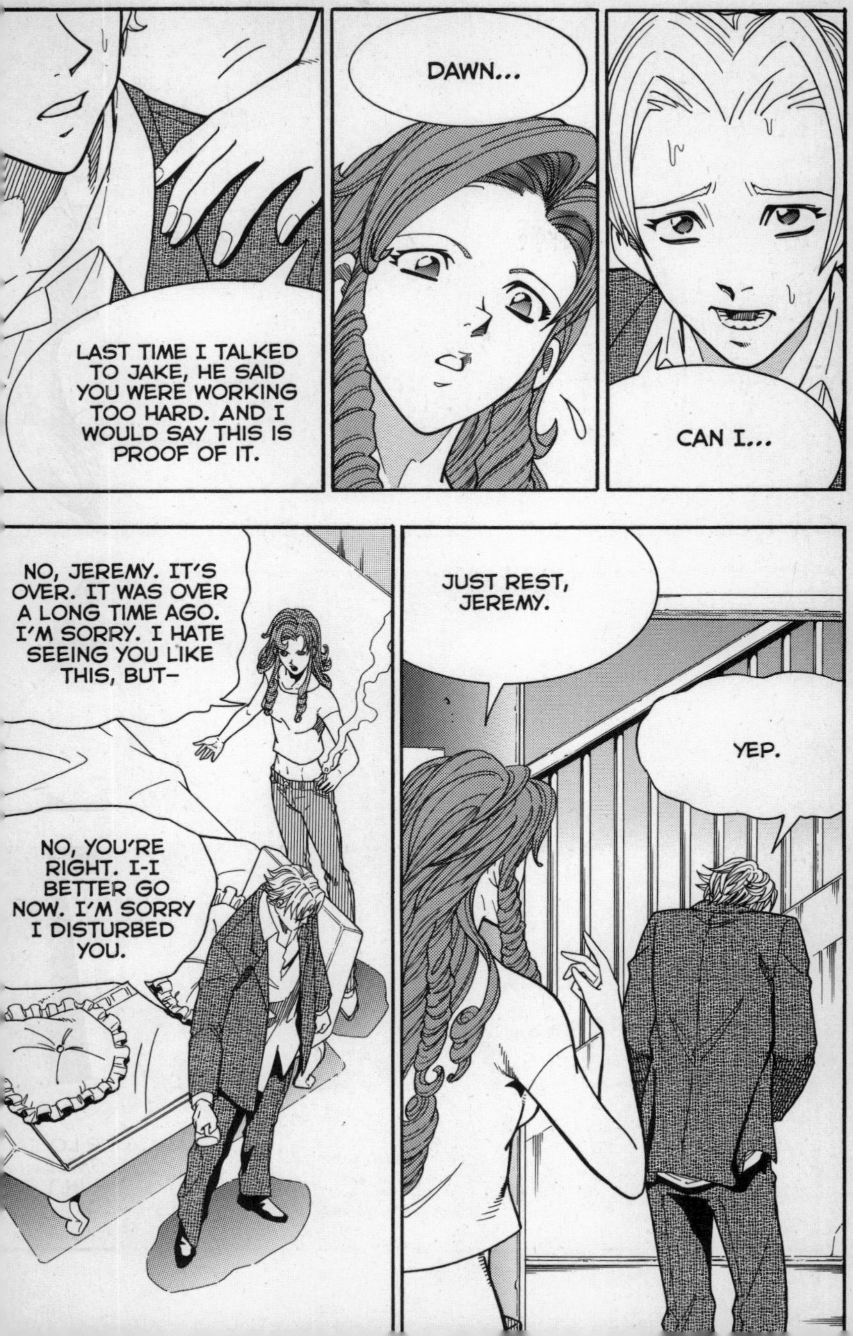
LAST TIME I TALKED TO JAKE, HE SAID YOU WERE WORKING TOO HARD. AND I WOULD SAY THIS IS PROOF OF IT.
DAWN...
CAN I...
NO, JEREMY. IT'S OVER. IT WAS OVER A LONG TIME AGO. I'M SORRY. I HATE SEEING YOU LIKE THIS, BUT–
NO, YOU'RE RIGHT. I-I BETTER GO NOW. I'M SORRY I DISTURBED YOU.
JUST REST, JEREMY.
YEP.

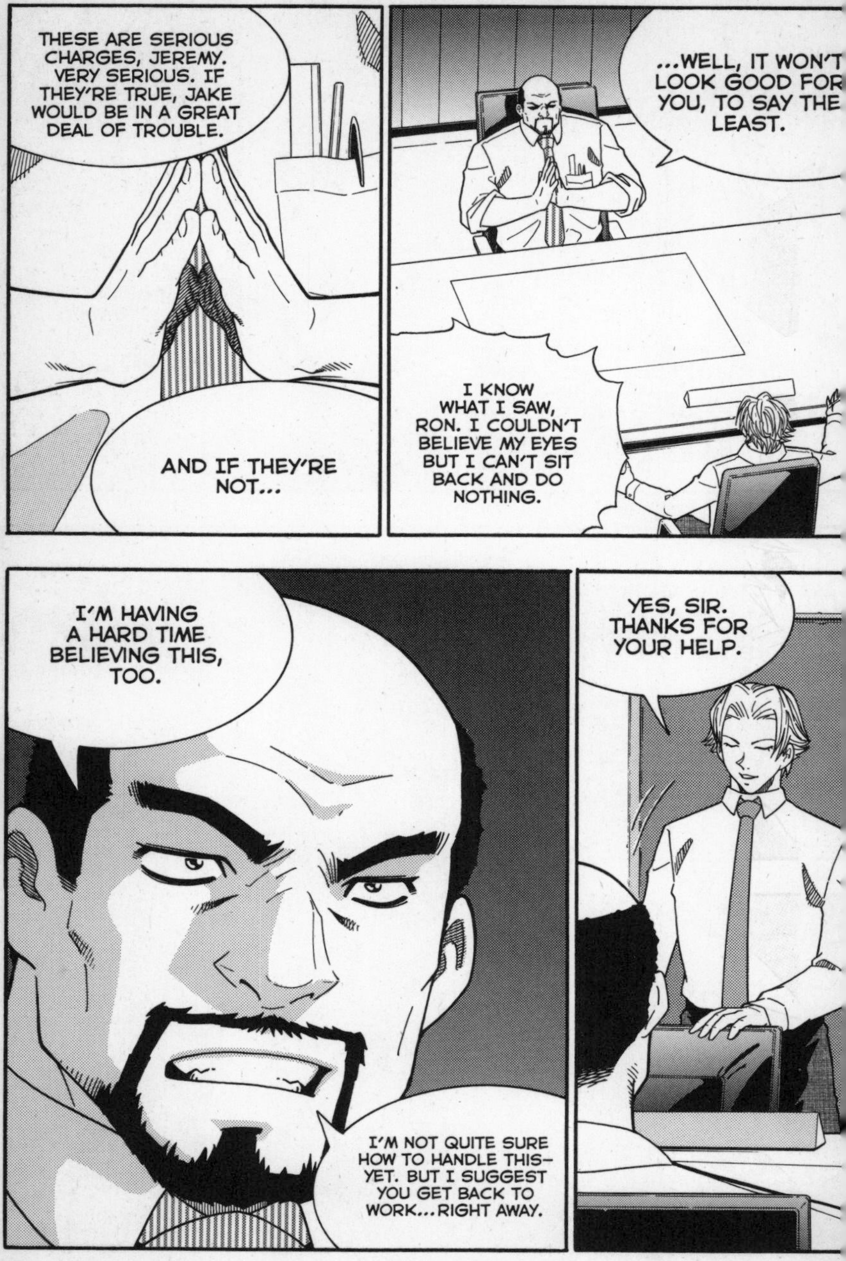

THESE ARE SERIOUS CHARGES, JEREMY. VERY SERIOUS. IF THEY'RE TRUE, JAKE WOULD BE IN A GREAT DEAL OF TROUBLE.
AND IF THEY'RE NOT...
...WELL, IT WON'T LOOK GOOD FOR YOU, TO SAY THE LEAST.
I KNOW WHAT I SAW, RON. I COULDN'T BELIEVE MY EYES BUT I CAN'T SIT BACK AND DO NOTHING.
I'M HAVING A HARD TIME BELIEVING THIS, TOO.
I'M NOT QUITE SURE HOW TO HANDLE THIS-YET. BUT I SUGGEST YOU GET BACK TO WORK...RIGHT AWAY.
YES, SIR. THANKS FOR YOUR HELP.

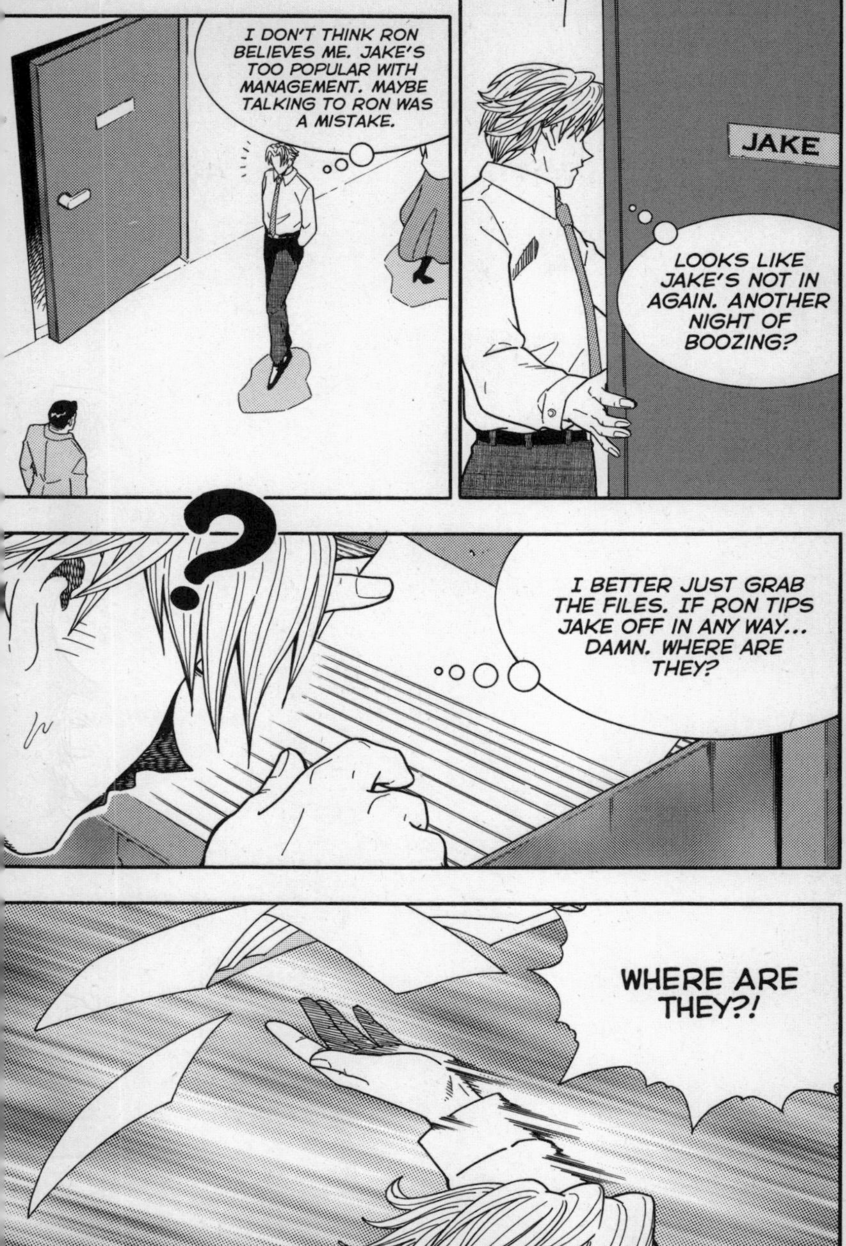
I DON'T THINK RON BELIEVES ME. JAKE'S TOO POPULAR WITH MANAGEMENT. MAYBE TALKING TO RON WAS A MISTAKE.
JAKE
LOOKS LIKE JAKE'S NOT IN AGAIN. ANOTHER NIGHT OF BOOZING?
I BETTER JUST GRAB THE FILES. IF RON TIPS JAKE OFF IN ANY WAY... DAMN. WHERE ARE THEY?
WHERE ARE THEY?!

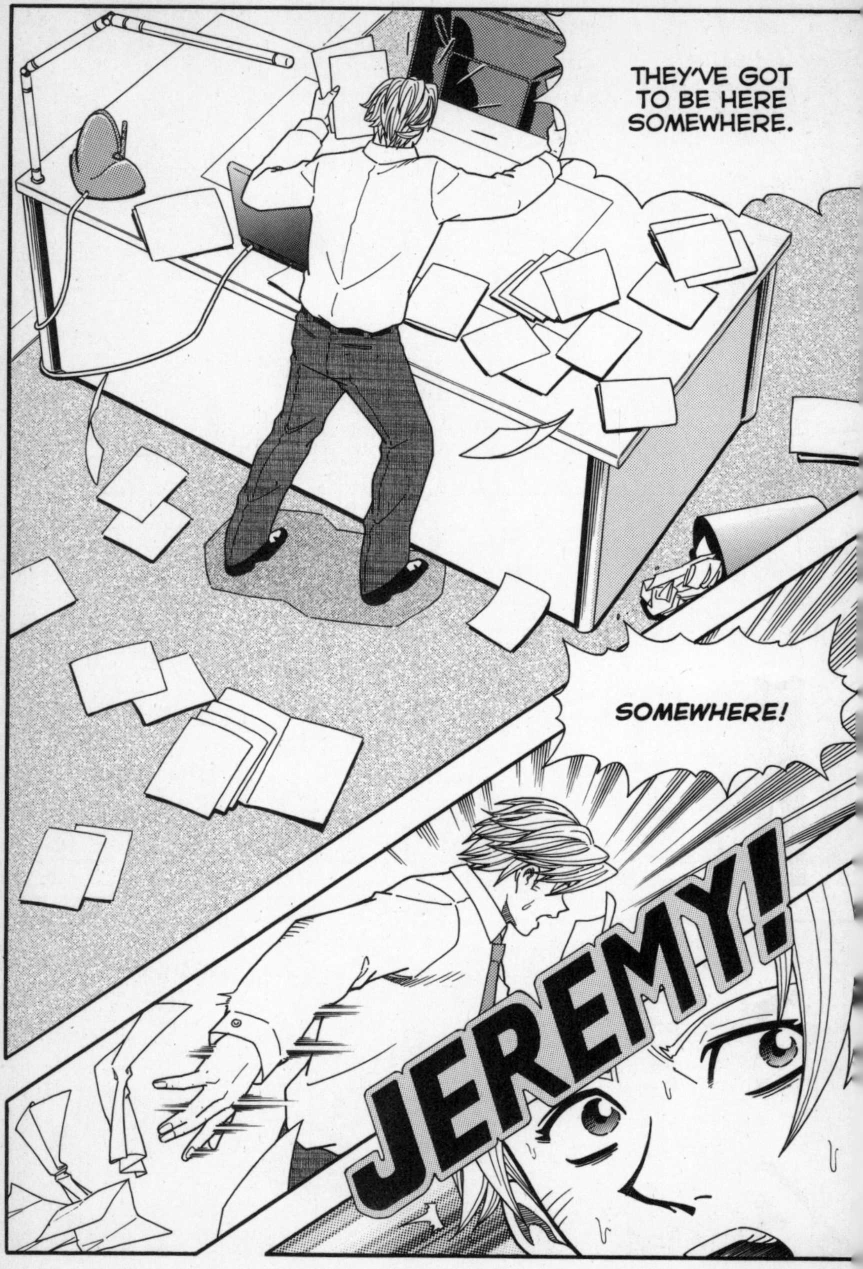
THEY'VE GOT TO BE HERE SOMEWHERE.
SOMEWHERE!
JEREMY!

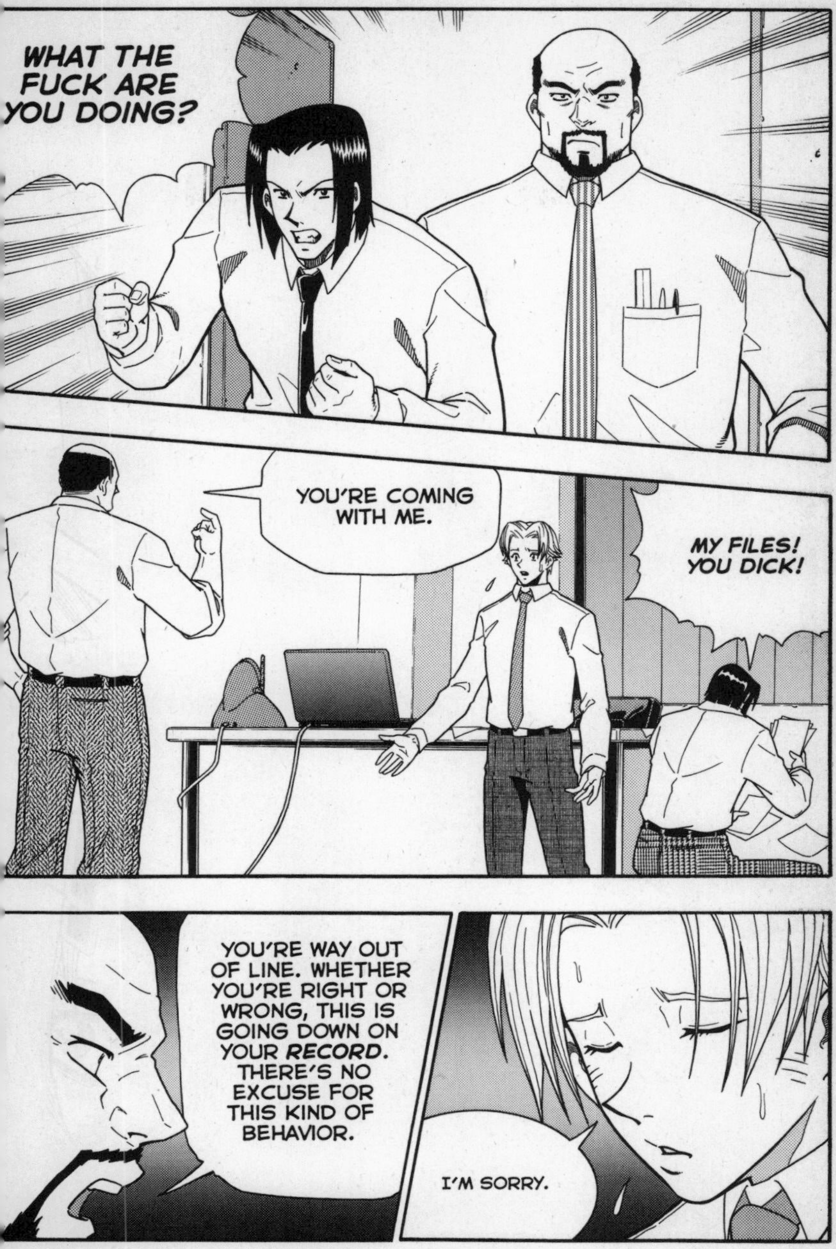
WHAT THE FUCK ARE YOU DOING?
YOU'RE COMING WITH ME.
MY FILES! YOU DICK!
YOU'RE WAY OUT OF LINE. WHETHER YOU'RE RIGHT OR WRONG, THIS IS GOING DOWN ON YOUR *RECORD*. THERE'S NO EXCUSE FOR THIS KIND OF BEHAVIOR.
I'M SORRY.

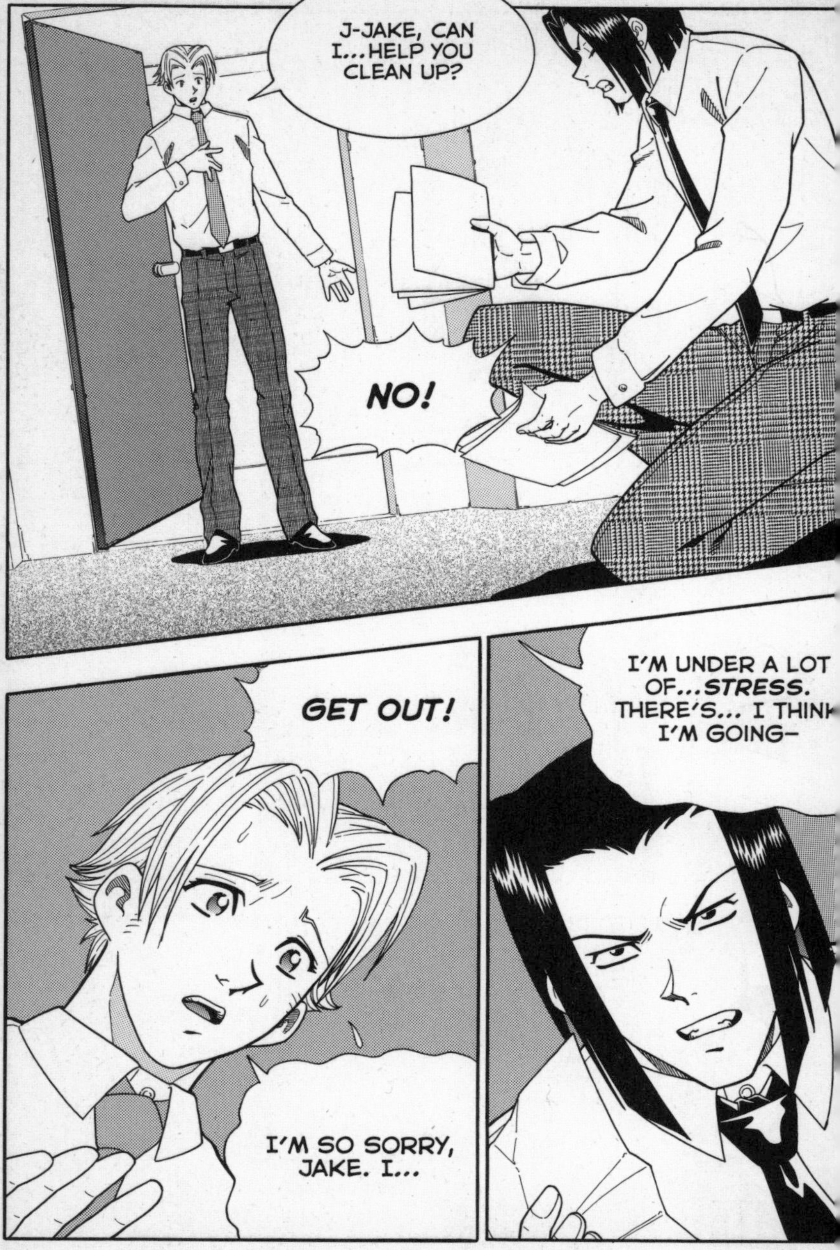

J-JAKE, CAN I...HELP YOU CLEAN UP?
NO!
GET OUT!
I'M SO SORRY, JAKE. I...
I'M UNDER A LOT OF...*STRESS*. THERE'S... I THINK I'M GOING–

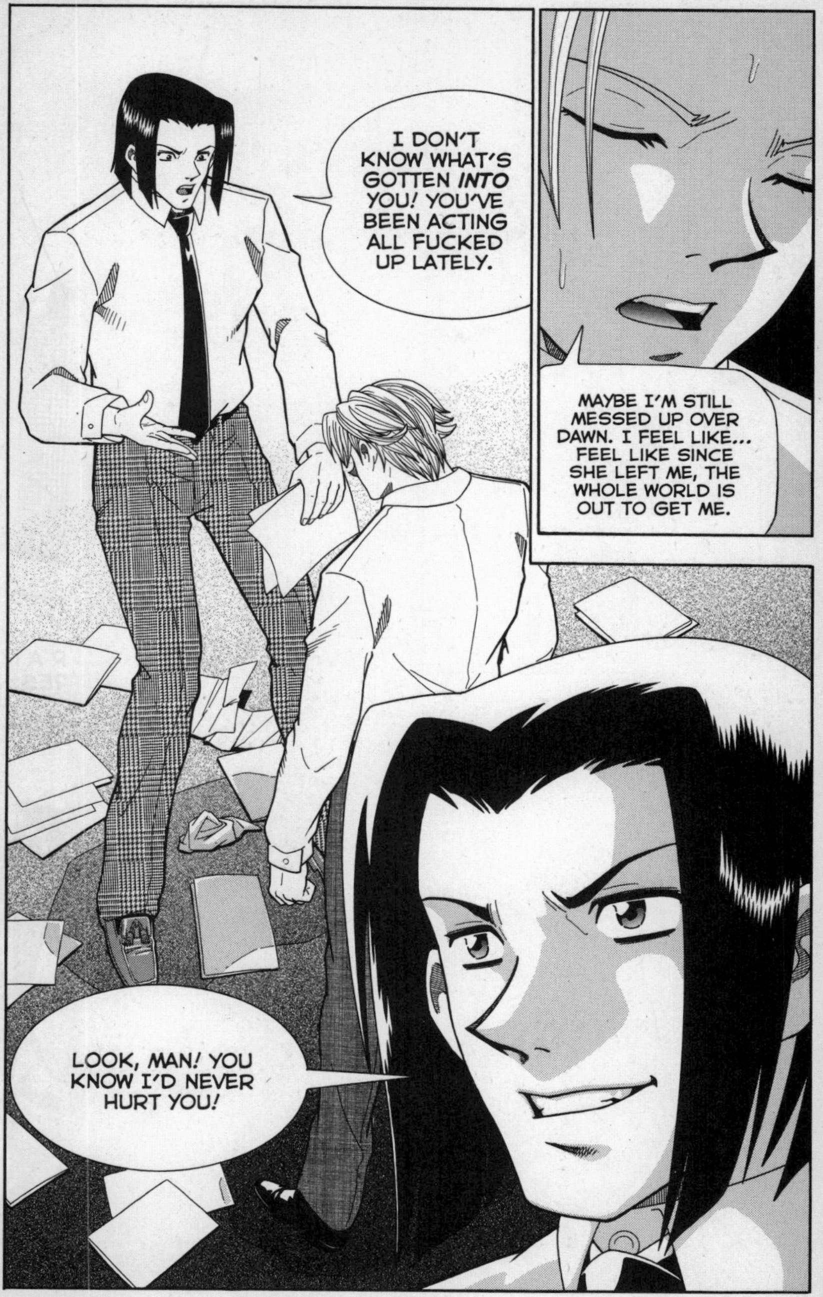
I DON'T KNOW WHAT'S GOTTEN *INTO* YOU! YOU'VE BEEN ACTING ALL FUCKED UP LATELY.
MAYBE I'M STILL MESSED UP OVER DAWN. I FEEL LIKE... FEEL LIKE SINCE SHE LEFT ME, THE WHOLE WORLD IS OUT TO GET ME.
LOOK, MAN! YOU KNOW I'D NEVER HURT YOU!

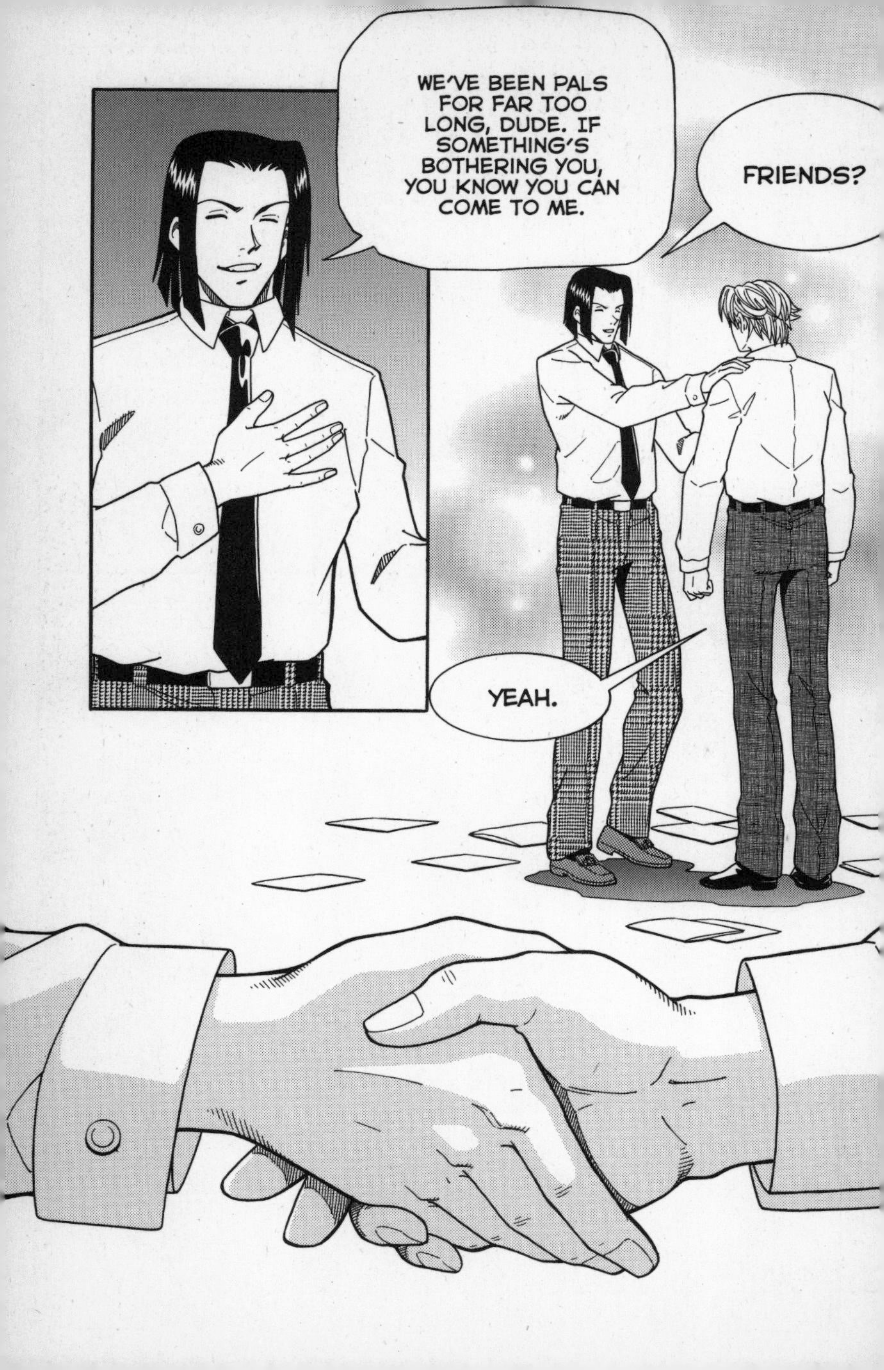
WE'VE BEEN PALS FOR FAR TOO LONG, DUDE. IF SOMETHING'S BOTHERING YOU, YOU KNOW YOU CAN COME TO ME.
FRIENDS?
YEAH.

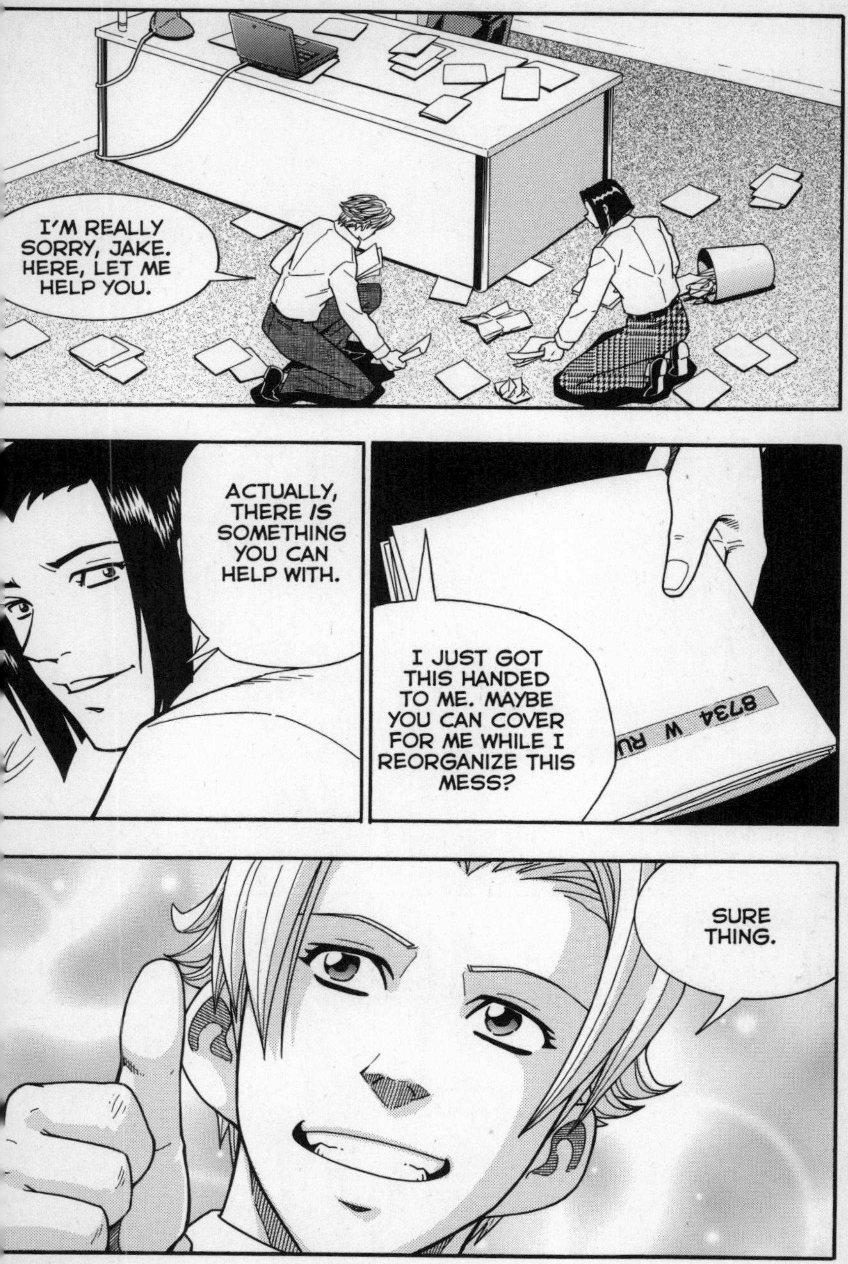
I'M REALLY SORRY, JAKE. HERE, LET ME HELP YOU.
ACTUALLY, THERE *IS* SOMETHING YOU CAN HELP WITH.
I JUST GOT THIS HANDED TO ME. MAYBE YOU CAN COVER FOR ME WHILE I REORGANIZE THIS MESS?
8734 W RU
SURE THING.

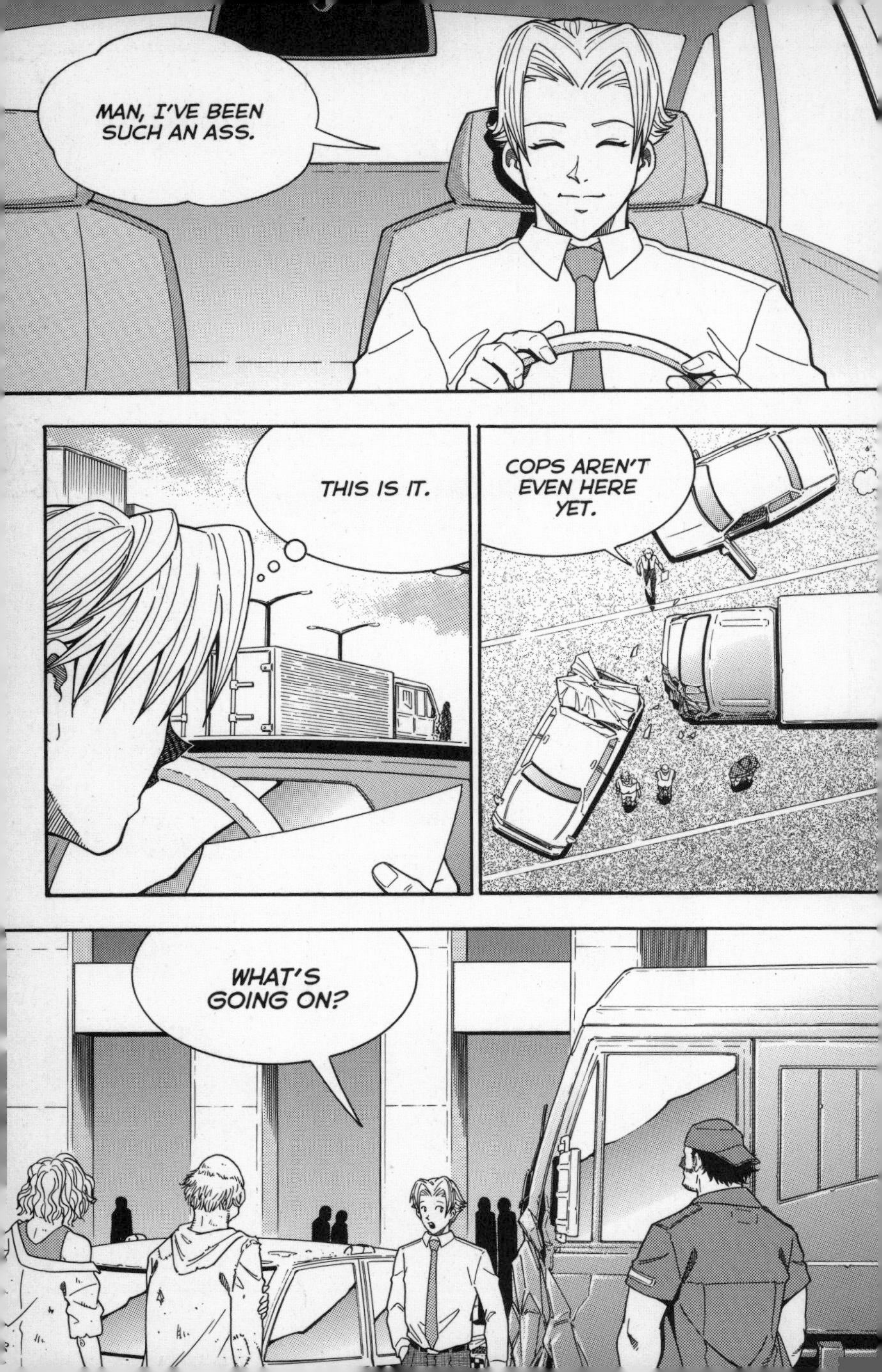
MAN, I'VE BEEN SUCH AN ASS.
THIS IS IT.
COPS AREN'T EVEN HERE YET.
WHAT'S GOING ON?

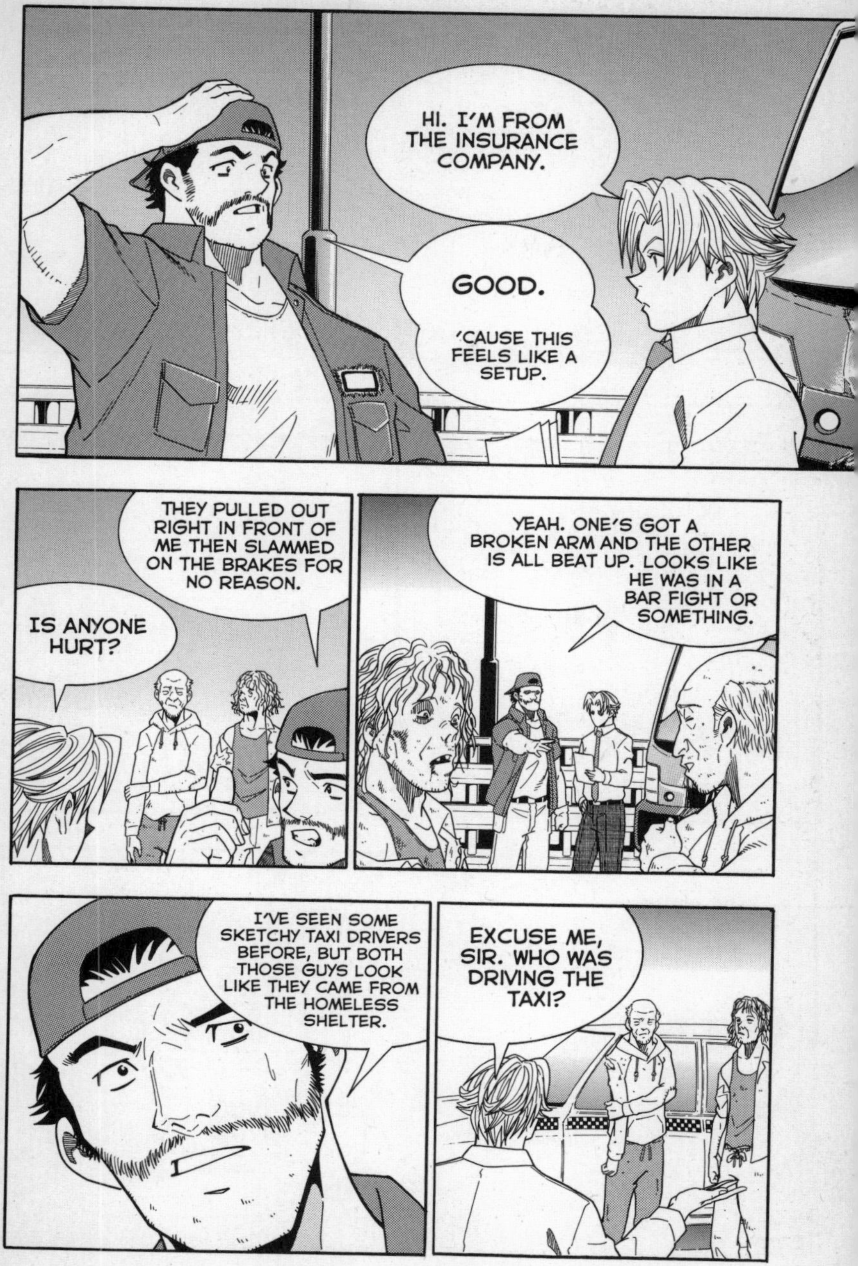
HI. I'M FROM THE INSURANCE COMPANY.
GOOD.
'CAUSE THIS FEELS LIKE A SETUP.
THEY PULLED OUT RIGHT IN FRONT OF ME THEN SLAMMED ON THE BRAKES FOR NO REASON.
IS ANYONE HURT?
YEAH. ONE'S GOT A BROKEN ARM AND THE OTHER IS ALL BEAT UP. LOOKS LIKE HE WAS IN A BAR FIGHT OR SOMETHING.
I'VE SEEN SOME SKETCHY TAXI DRIVERS BEFORE, BUT BOTH THOSE GUYS LOOK LIKE THEY CAME FROM THE HOMELESS SHELTER.
EXCUSE ME, SIR. WHO WAS DRIVING THE TAXI?

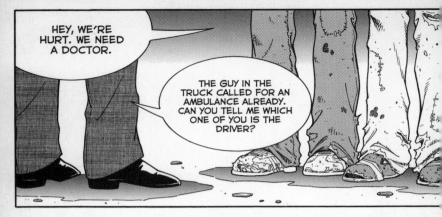

HEY, WE'RE HURT. WE NEED A DOCTOR.

THE GUY IN THE TRUCK CALLED FOR AN AMBULANCE ALREADY. CAN YOU TELL ME WHICH ONE OF YOU IS THE DRIVER?

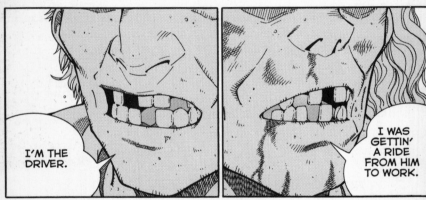

I'M THE DRIVER.

I WAS GETTIN' A RIDE FROM HIM TO WORK.

THIS ISN'T MAKING ANY SENSE.

100

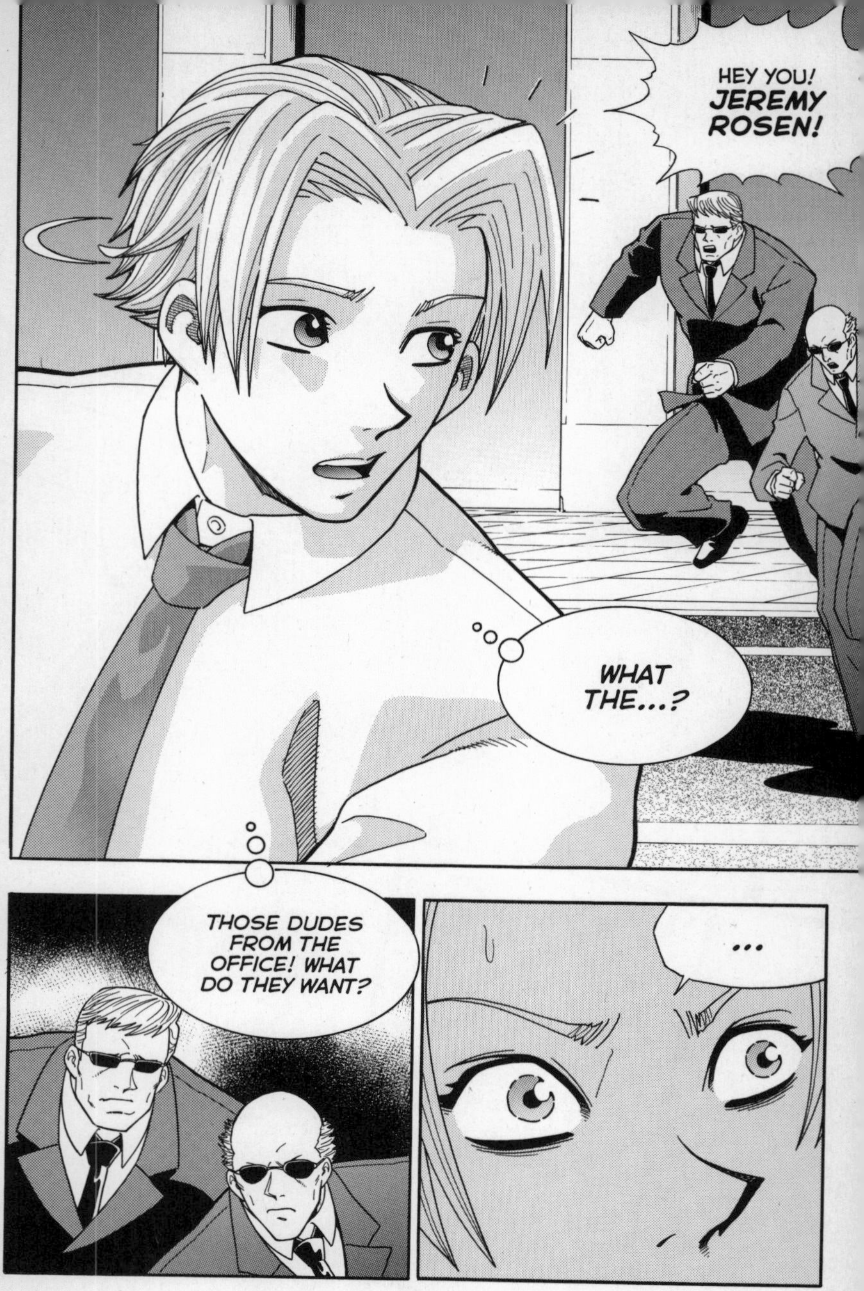
HEY YOU! JEREMY ROSEN!
WHAT THE...?
THOSE DUDES FROM THE OFFICE! WHAT DO THEY WANT?
...

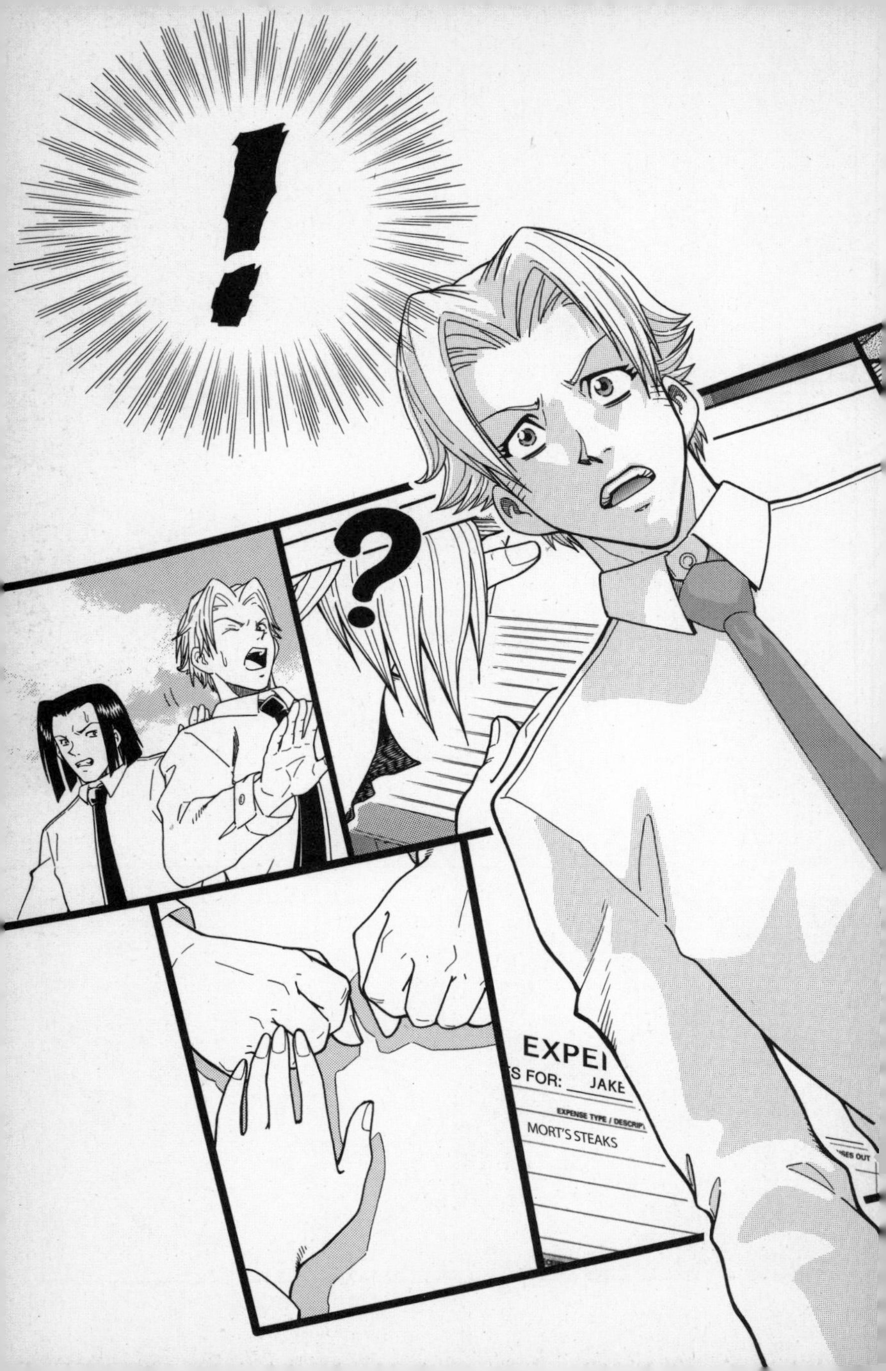
!
?
EXPE
S FOR: JAKE
EXPENSE TYPE / DESCRI
MORT'S STEAKS

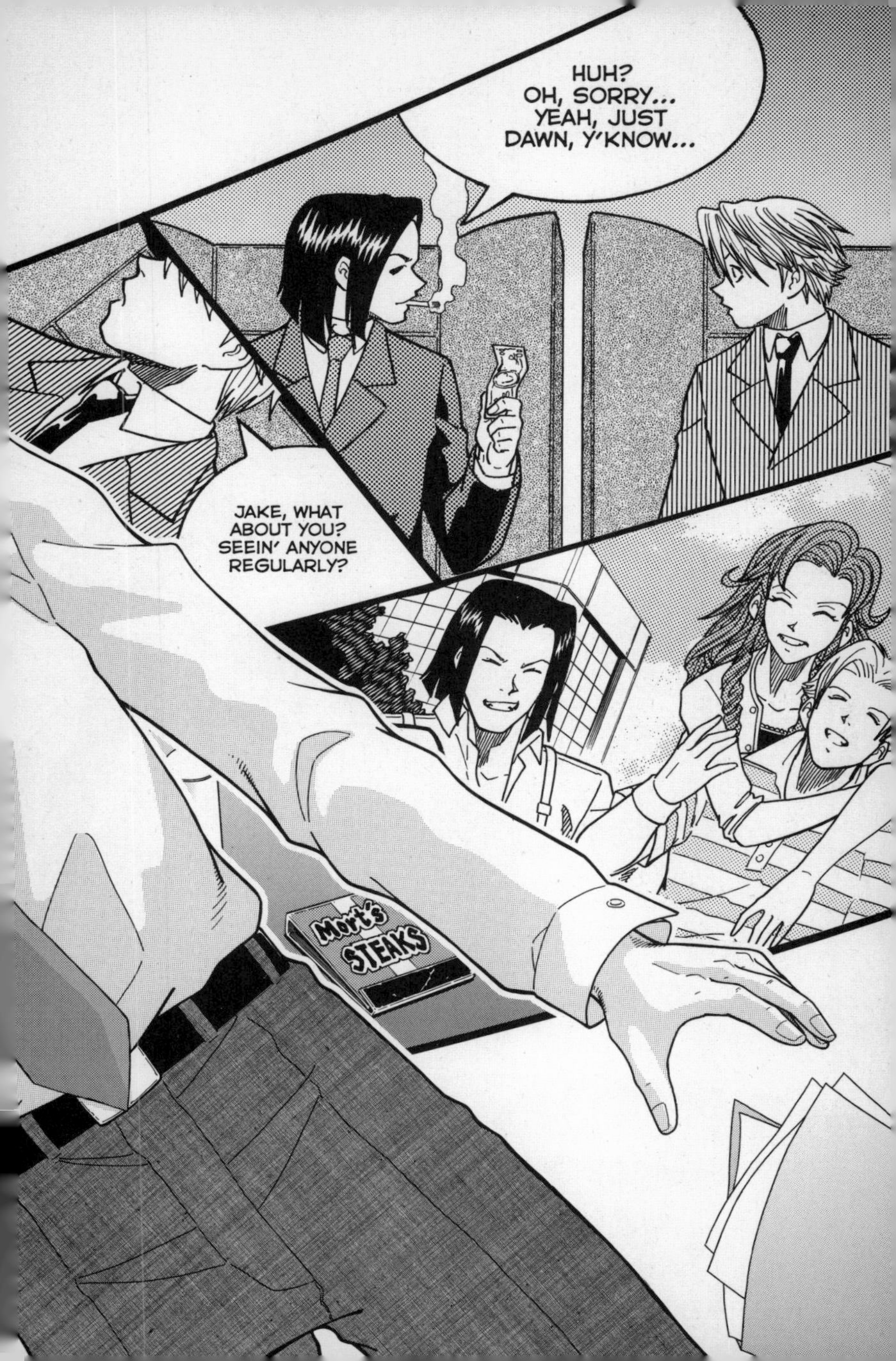
HUH? OH, SORRY... YEAH, JUST DAWN, Y'KNOW...
JAKE, WHAT ABOUT YOU? SEEIN' ANYONE REGULARLY?
Mort's STEAKS

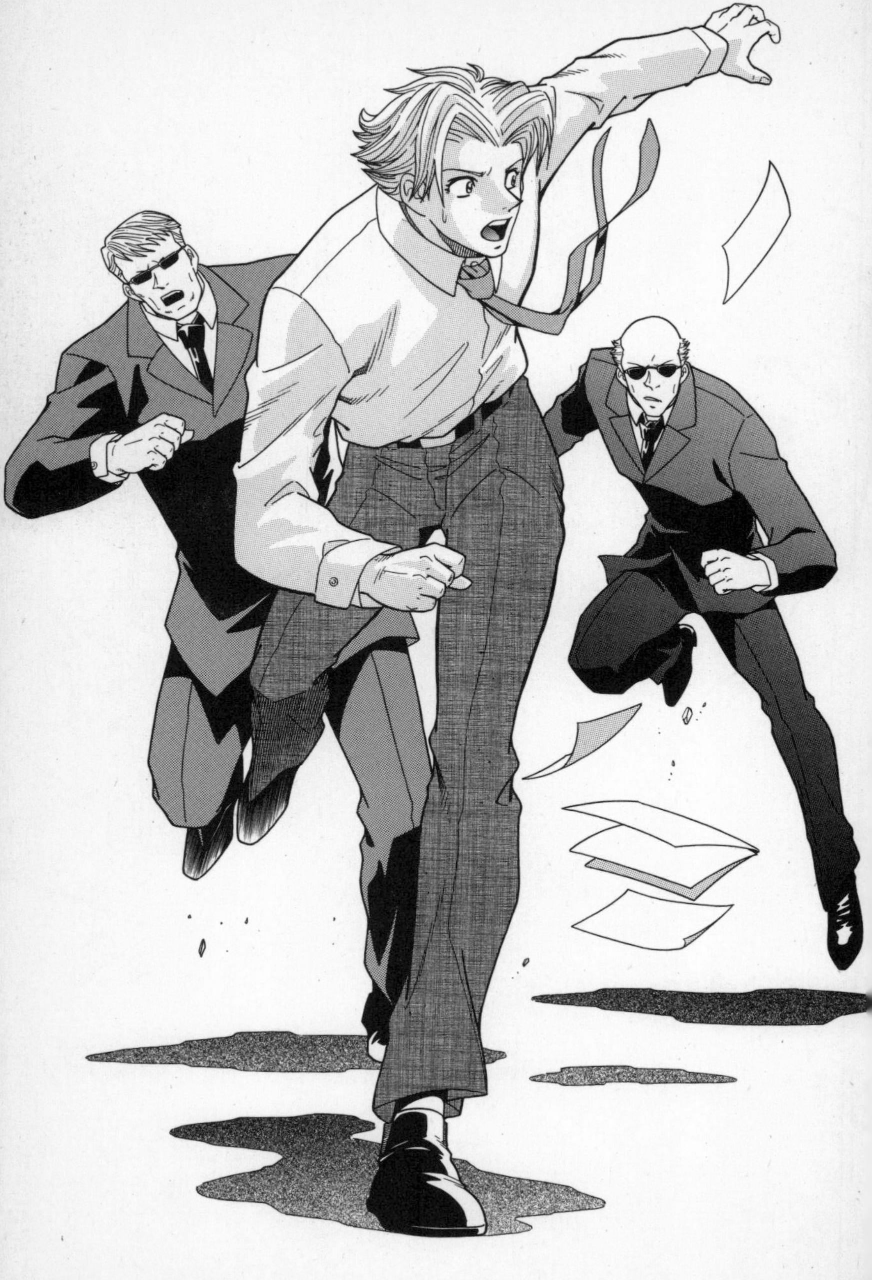

# Juror 13™

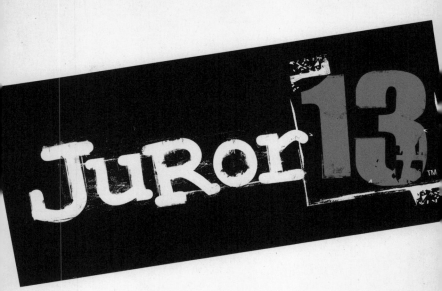

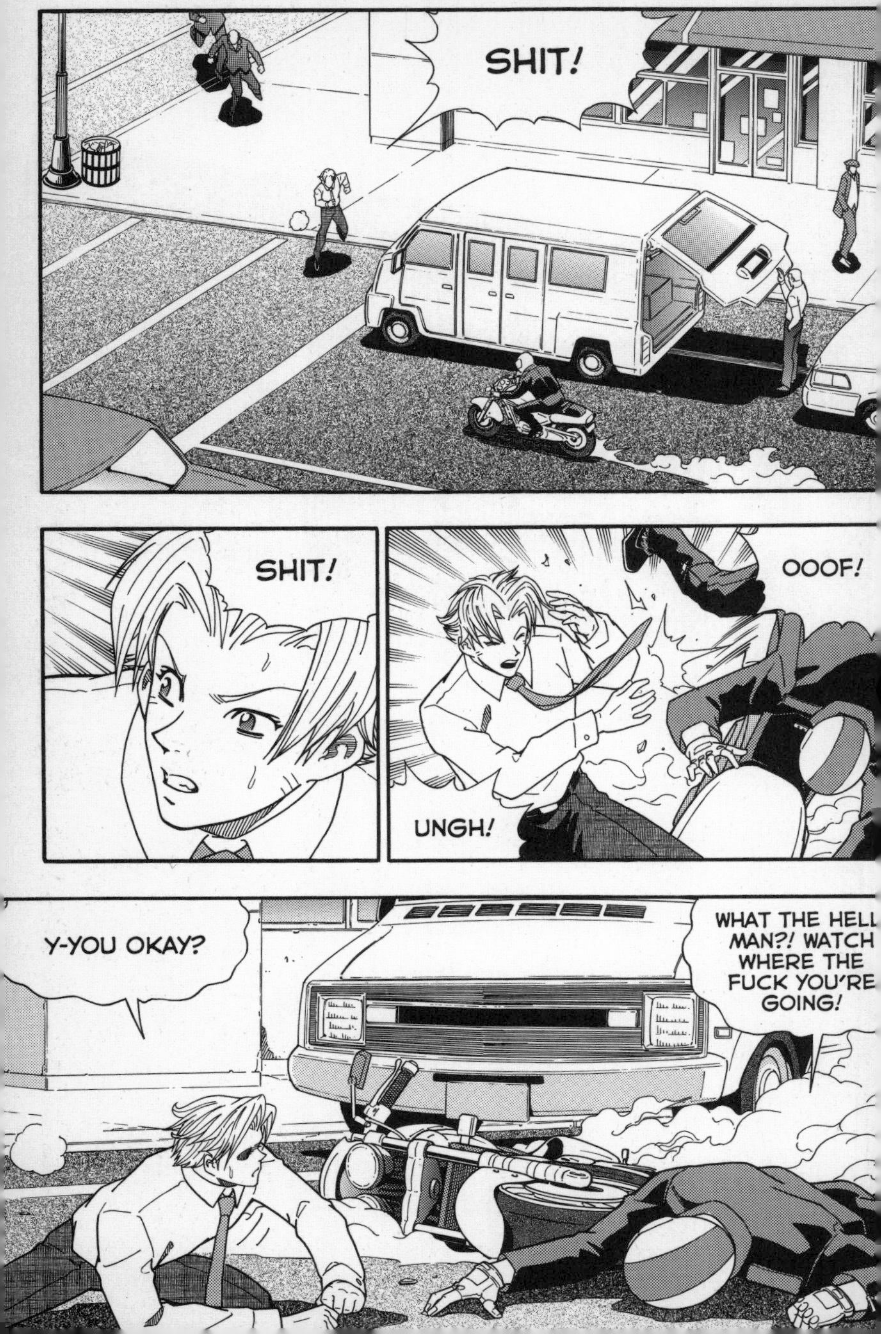
SHIT!
SHIT!
OOOF!
UNGH!
Y-YOU OKAY?
WHAT THE HELL MAN?! WATCH WHERE THE FUCK YOU'RE GOING!

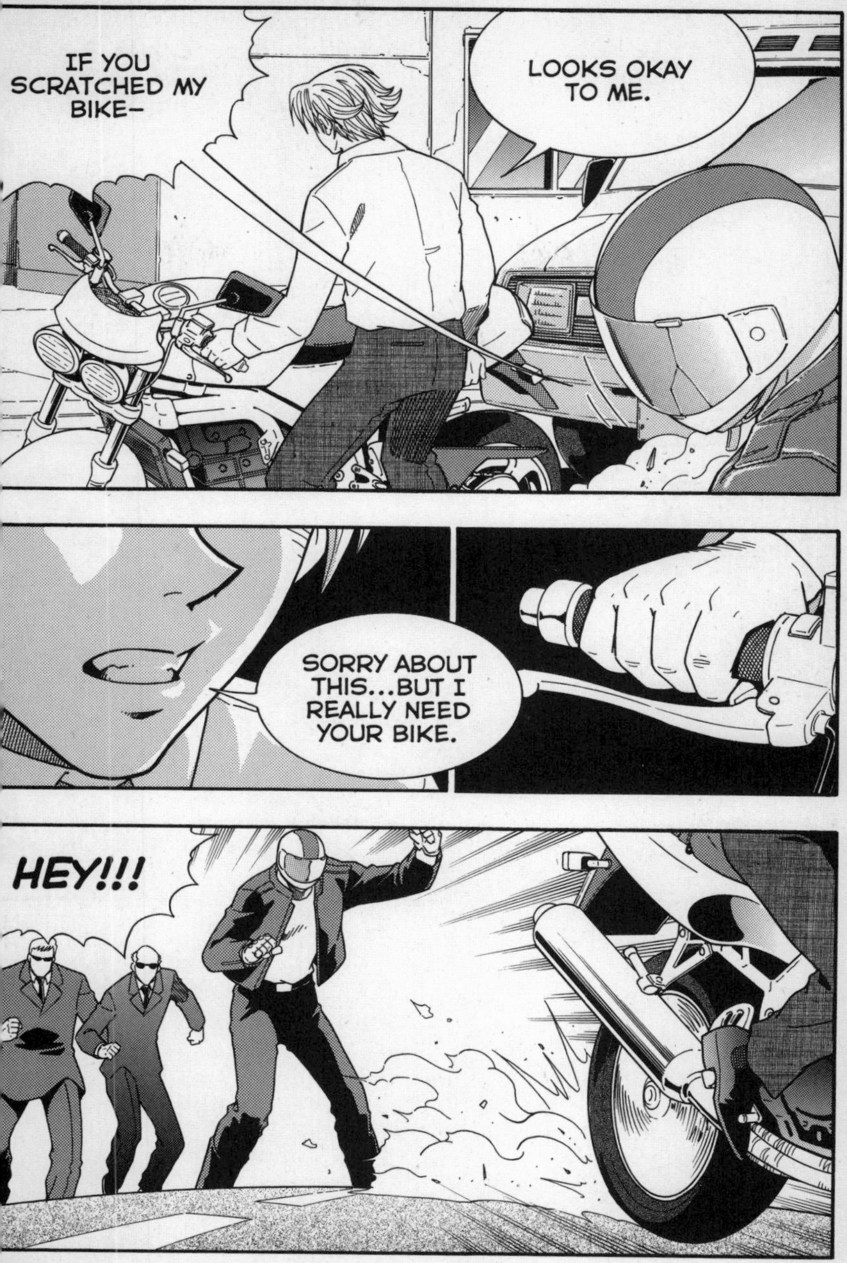

IF YOU SCRATCHED MY BIKE–
LOOKS OKAY TO ME.
SORRY ABOUT THIS...BUT I REALLY NEED YOUR BIKE.
HEY!!!

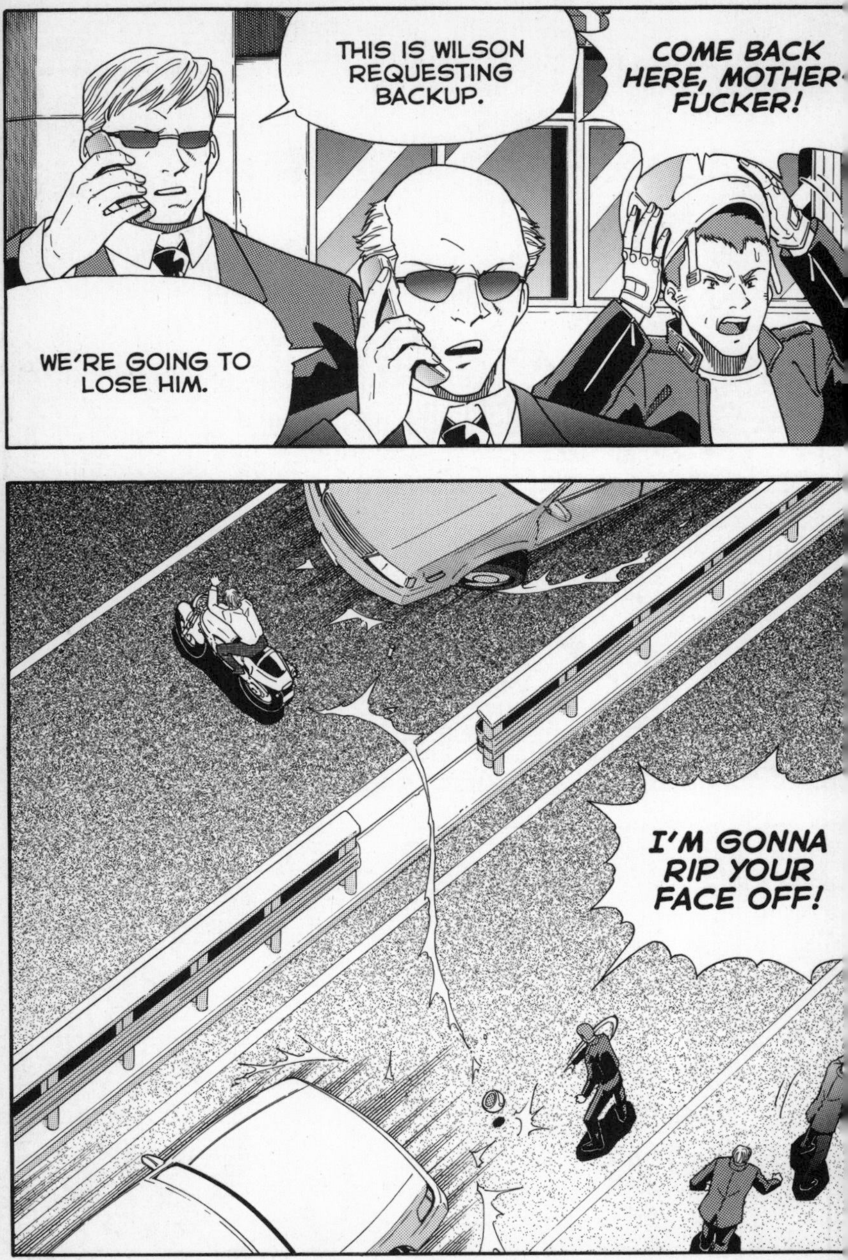
THIS IS WILSON REQUESTING BACKUP.
COME BACK HERE, MOTHER-FUCKER!
WE'RE GOING TO LOSE HIM.
I'M GONNA RIP YOUR FACE OFF!

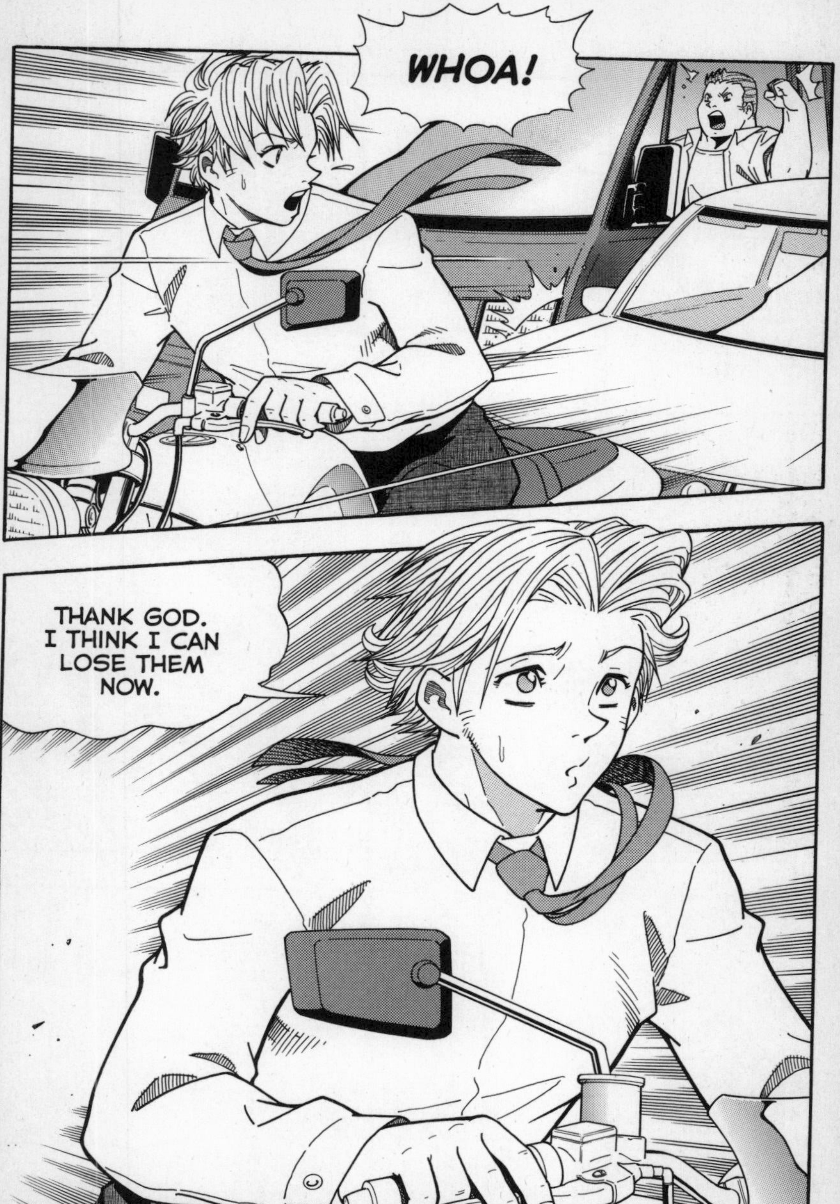
WHOA!
THANK GOD. I THINK I CAN LOSE THEM NOW.

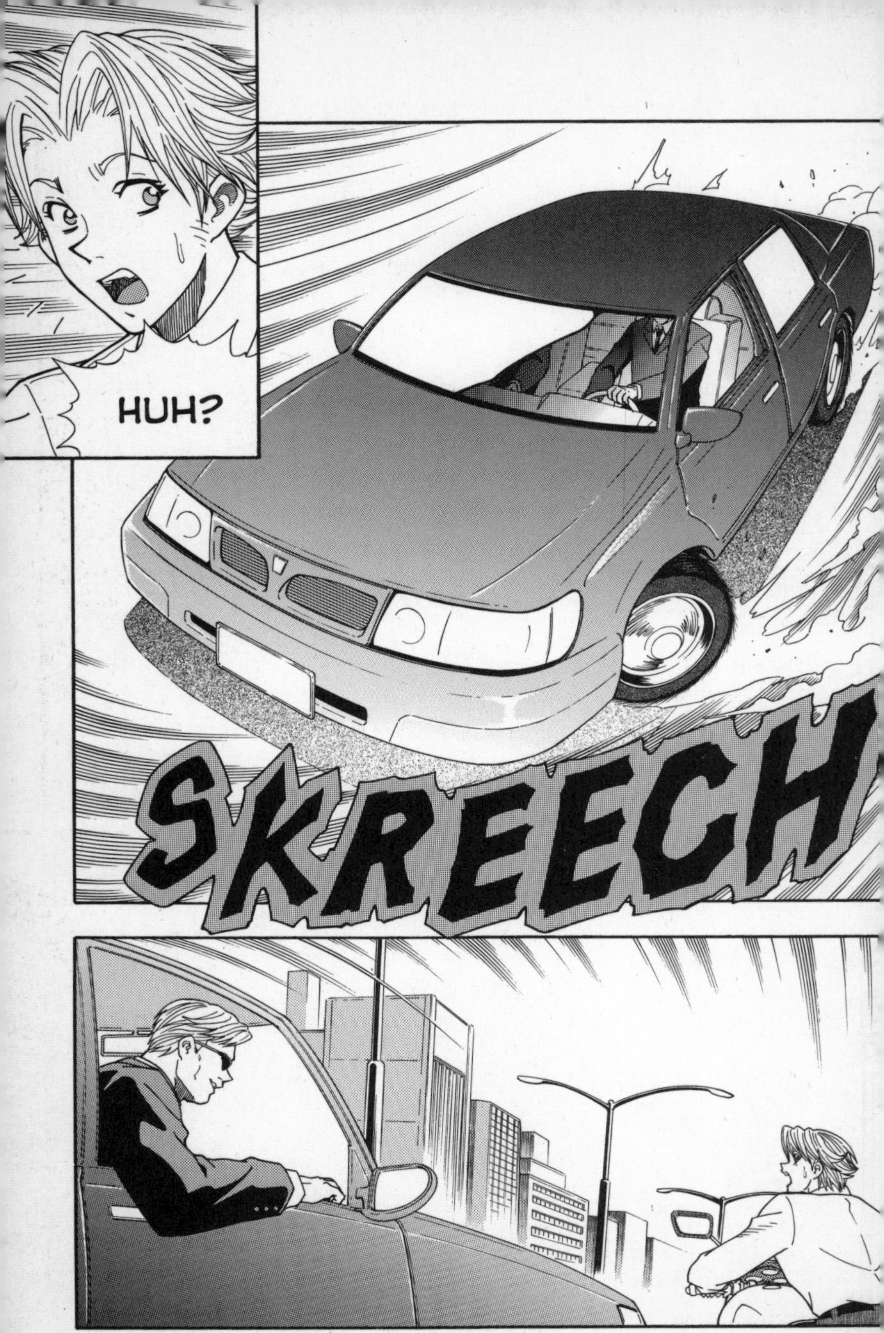
HUH?
SKREECH

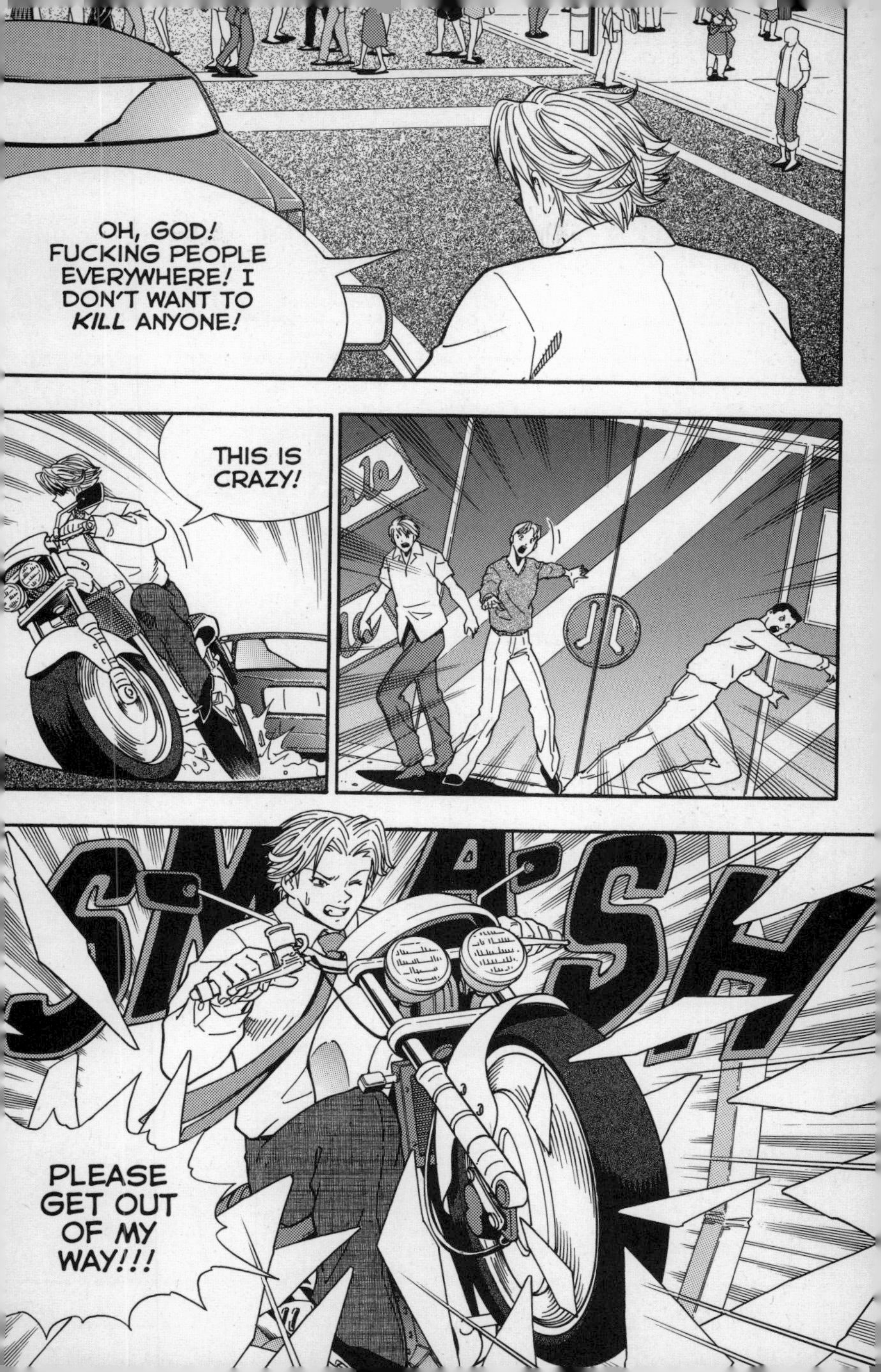
OH, GOD! FUCKING PEOPLE EVERYWHERE! I DON'T WANT TO *KILL* ANYONE!
THIS IS CRAZY!
SMASH
PLEASE GET OUT OF MY WAY!!!

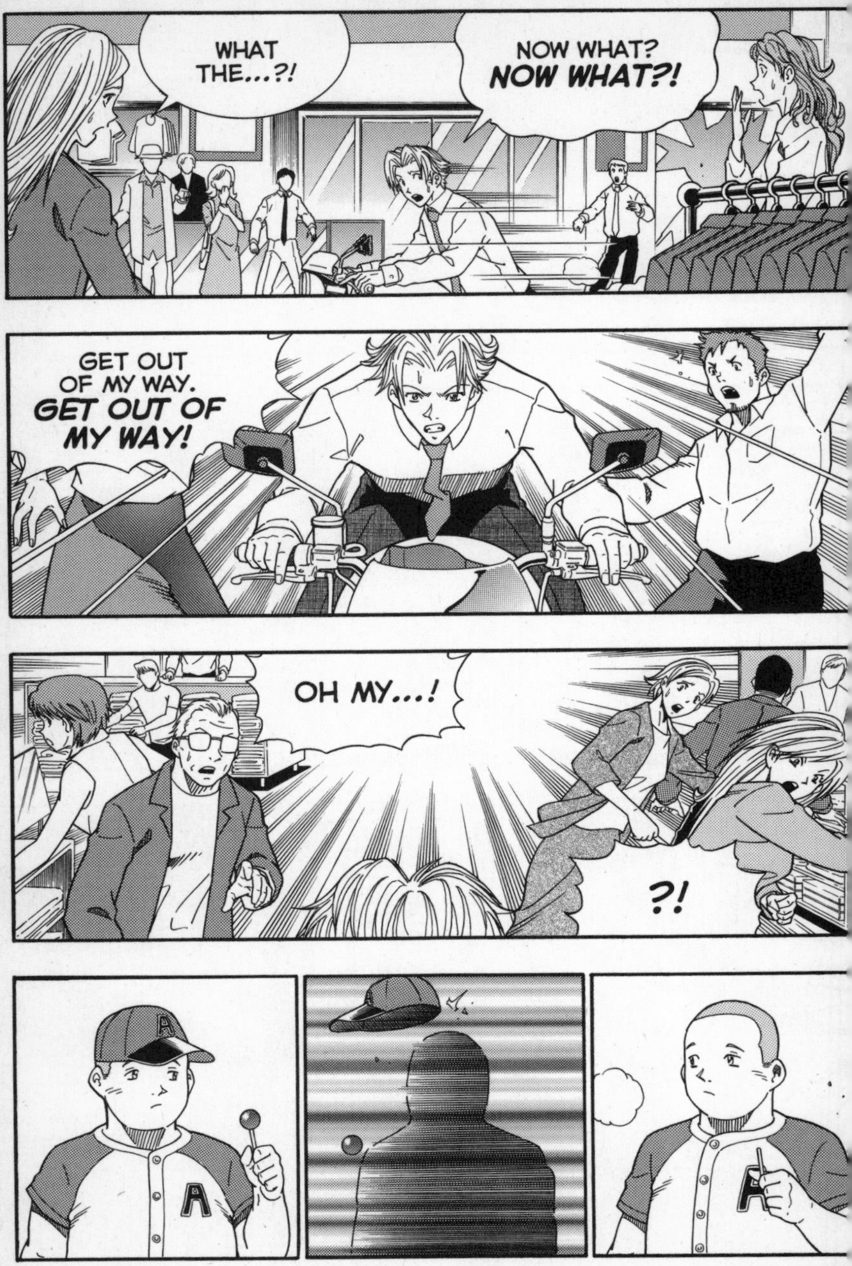
WHAT THE...?!
NOW WHAT? NOW WHAT?!
GET OUT OF MY WAY. GET OUT OF MY WAY!
OH MY...!
?!

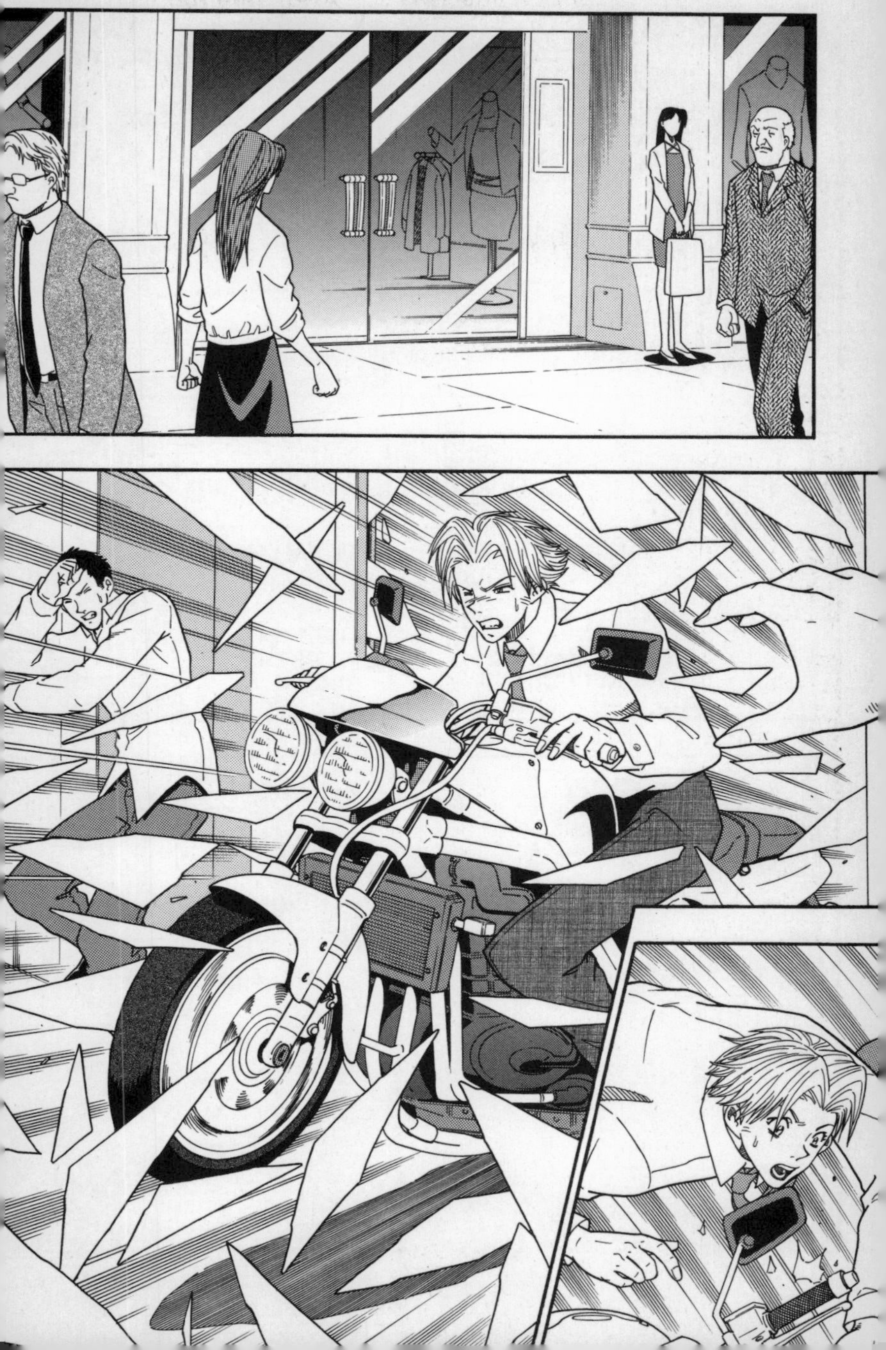

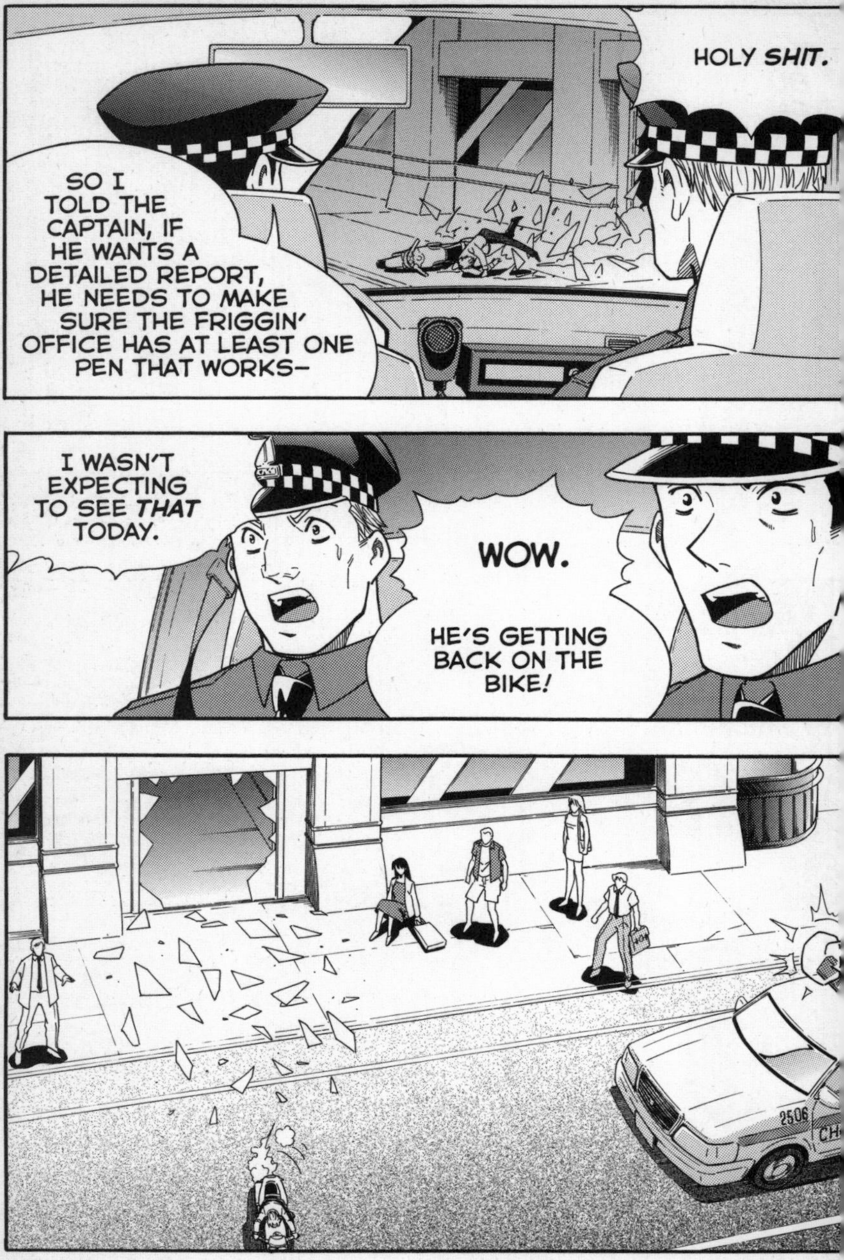
SO I TOLD THE CAPTAIN, IF HE WANTS A DETAILED REPORT, HE NEEDS TO MAKE SURE THE FRIGGIN' OFFICE HAS AT LEAST ONE PEN THAT WORKS–
HOLY *SHIT.*
I WASN'T EXPECTING TO SEE *THAT* TODAY.
WOW.
HE'S GETTING BACK ON THE BIKE!
2506

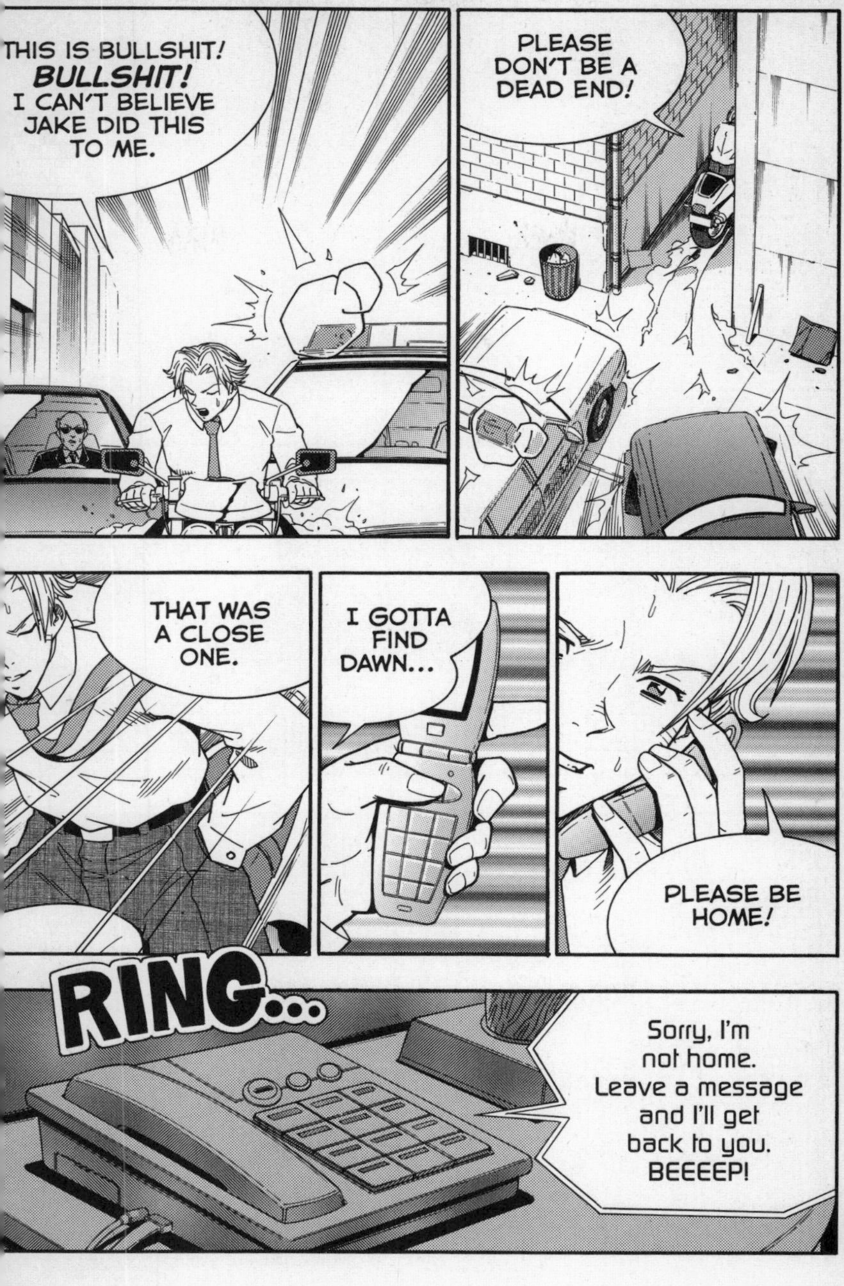

THIS IS BULLSHIT! ***BULLSHIT!*** I CAN'T BELIEVE JAKE DID THIS TO ME.
PLEASE DON'T BE A DEAD END!
THAT WAS A CLOSE ONE.
I GOTTA FIND DAWN...
PLEASE BE HOME!
RING...
Sorry, I'm not home. Leave a message and I'll get back to you. BEEEEP!

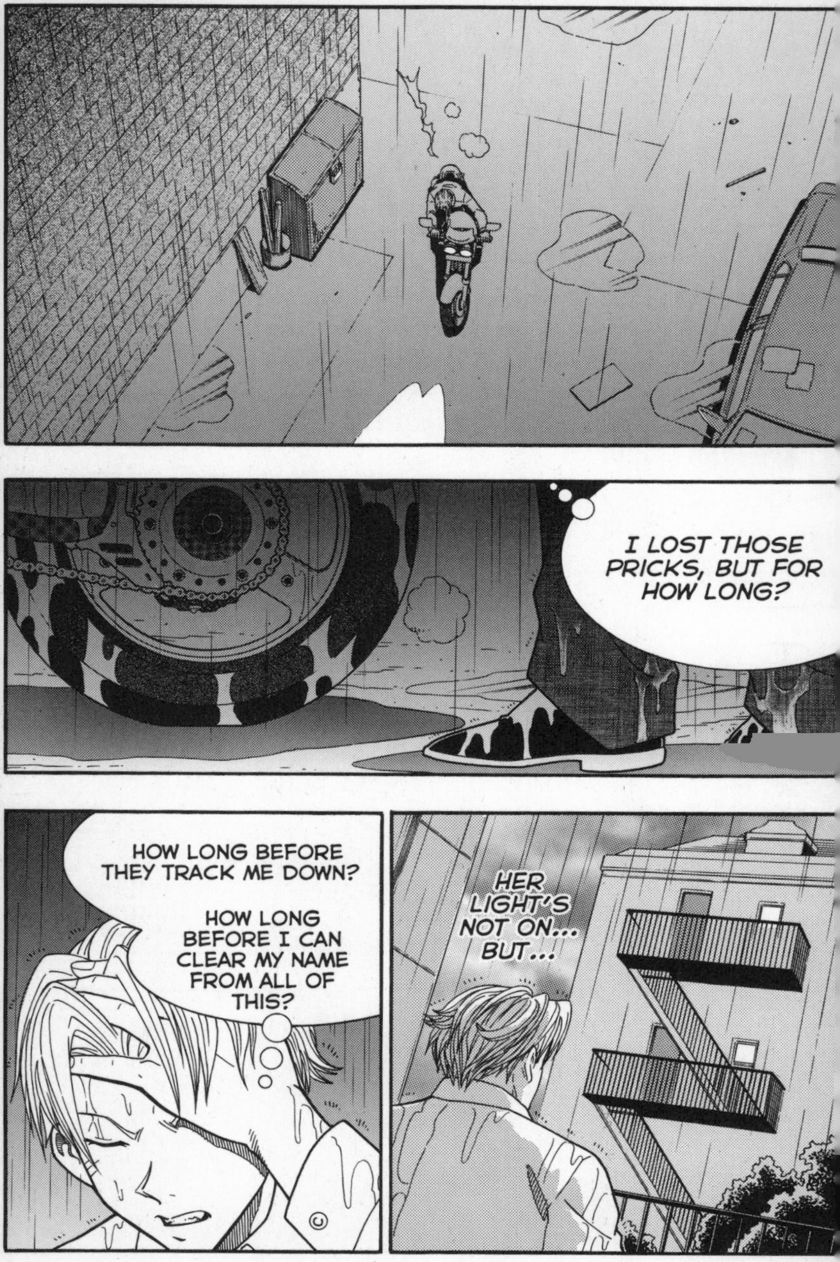
I LOST THOSE PRICKS, BUT FOR HOW LONG?
HOW LONG BEFORE THEY TRACK ME DOWN?
HOW LONG BEFORE I CAN CLEAR MY NAME FROM ALL OF THIS?
HER LIGHT'S NOT ON... BUT...

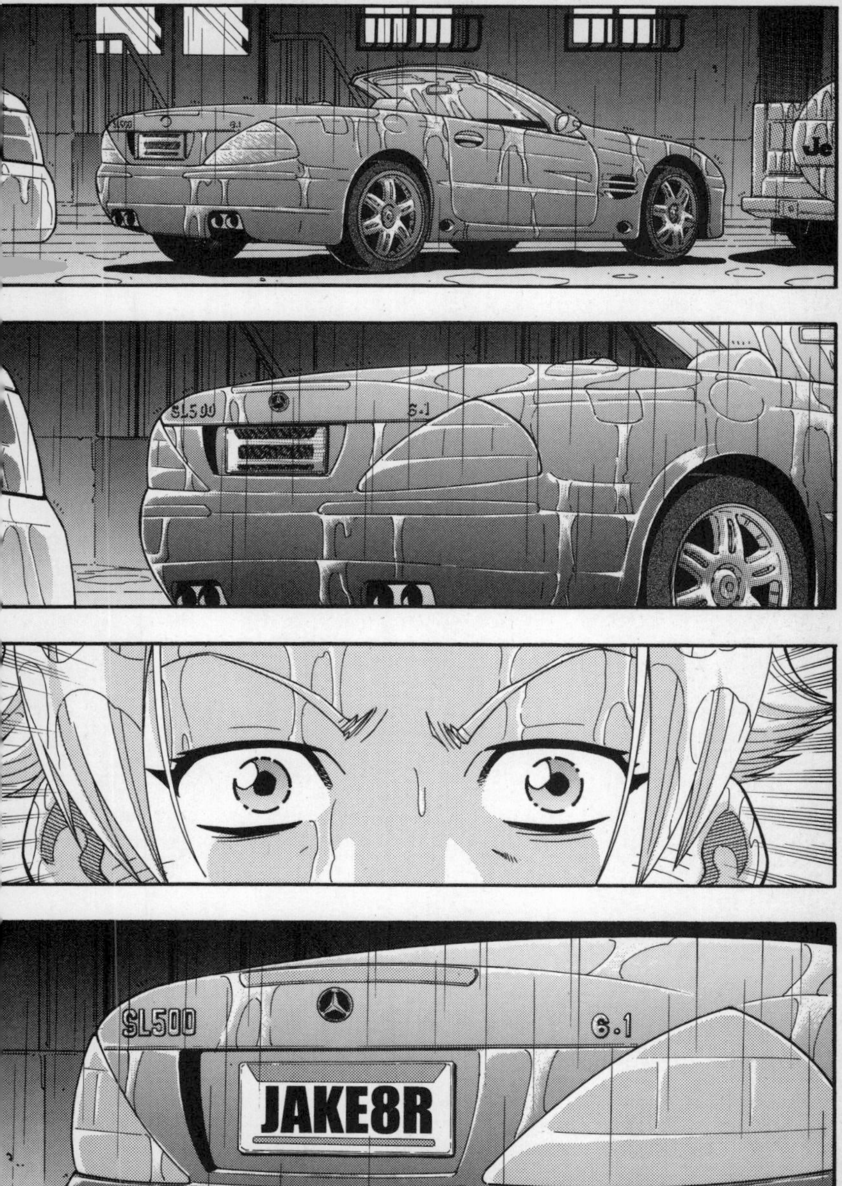
SL500
6.1
SL500
6.1
JAKE8R

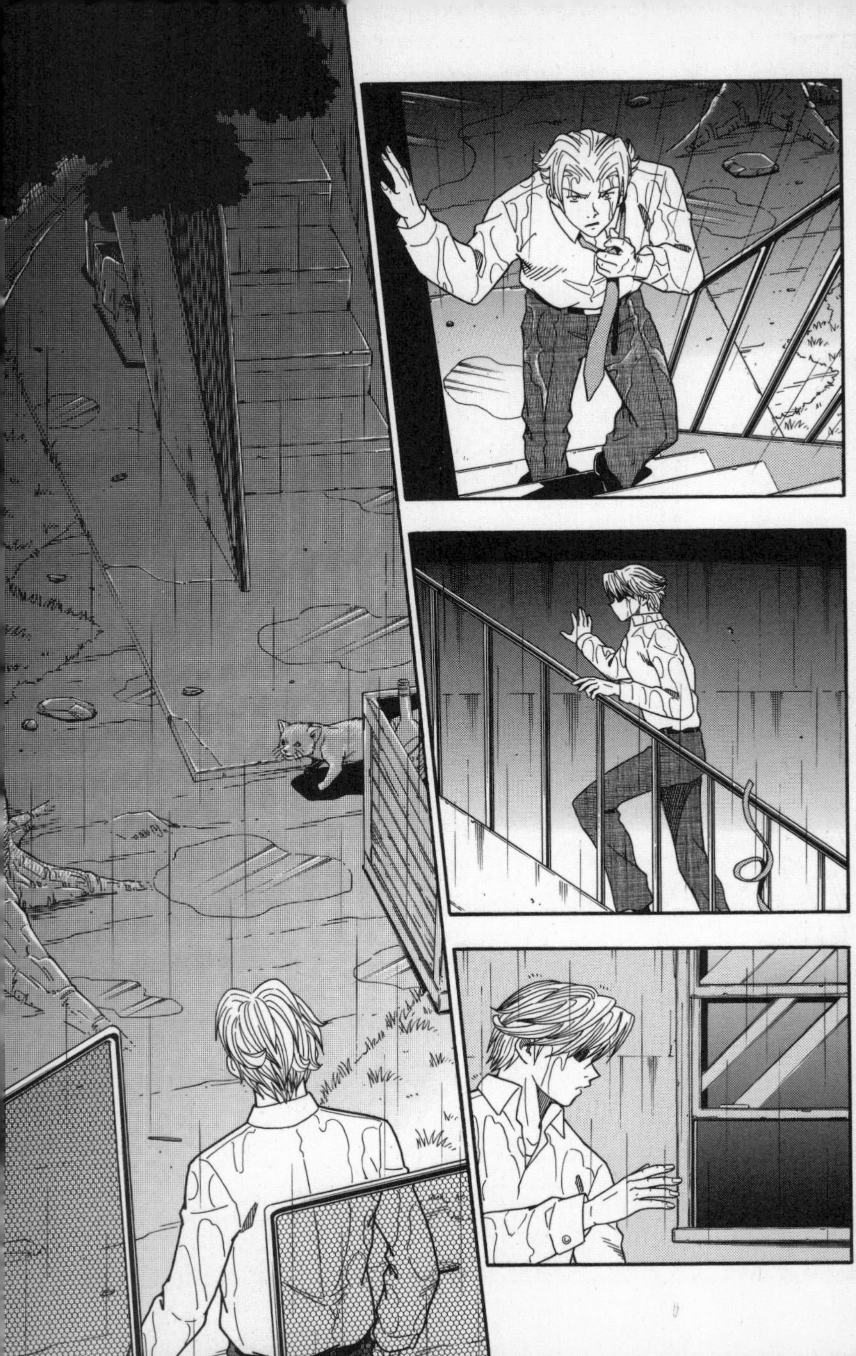

ARE YOU SURE EVERYTHING'S COOL?

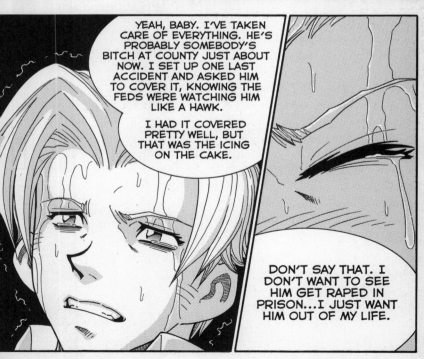

YEAH, BABY. I'VE TAKEN CARE OF EVERYTHING. HE'S PROBABLY SOMEBODY'S BITCH AT COUNTY JUST ABOUT NOW. I SET UP ONE LAST ACCIDENT AND ASKED HIM TO COVER IT, KNOWING THE FEDS WERE WATCHING HIM LIKE A HAWK.

I HAD IT COVERED PRETTY WELL, BUT THAT WAS THE ICING ON THE CAKE.

DON'T SAY THAT. I DON'T WANT TO SEE HIM GET RAPED IN PRISON...I JUST WANT HIM OUT OF MY LIFE.

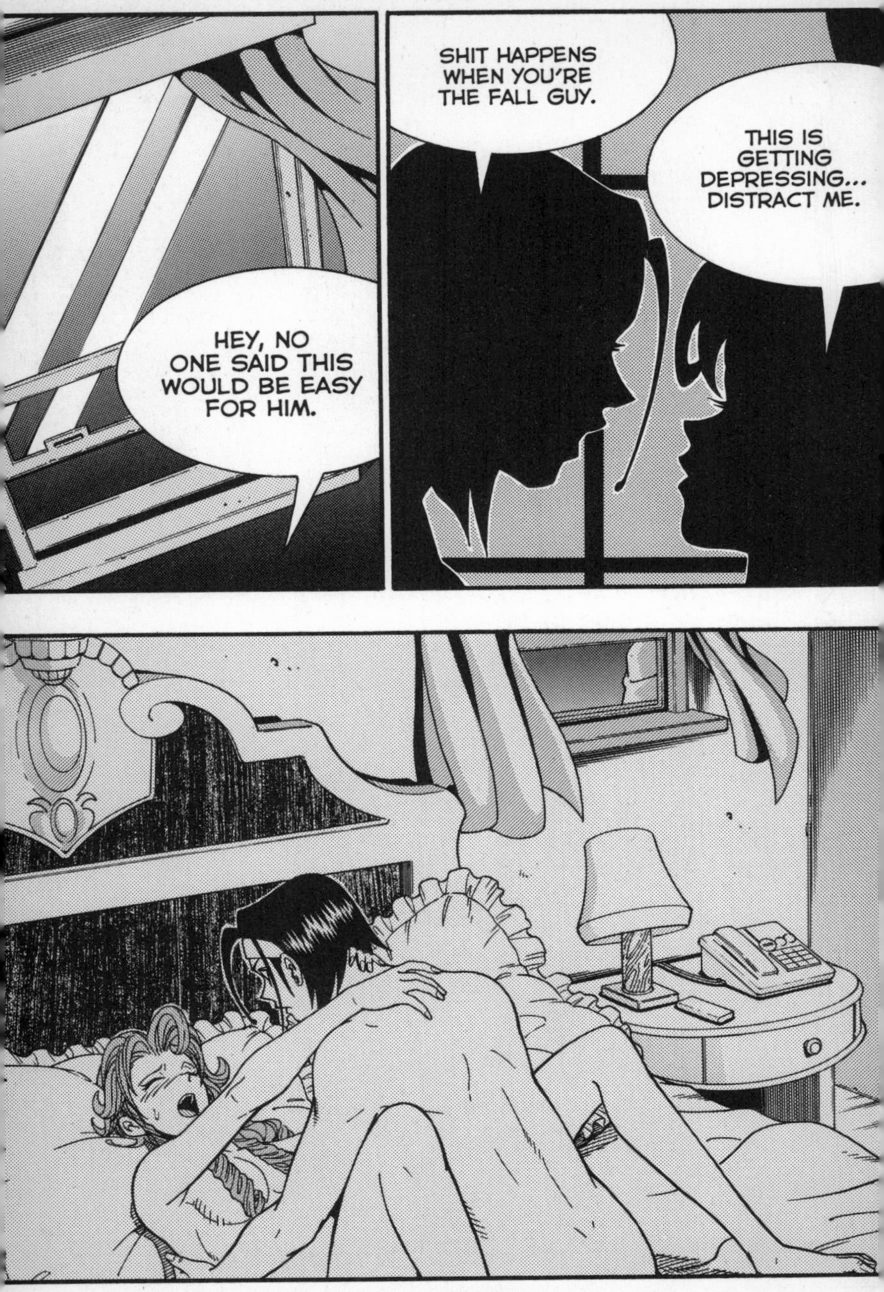
HEY, NO ONE SAID THIS WOULD BE EASY FOR HIM.
SHIT HAPPENS WHEN YOU'RE THE FALL GUY.
THIS IS GETTING DEPRESSING... DISTRACT ME.

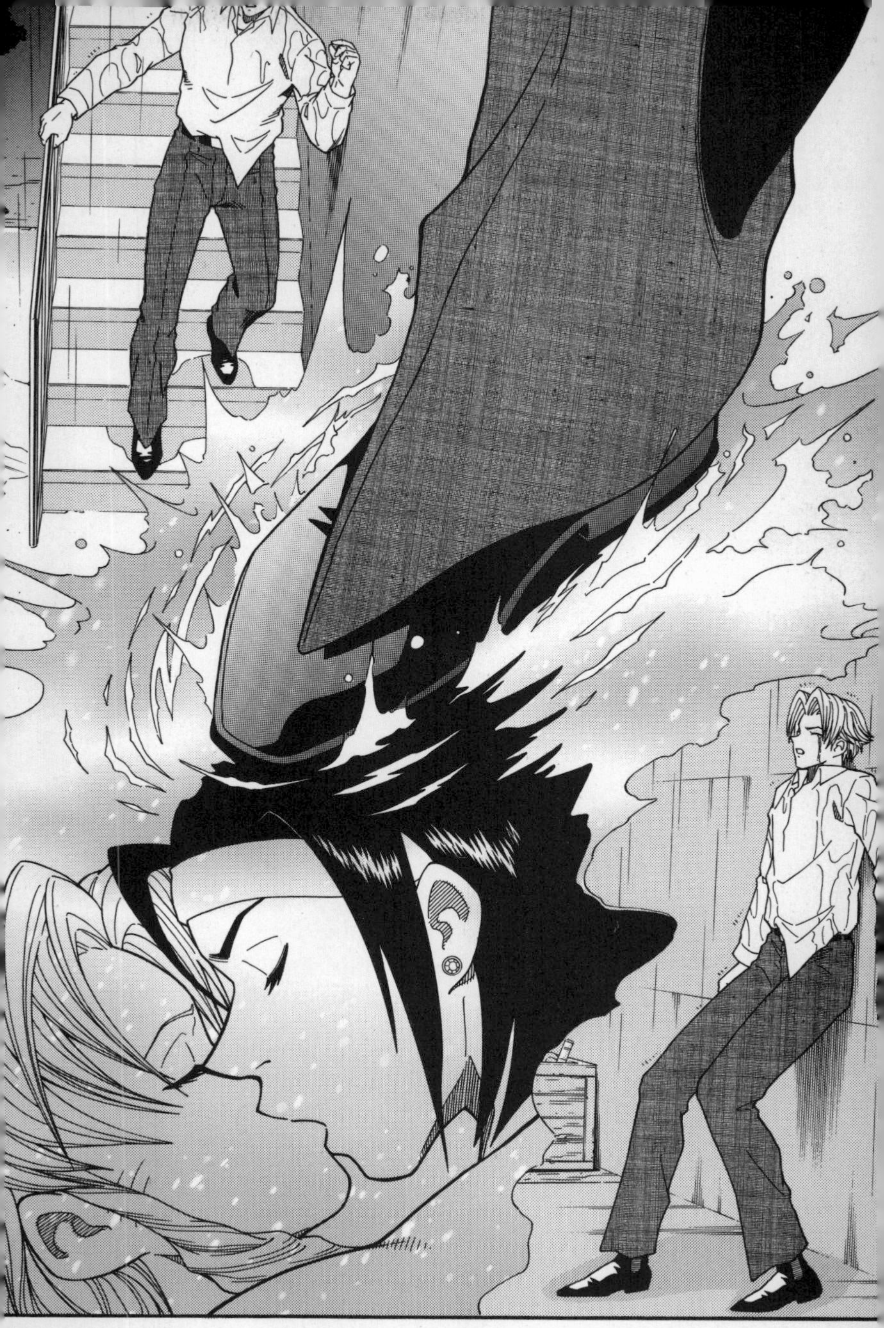

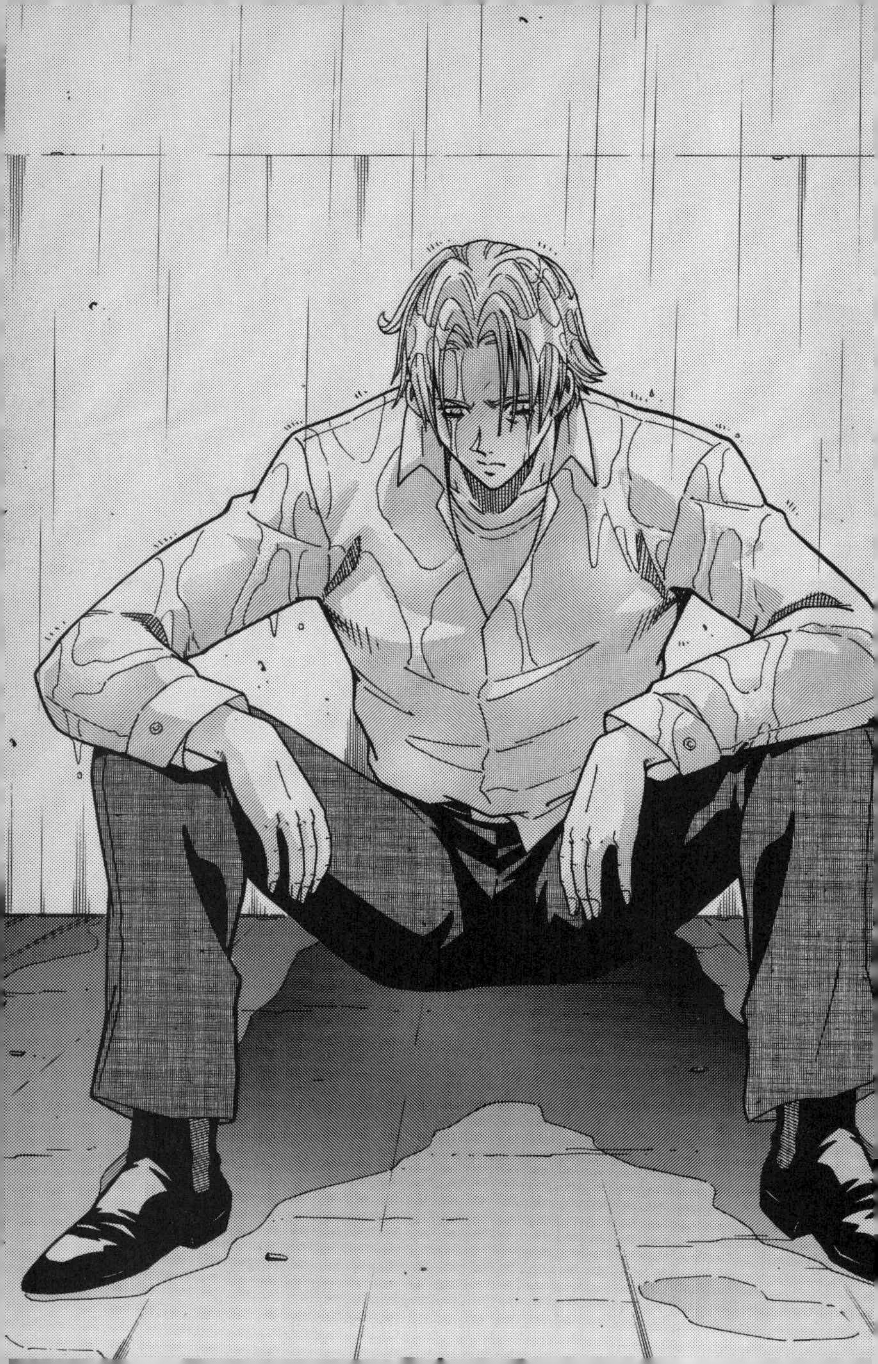

Juror 13™

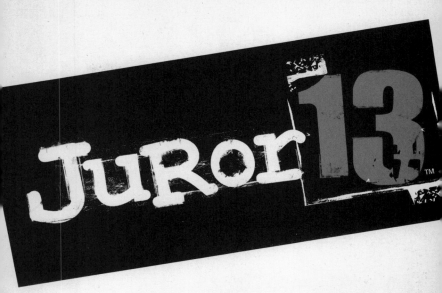

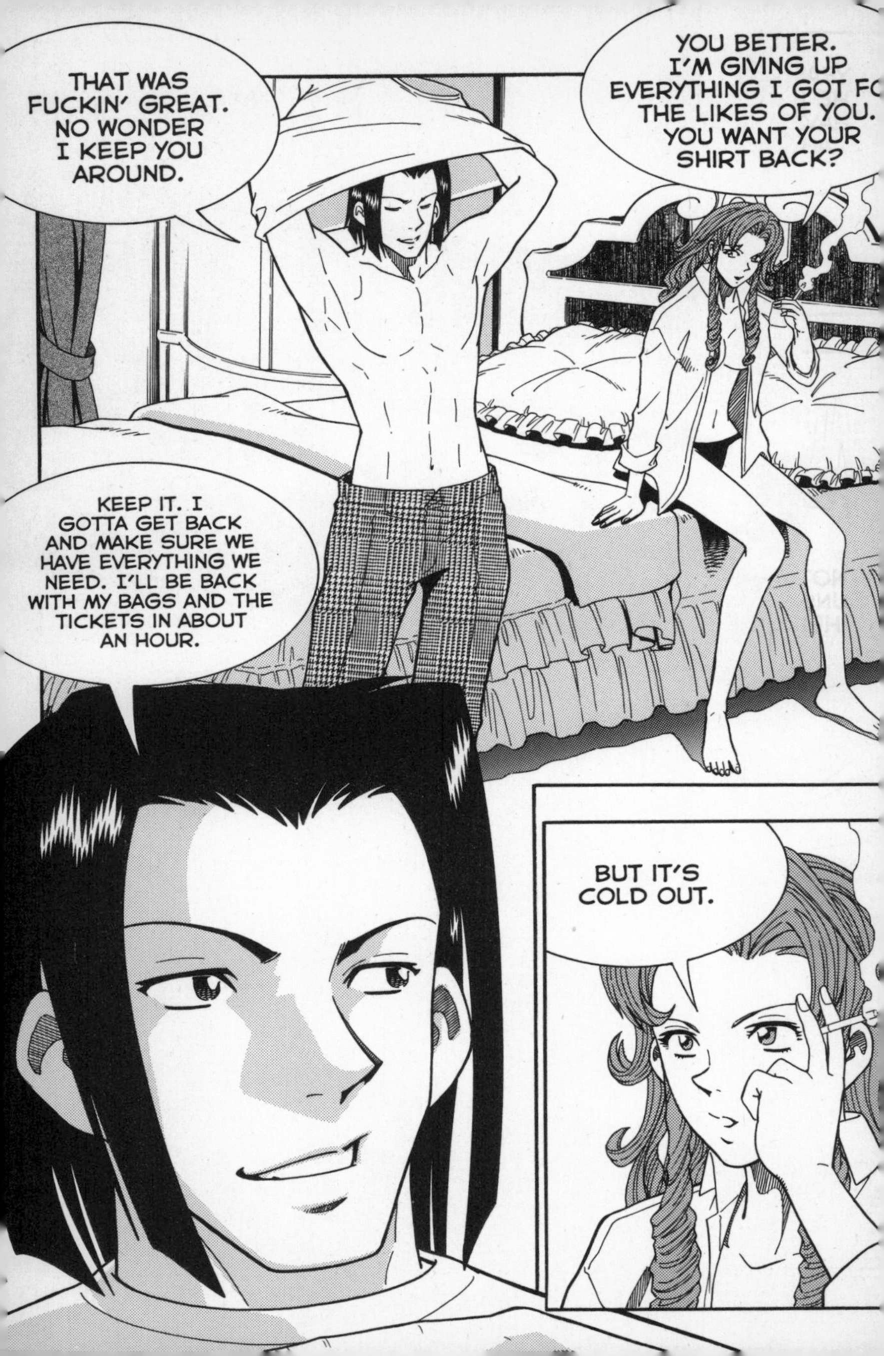
THAT WAS FUCKIN' GREAT. NO WONDER I KEEP YOU AROUND.
YOU BETTER. I'M GIVING UP EVERYTHING I GOT FO THE LIKES OF YOU. YOU WANT YOUR SHIRT BACK?
KEEP IT. I GOTTA GET BACK AND MAKE SURE WE HAVE EVERYTHING WE NEED. I'LL BE BACK WITH MY BAGS AND THE TICKETS IN ABOUT AN HOUR.
BUT IT'S COLD OUT.

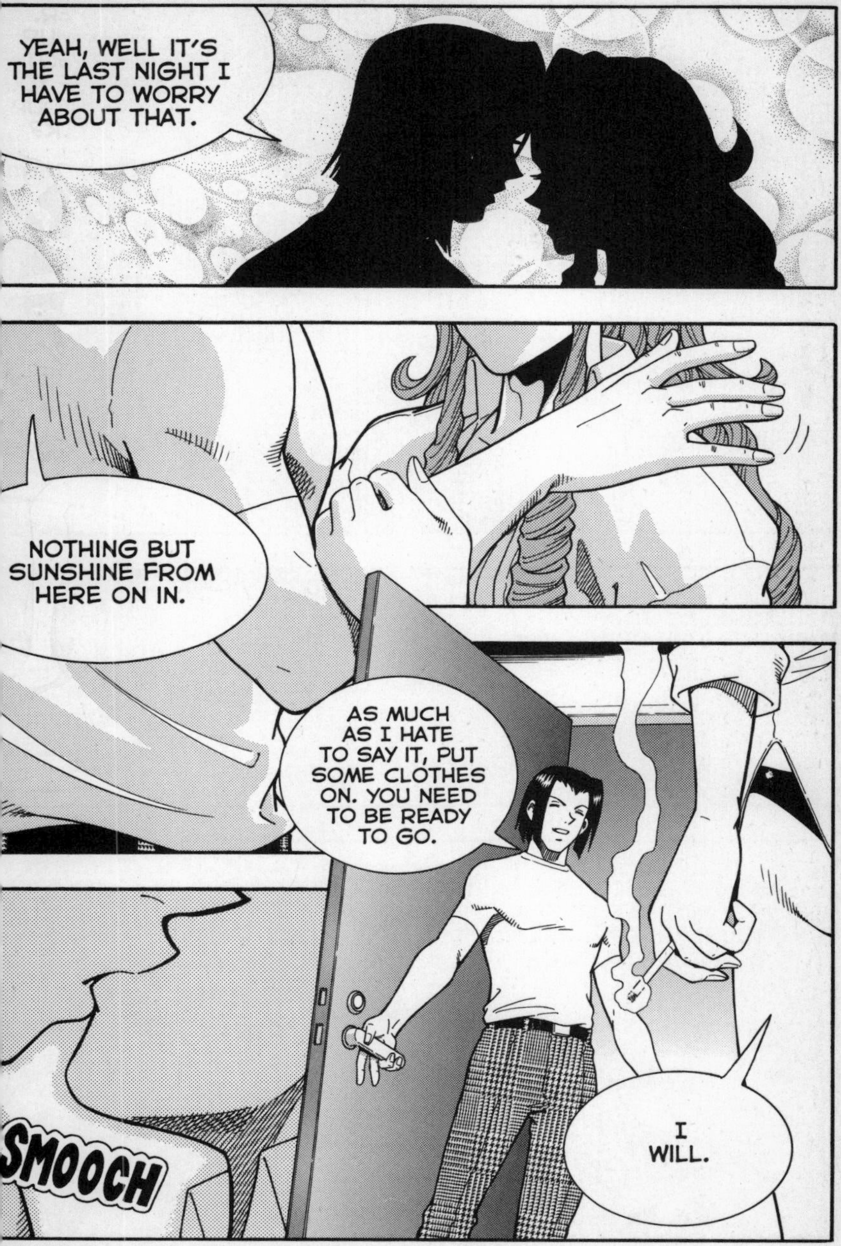
YEAH, WELL IT'S THE LAST NIGHT I HAVE TO WORRY ABOUT THAT.
NOTHING BUT SUNSHINE FROM HERE ON IN.
AS MUCH AS I HATE TO SAY IT, PUT SOME CLOTHES ON. YOU NEED TO BE READY TO GO.
SMOOCH
I WILL.

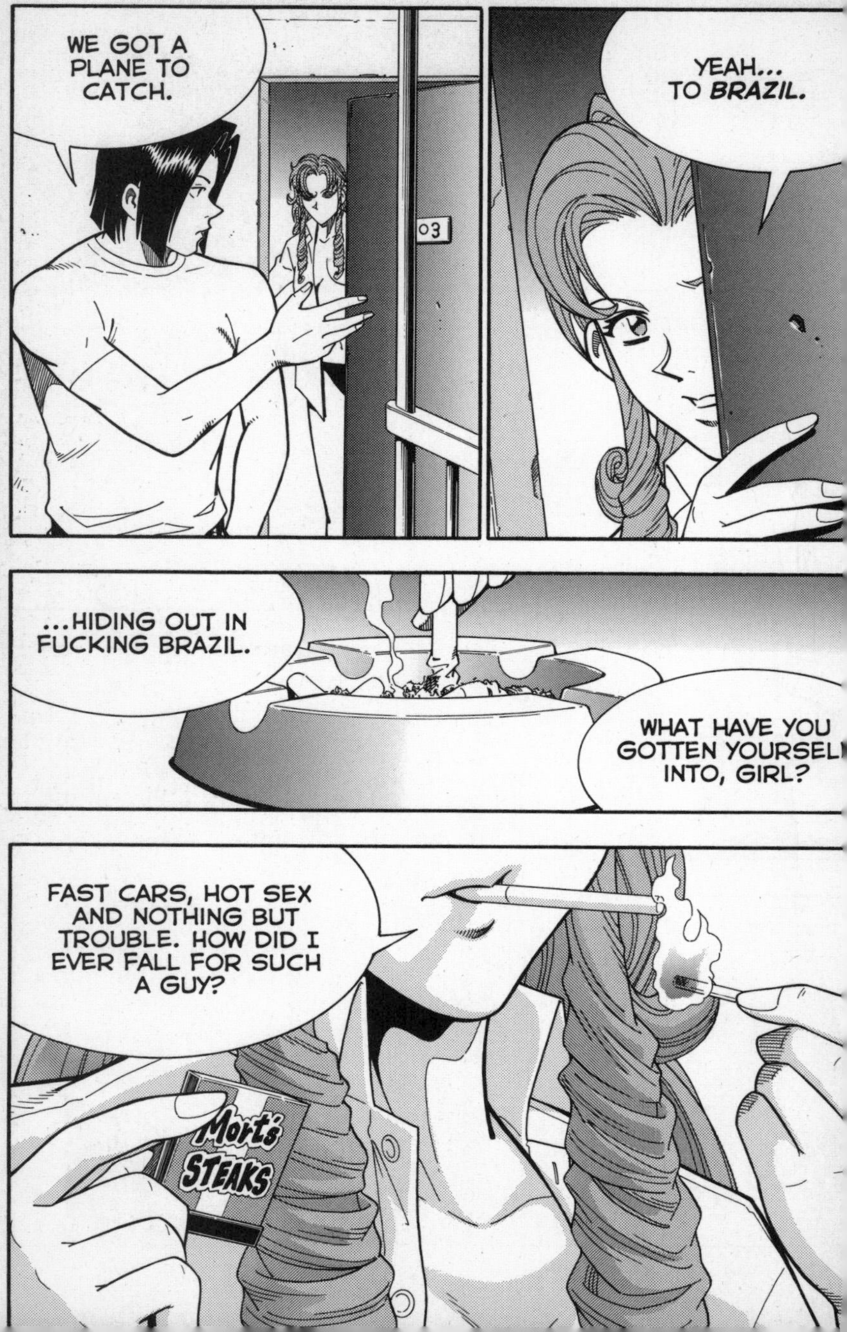
WE GOT A PLANE TO CATCH.
YEAH... TO *BRAZIL.*
03
...HIDING OUT IN FUCKING BRAZIL.
WHAT HAVE YOU GOTTEN YOURSELF INTO, GIRL?
FAST CARS, HOT SEX AND NOTHING BUT TROUBLE. HOW DID I EVER FALL FOR SUCH A GUY?
Mort's STEAKS

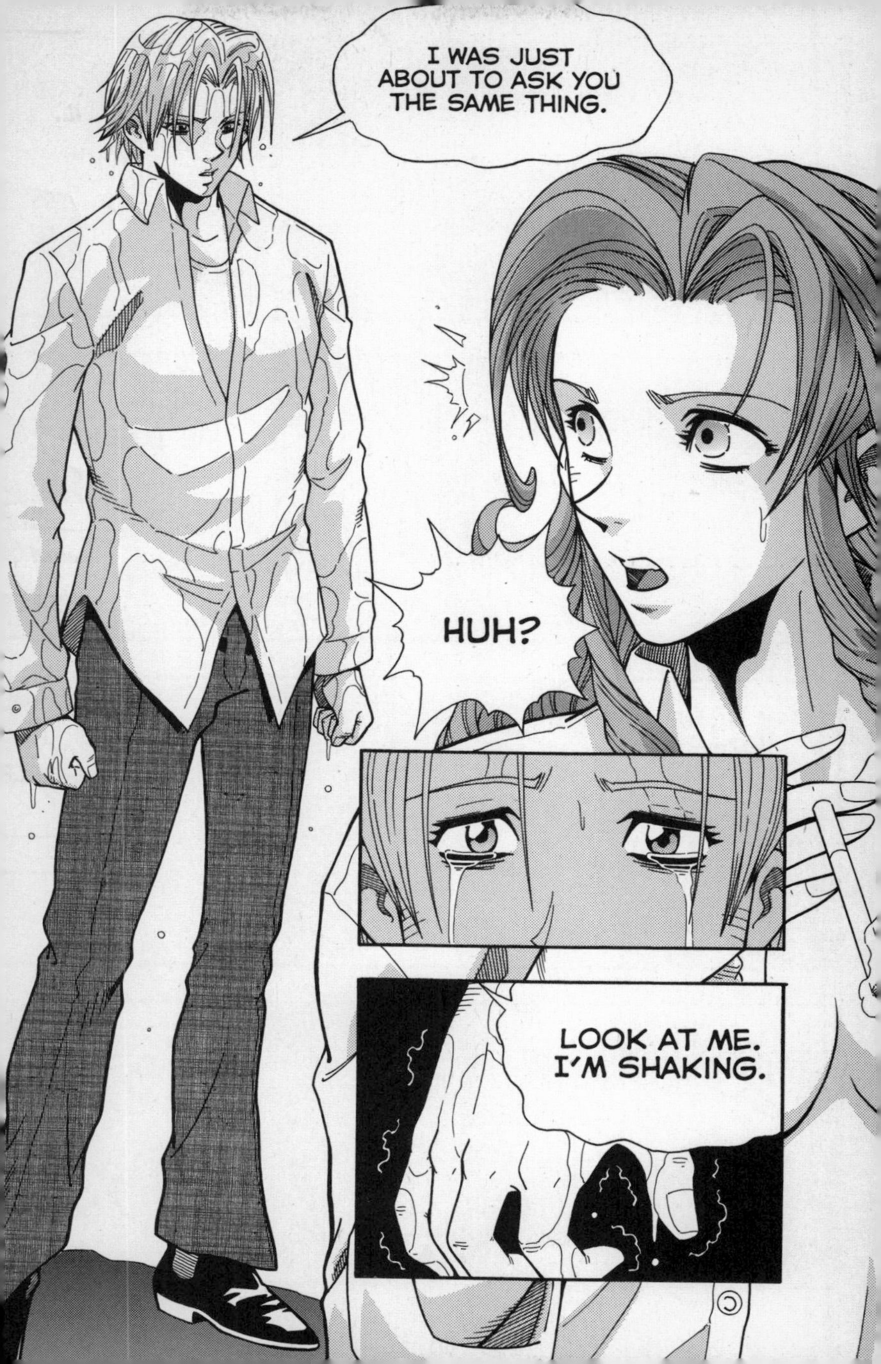
I WAS JUST ABOUT TO ASK YOU THE SAME THING.
HUH?
LOOK AT ME. I'M SHAKING.

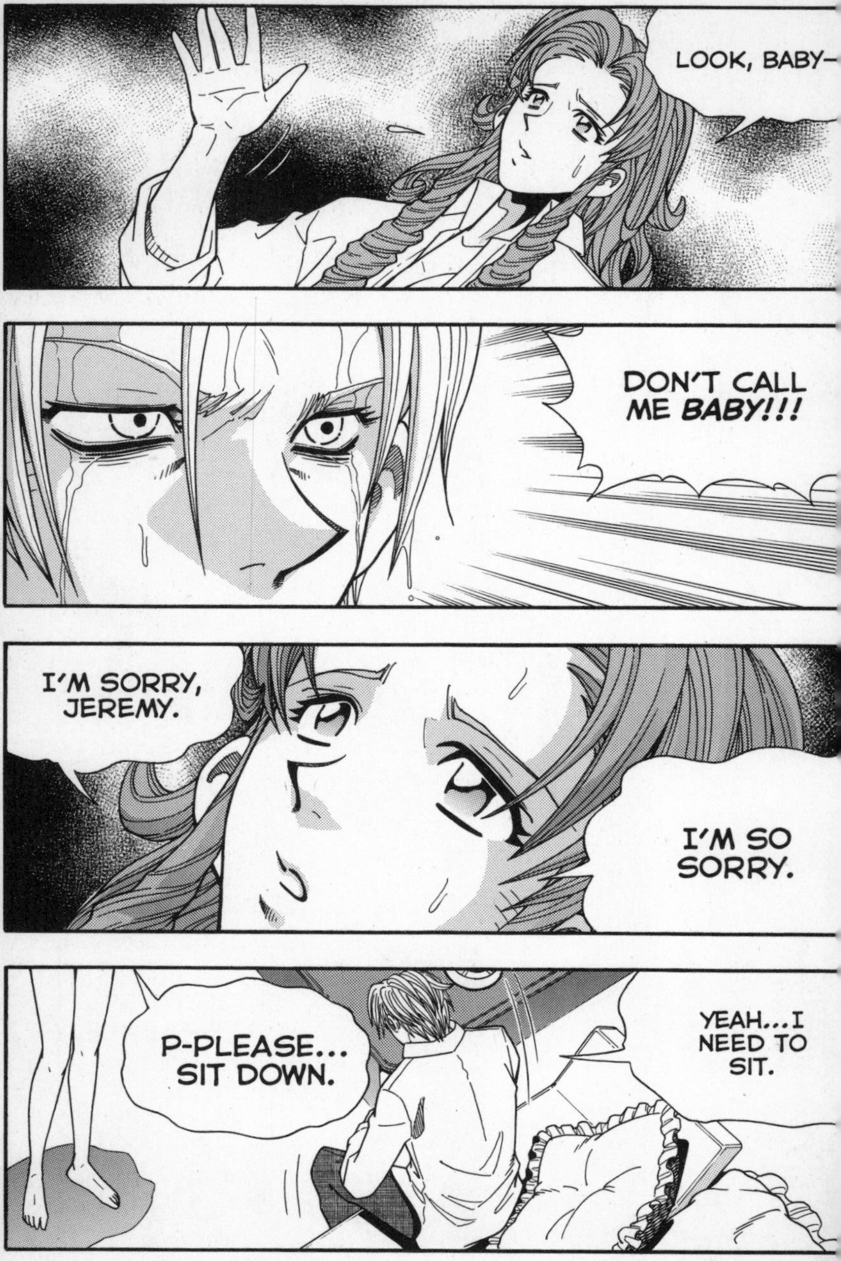

LOOK, BABY—
DON'T CALL ME *BABY!!!*
I'M SORRY, JEREMY.
I'M SO SORRY.
P-PLEASE... SIT DOWN.
YEAH...I NEED TO SIT.

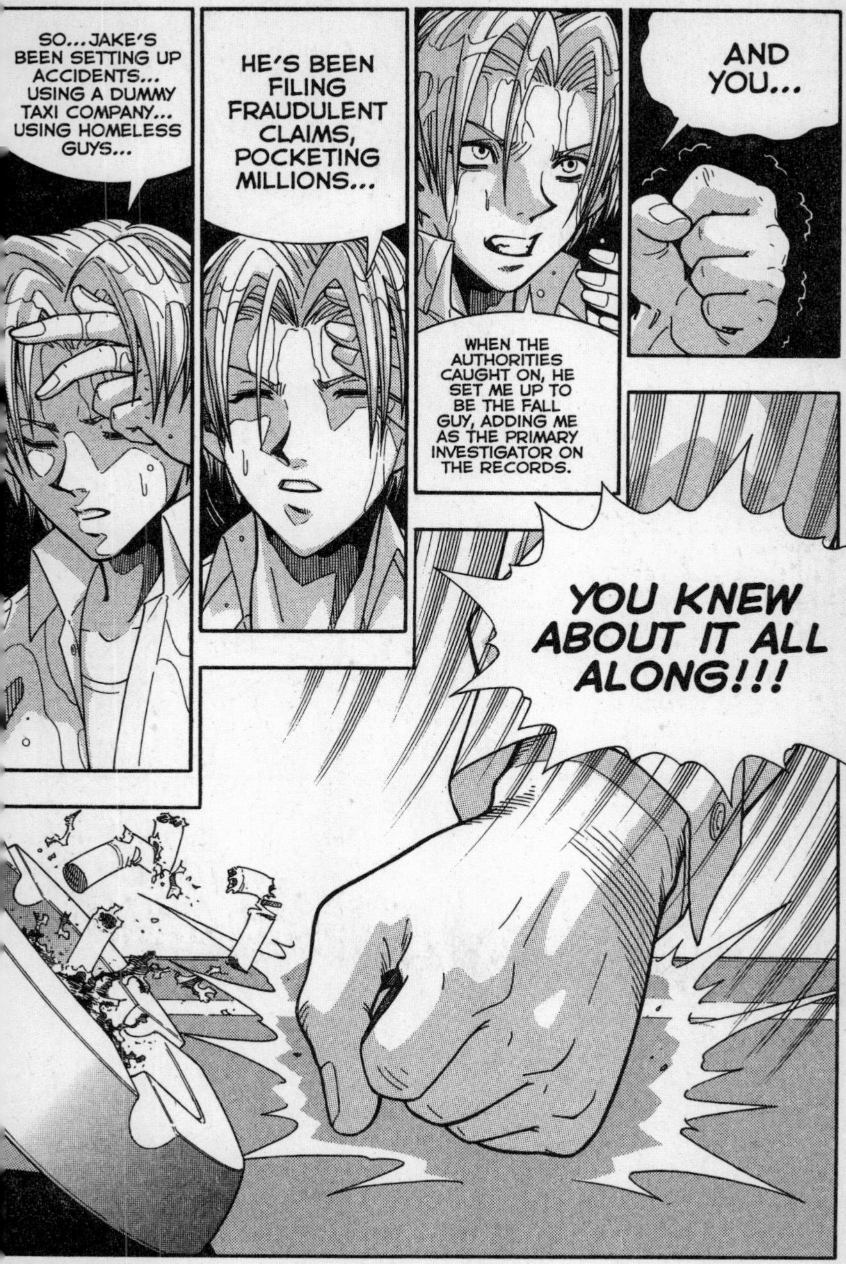
SO...JAKE'S BEEN SETTING UP ACCIDENTS... USING A DUMMY TAXI COMPANY... USING HOMELESS GUYS...
HE'S BEEN FILING FRAUDULENT CLAIMS, POCKETING MILLIONS...
WHEN THE AUTHORITIES CAUGHT ON, HE SET ME UP TO BE THE FALL GUY, ADDING ME AS THE PRIMARY INVESTIGATOR ON THE RECORDS.
AND YOU...
YOU KNEW ABOUT IT ALL ALONG!!!

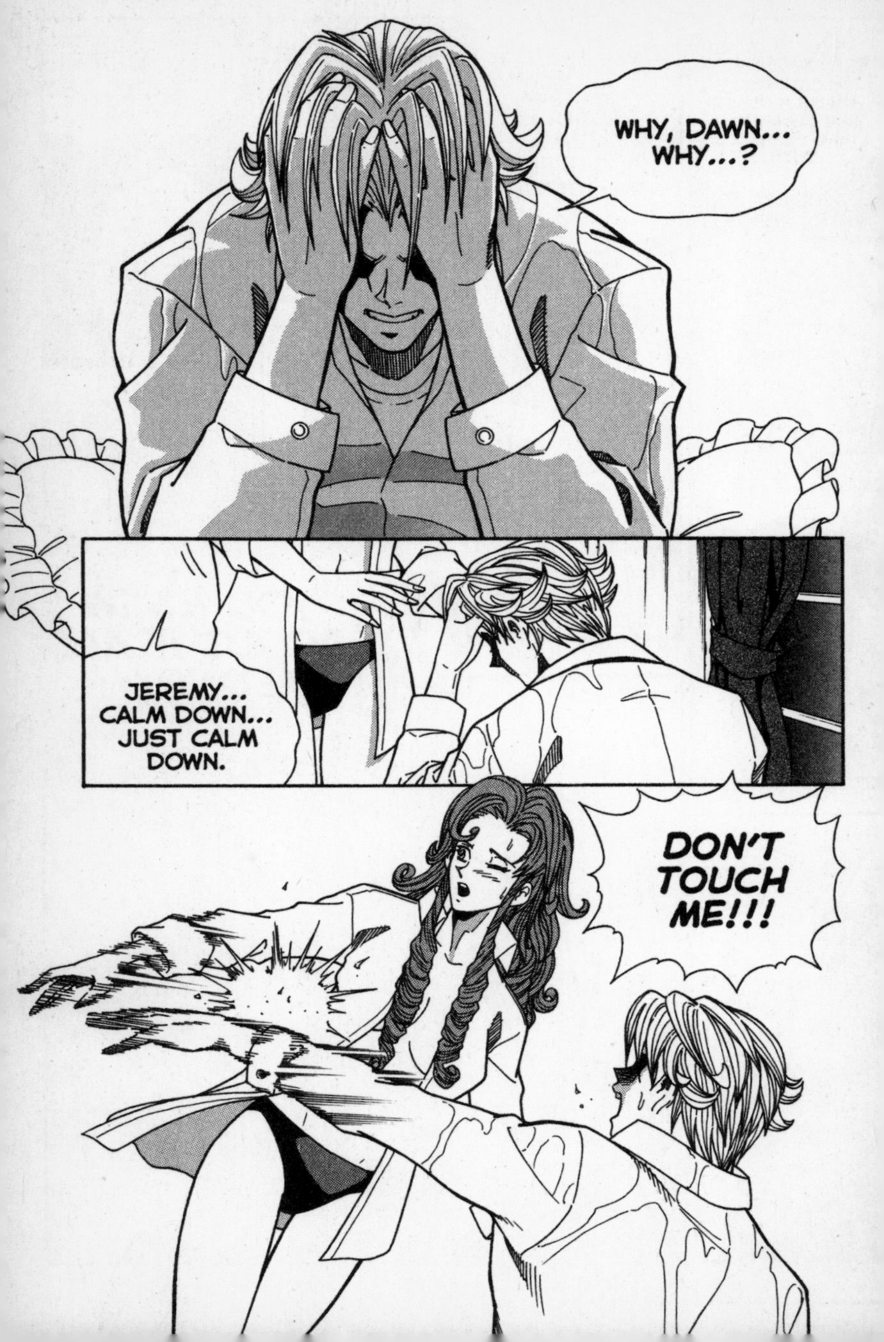
WHY, DAWN... WHY...?
JEREMY... CALM DOWN... JUST CALM DOWN.
DON'T TOUCH ME!!!

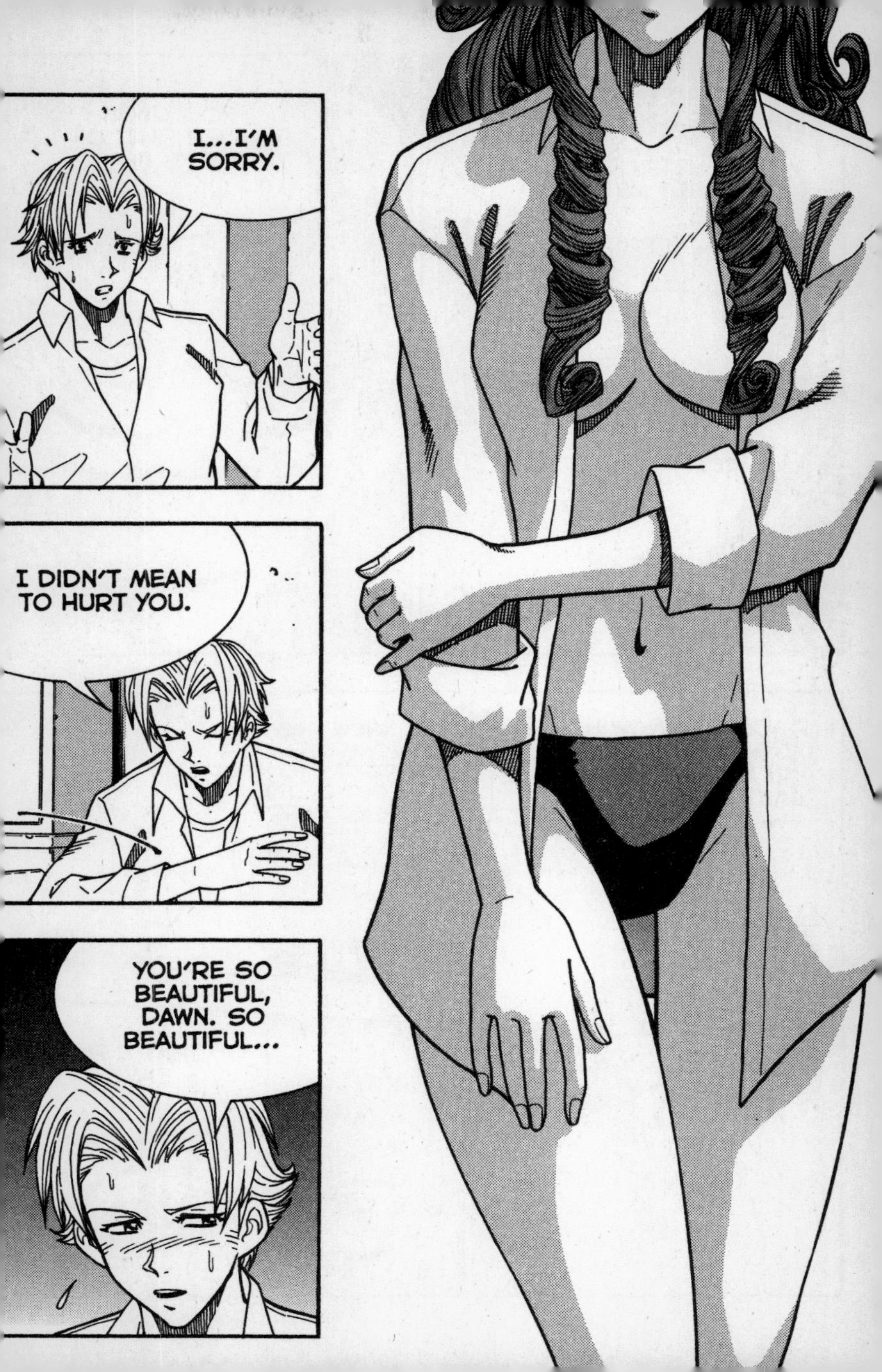
I...I'M SORRY.
I DIDN'T MEAN TO HURT YOU.
YOU'RE SO BEAUTIFUL, DAWN. SO BEAUTIFUL...

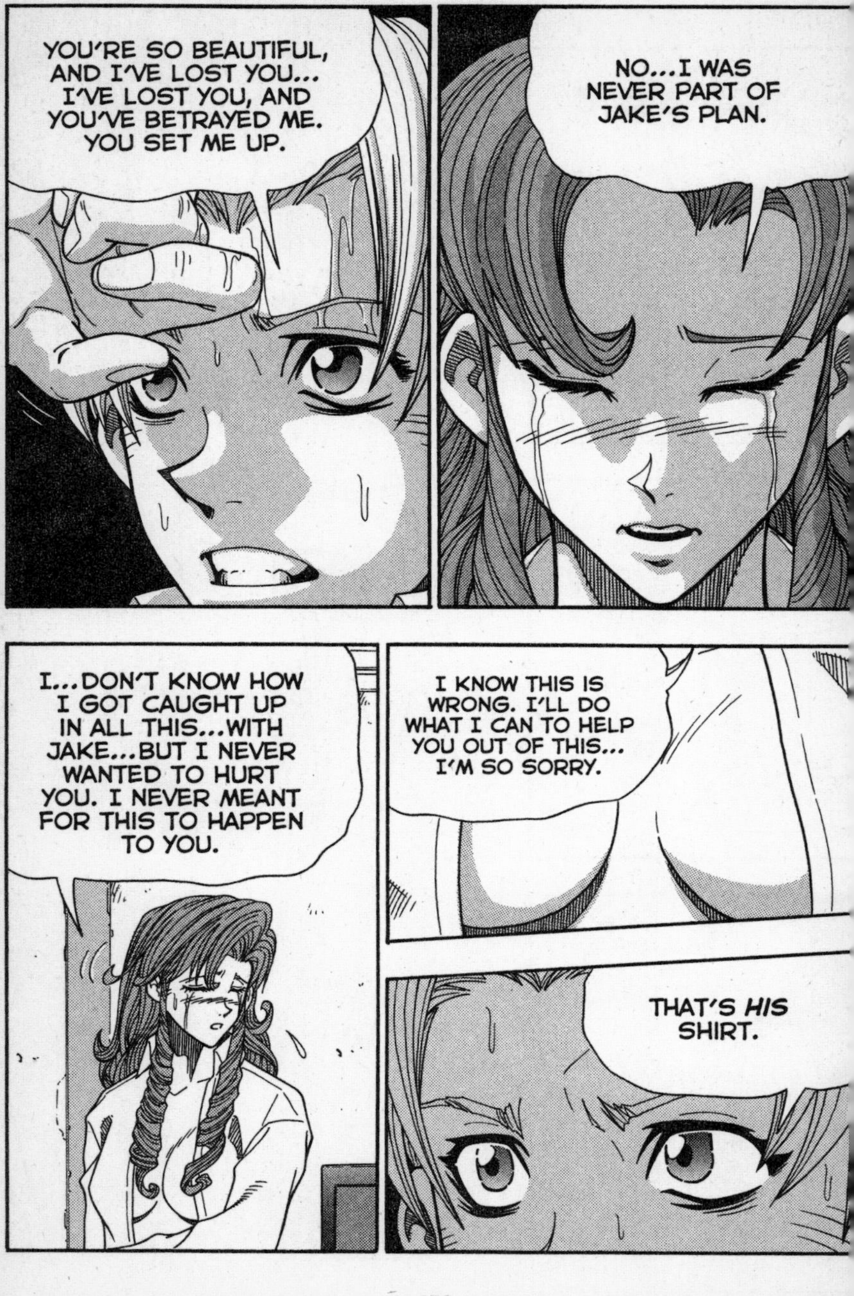
YOU'RE SO BEAUTIFUL, AND I'VE LOST YOU... I'VE LOST YOU, AND YOU'VE BETRAYED ME. YOU SET ME UP.
NO...I WAS NEVER PART OF JAKE'S PLAN.
I...DON'T KNOW HOW I GOT CAUGHT UP IN ALL THIS...WITH JAKE...BUT I NEVER WANTED TO HURT YOU. I NEVER MEANT FOR THIS TO HAPPEN TO YOU.
I KNOW THIS IS WRONG. I'LL DO WHAT I CAN TO HELP YOU OUT OF THIS... I'M SO SORRY.
THAT'S *HIS* SHIRT.

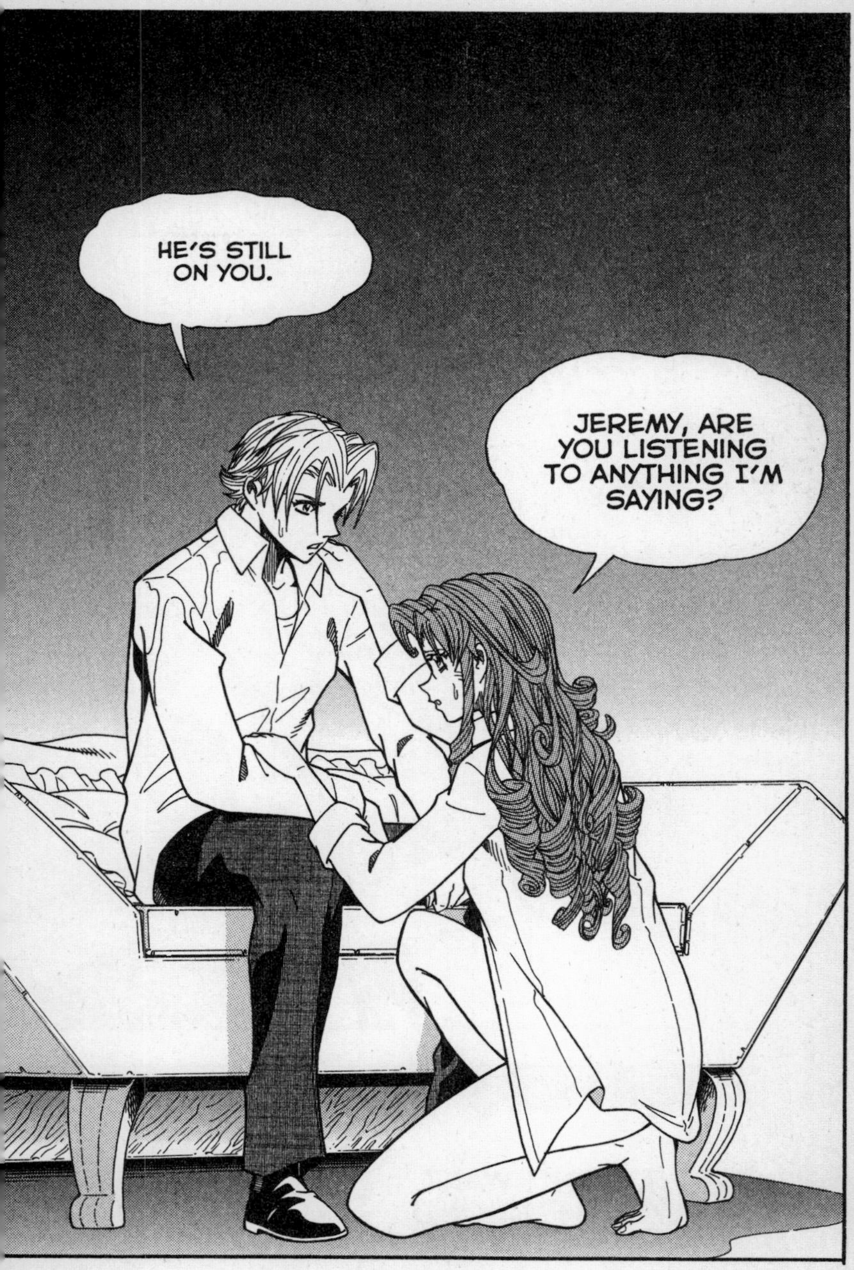
HE'S STILL ON YOU.
JEREMY, ARE YOU LISTENING TO ANYTHING I'M SAYING?

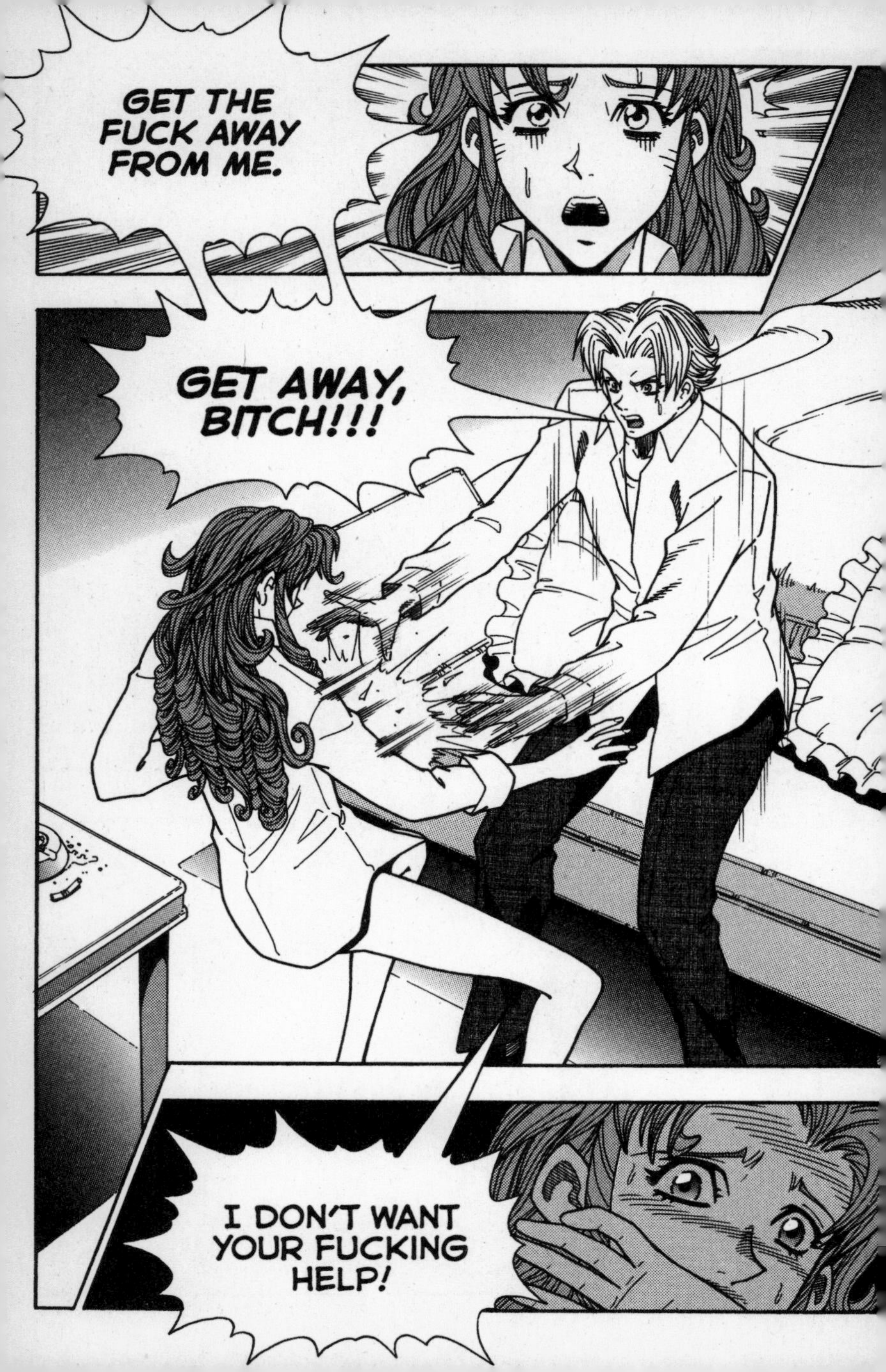
GET THE FUCK AWAY FROM ME.
GET AWAY, BITCH!!!
I DON'T WANT YOUR FUCKING HELP!

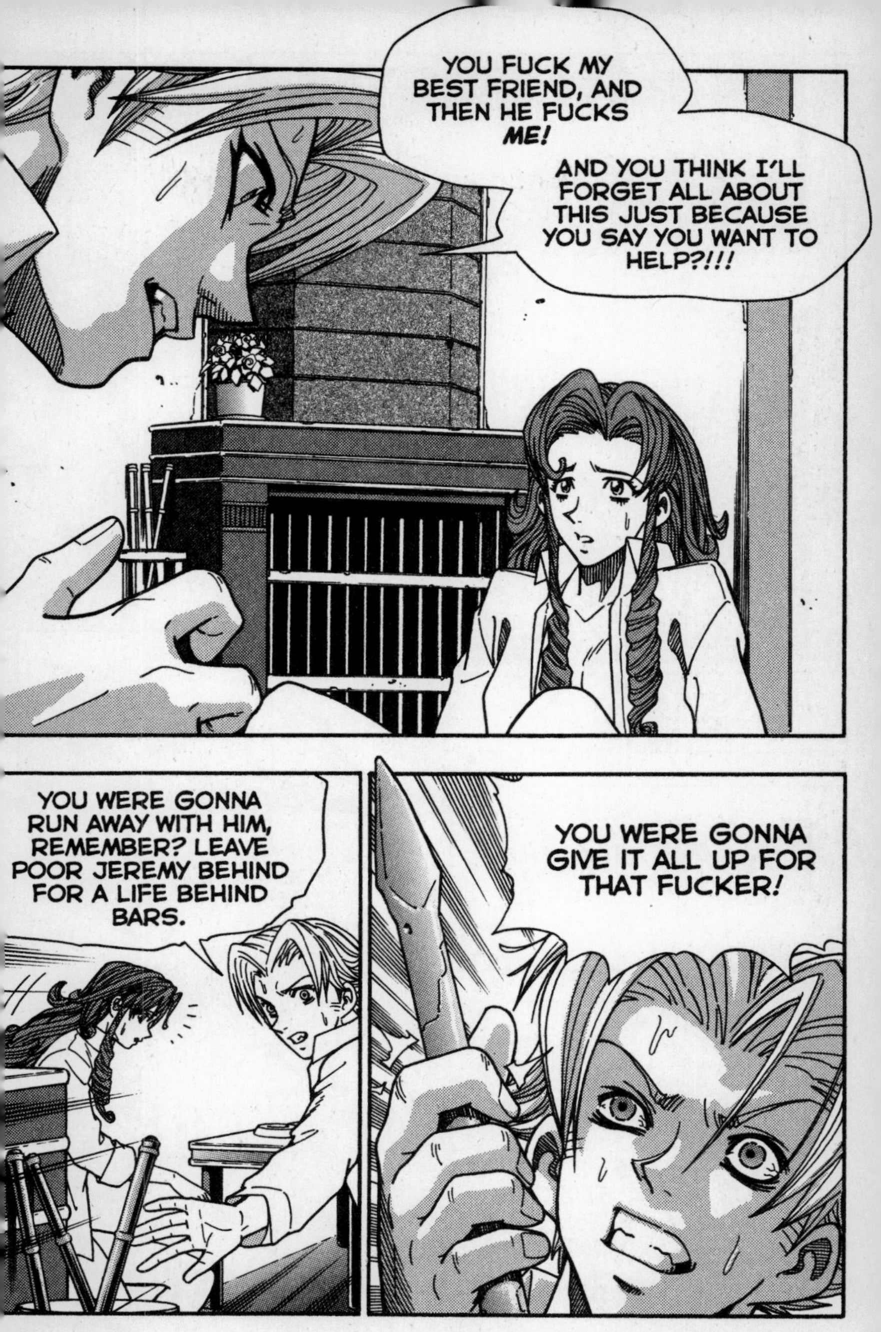
YOU FUCK MY BEST FRIEND, AND THEN HE FUCKS *ME!*
AND YOU THINK I'LL FORGET ALL ABOUT THIS JUST BECAUSE YOU SAY YOU WANT TO HELP?!!!
YOU WERE GONNA RUN AWAY WITH HIM, REMEMBER? LEAVE POOR JEREMY BEHIND FOR A LIFE BEHIND BARS.
YOU WERE GONNA GIVE IT ALL UP FOR THAT FUCKER*!*

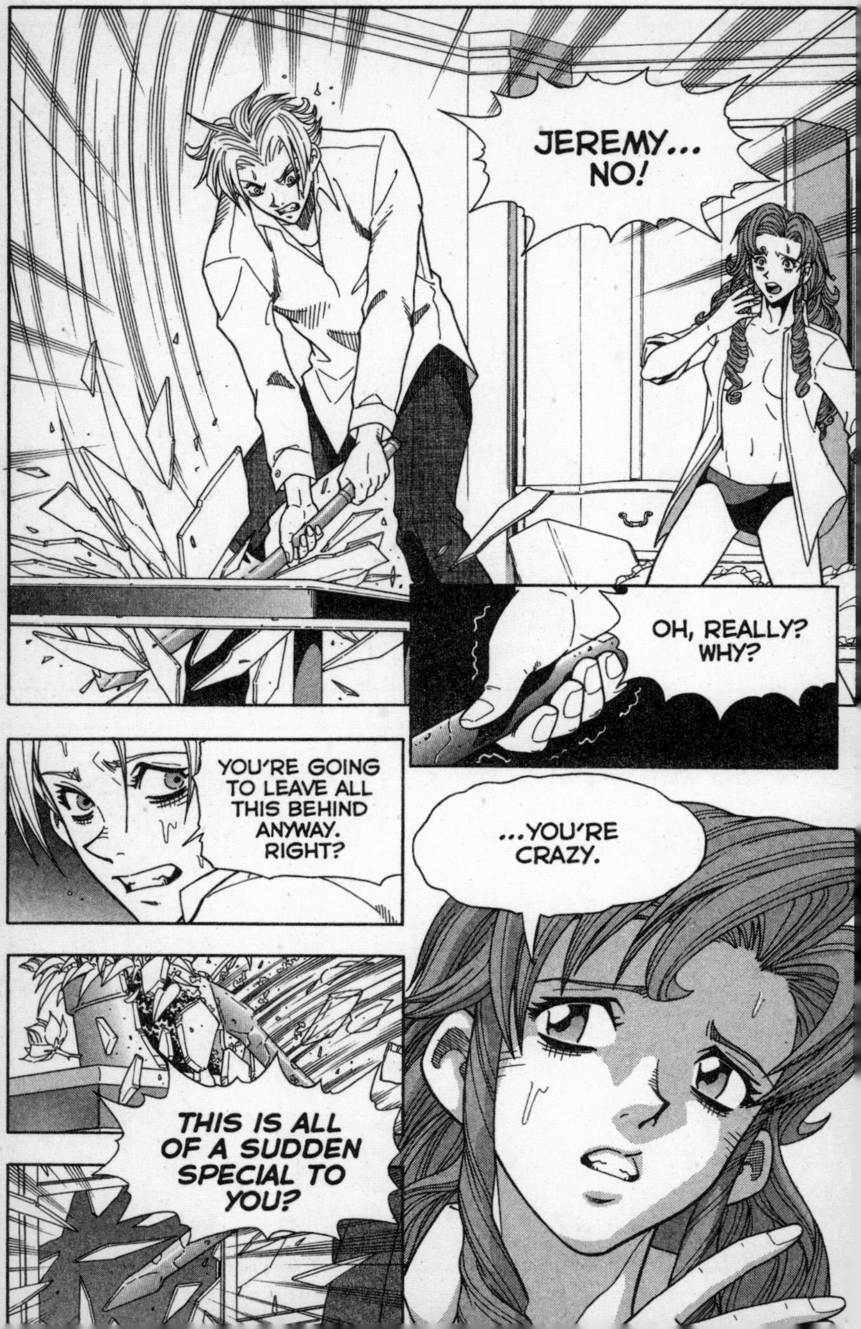
JEREMY... NO!
OH, REALLY? WHY?
YOU'RE GOING TO LEAVE ALL THIS BEHIND ANYWAY. RIGHT?
...YOU'RE CRAZY.
THIS IS ALL OF A SUDDEN SPECIAL TO YOU?

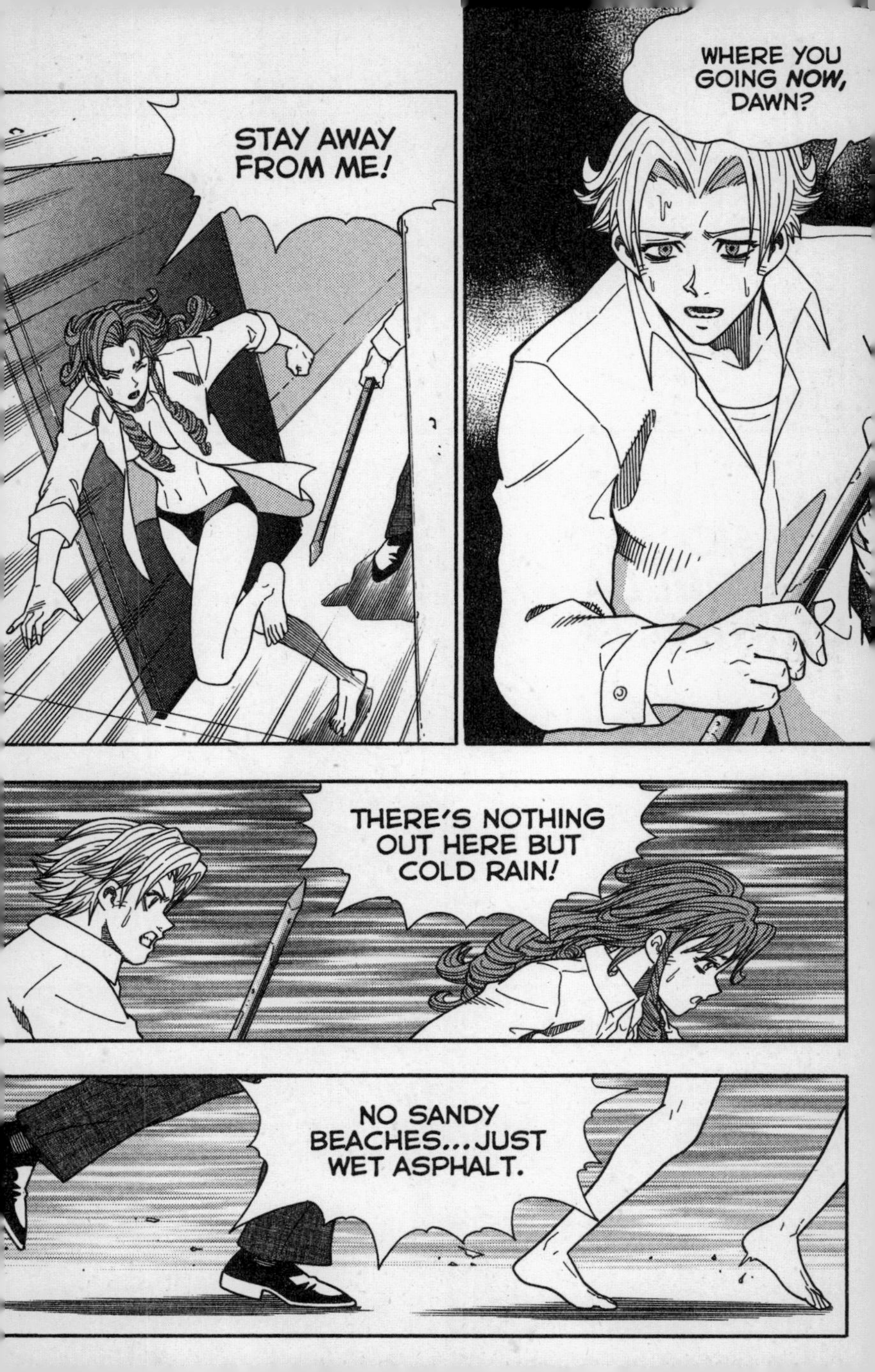
STAY AWAY FROM ME!
WHERE YOU GOING NOW, DAWN?
THERE'S NOTHING OUT HERE BUT COLD RAIN!
NO SANDY BEACHES...JUST WET ASPHALT.

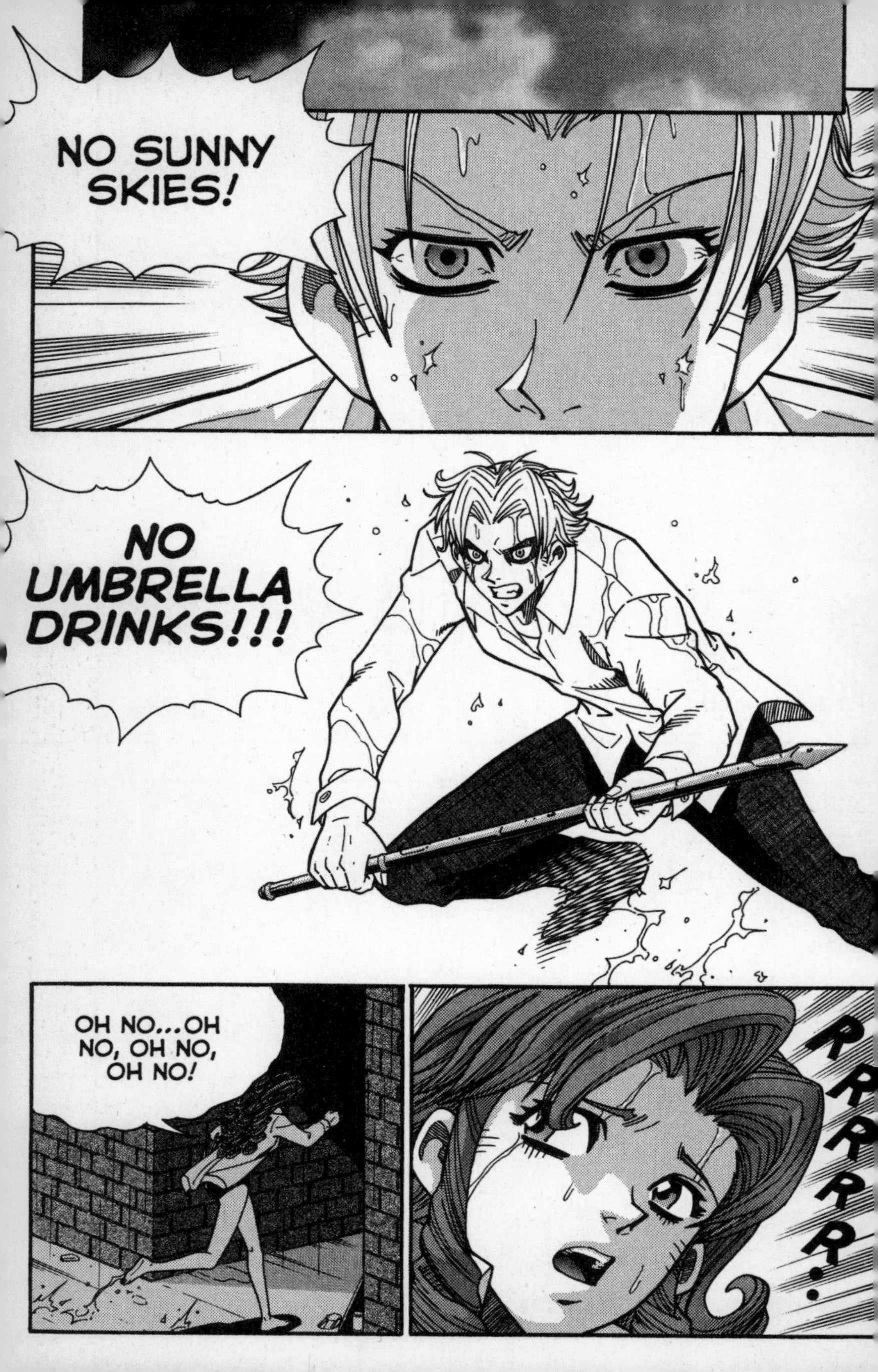
NO SUNNY SKIES!
NO UMBRELLA DRINKS!!!
OH NO...OH NO, OH NO, OH NO!
RRRRRR...

SCREECH

2506

THERE'S THE BIKE!

NOOOOo...

WHICH WAY?

HEAR THAT? THIS WAY!

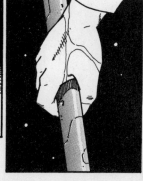

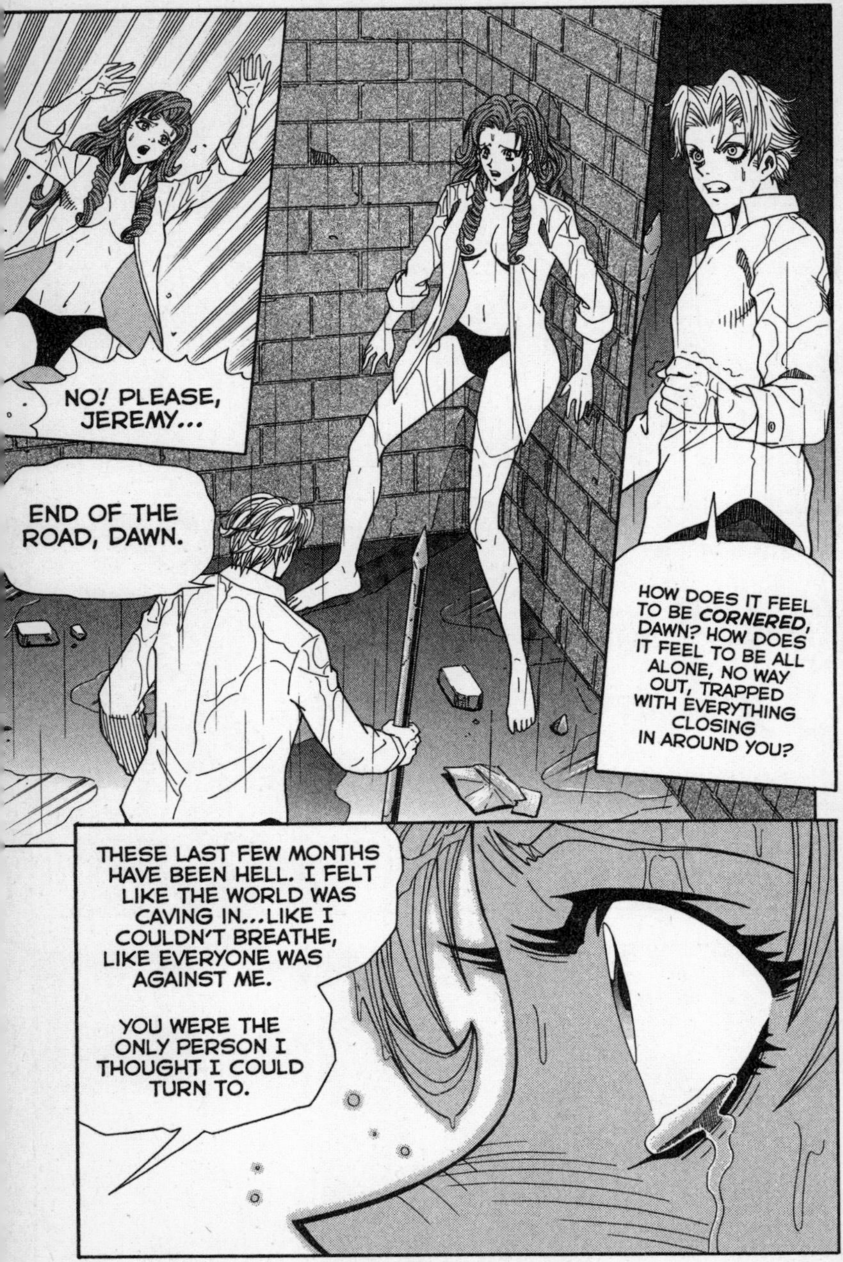
NO! PLEASE, JEREMY...
END OF THE ROAD, DAWN.
HOW DOES IT FEEL TO BE *CORNERED*, DAWN? HOW DOES IT FEEL TO BE ALL ALONE, NO WAY OUT, TRAPPED WITH EVERYTHING CLOSING IN AROUND YOU?
THESE LAST FEW MONTHS HAVE BEEN HELL. I FELT LIKE THE WORLD WAS CAVING IN...LIKE I COULDN'T BREATHE, LIKE EVERYONE WAS AGAINST ME.
YOU WERE THE ONLY PERSON I THOUGHT I COULD TURN TO.

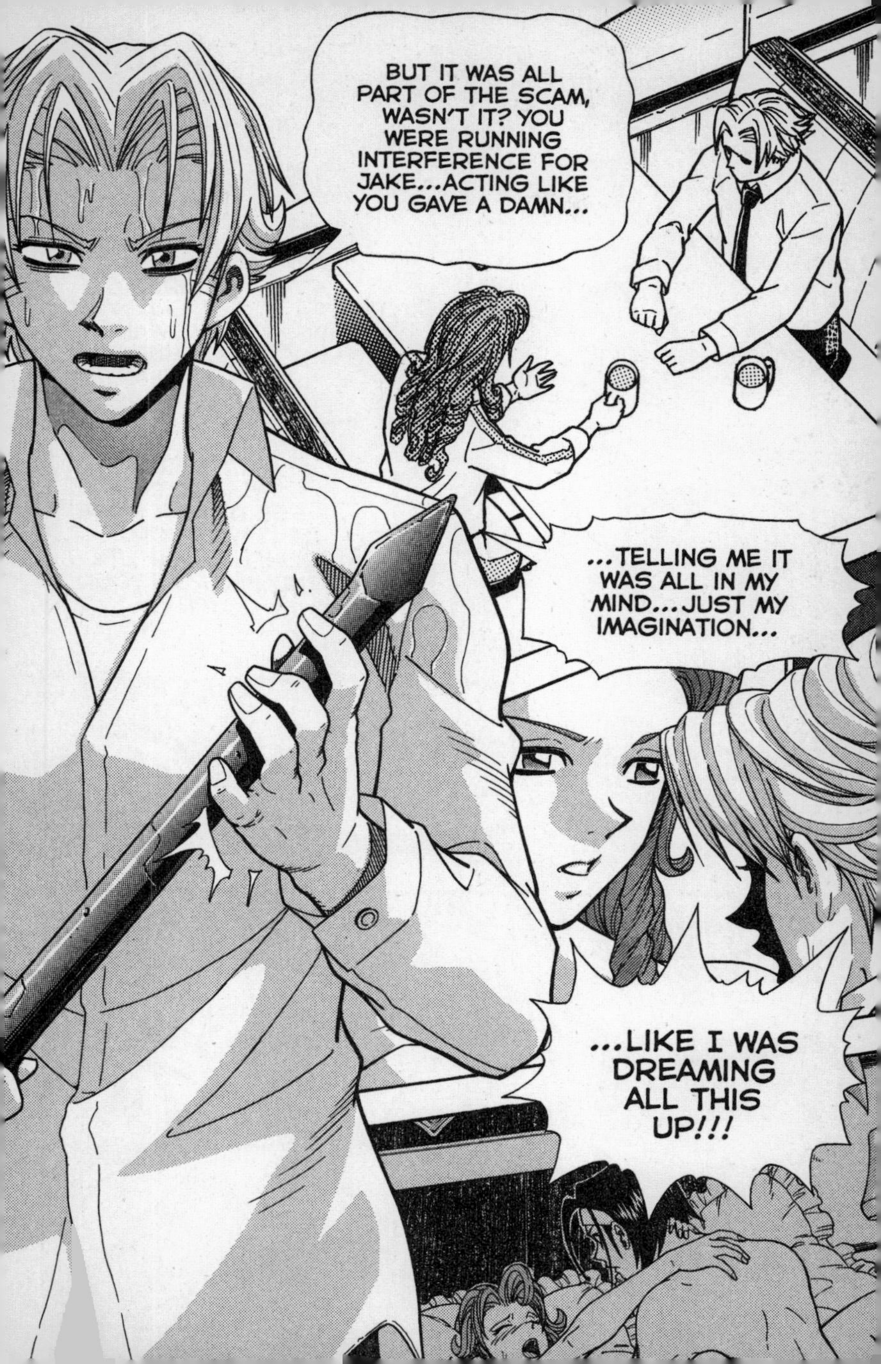
BUT IT WAS ALL PART OF THE SCAM, WASN'T IT? YOU WERE RUNNING INTERFERENCE FOR JAKE...ACTING LIKE YOU GAVE A DAMN...
...TELLING ME IT WAS ALL IN MY MIND...JUST MY IMAGINATION...
...LIKE I WAS DREAMING ALL THIS UP!!!

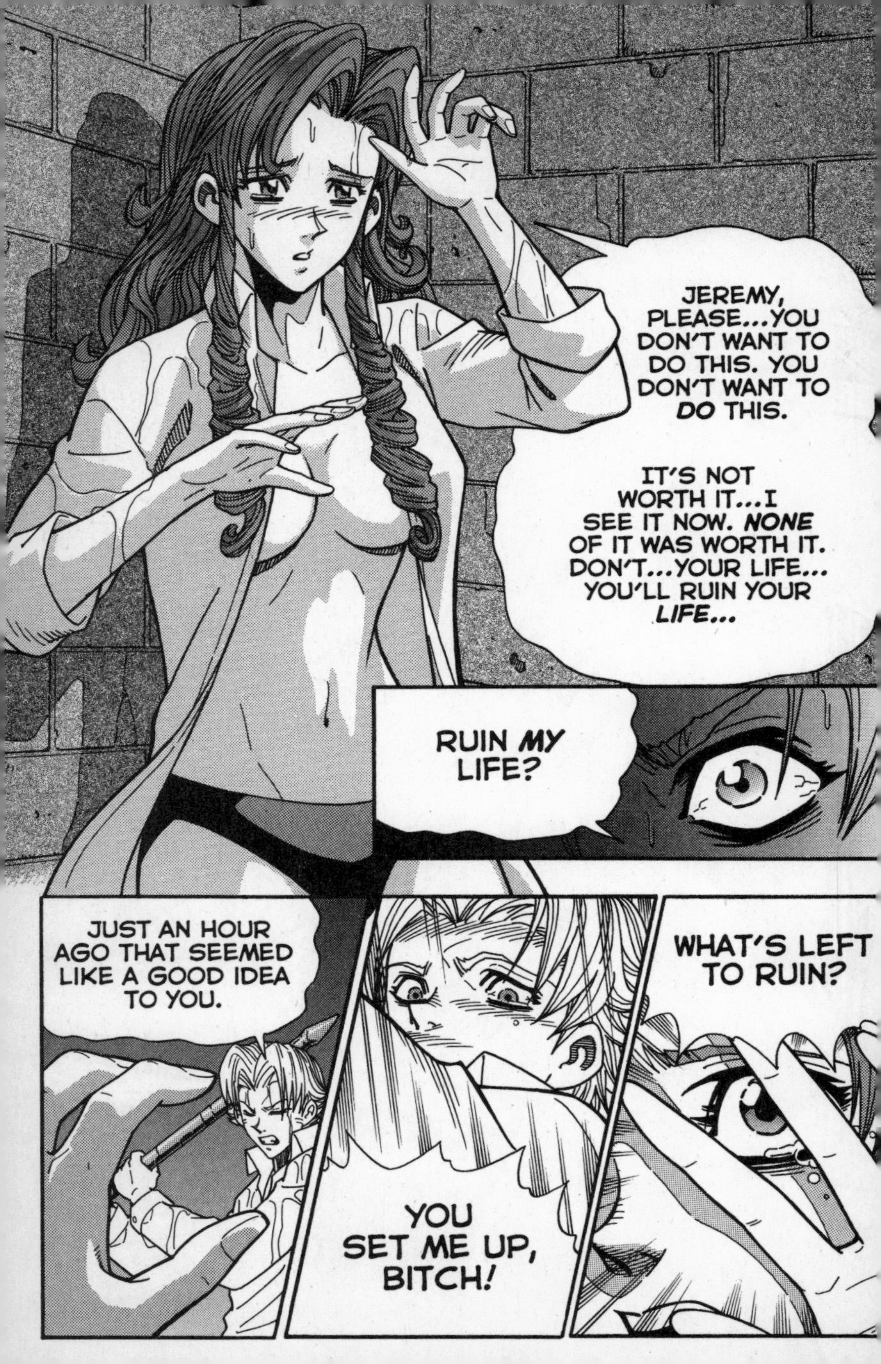
JEREMY, PLEASE...YOU DON'T WANT TO DO THIS. YOU DON'T WANT TO *DO* THIS.
IT'S NOT WORTH IT...I SEE IT NOW. *NONE* OF IT WAS WORTH IT. DON'T...YOUR LIFE... YOU'LL RUIN YOUR *LIFE...*
RUIN *MY* LIFE?
JUST AN HOUR AGO THAT SEEMED LIKE A GOOD IDEA TO YOU.
YOU SET ME UP, BITCH!
WHAT'S LEFT TO RUIN?

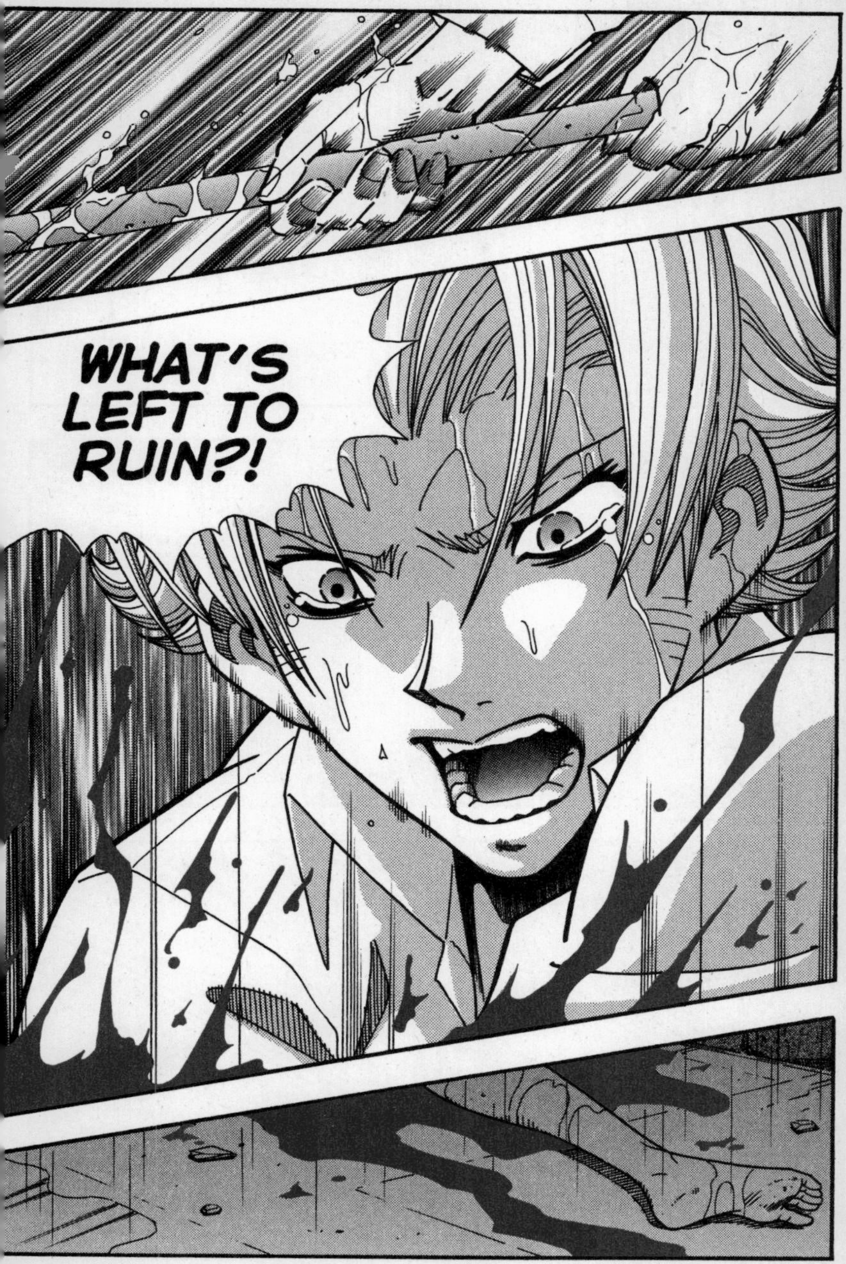
WHAT'S LEFT TO RUIN?!

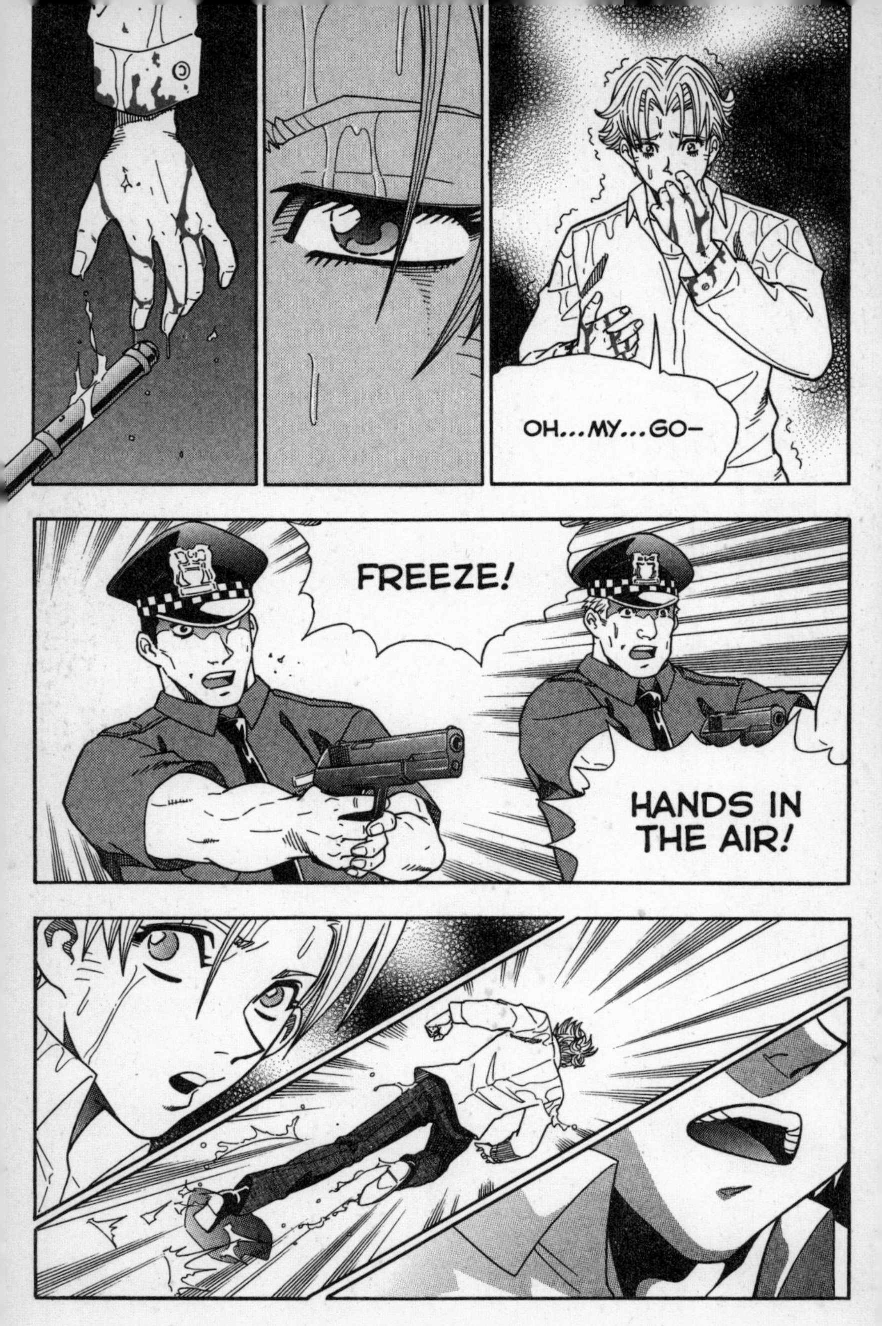
OH...MY...GO-
FREEZE!
HANDS IN THE AIR!

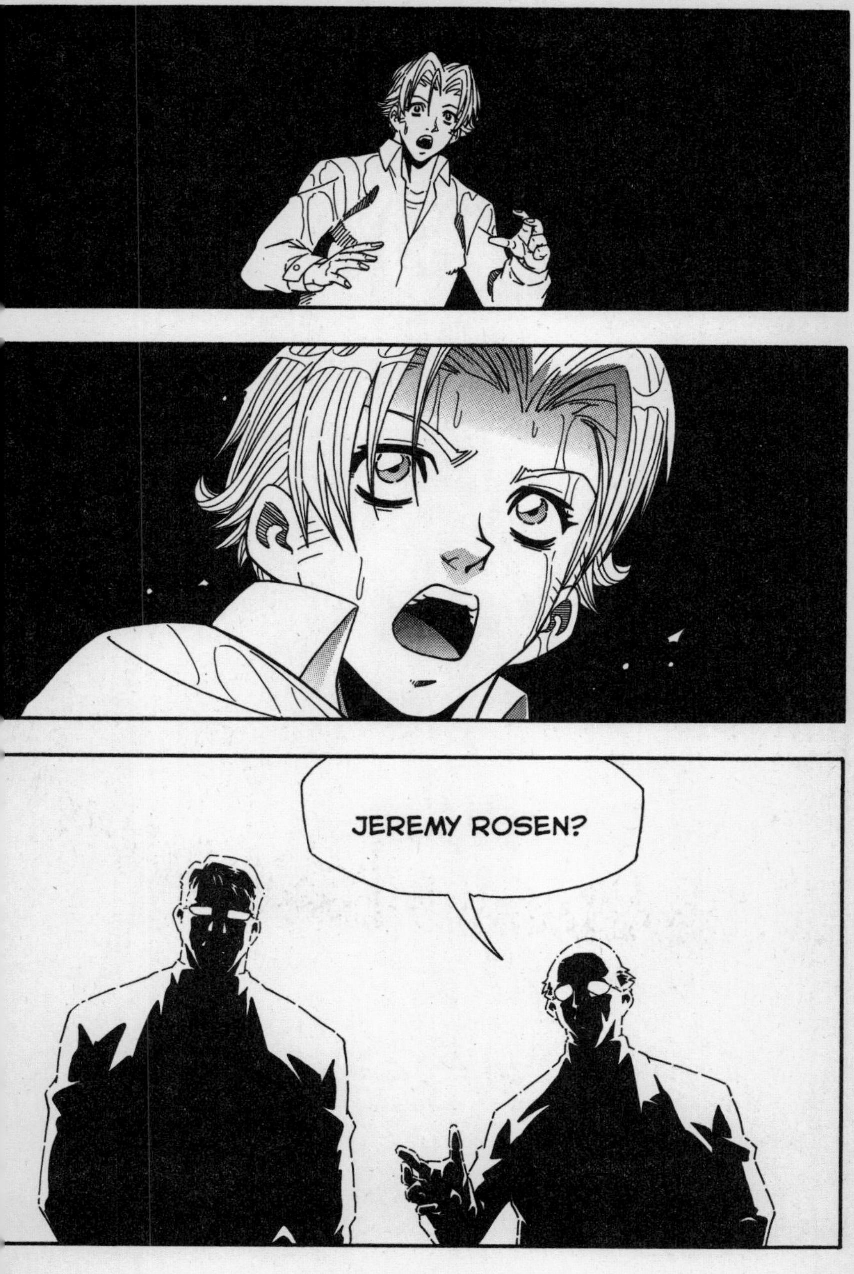
JEREMY ROSEN?

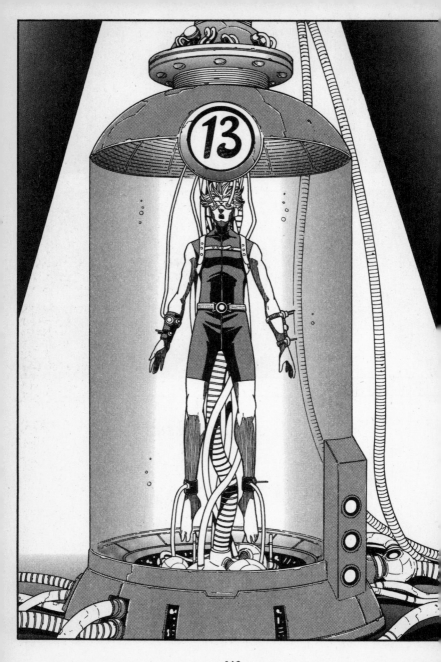

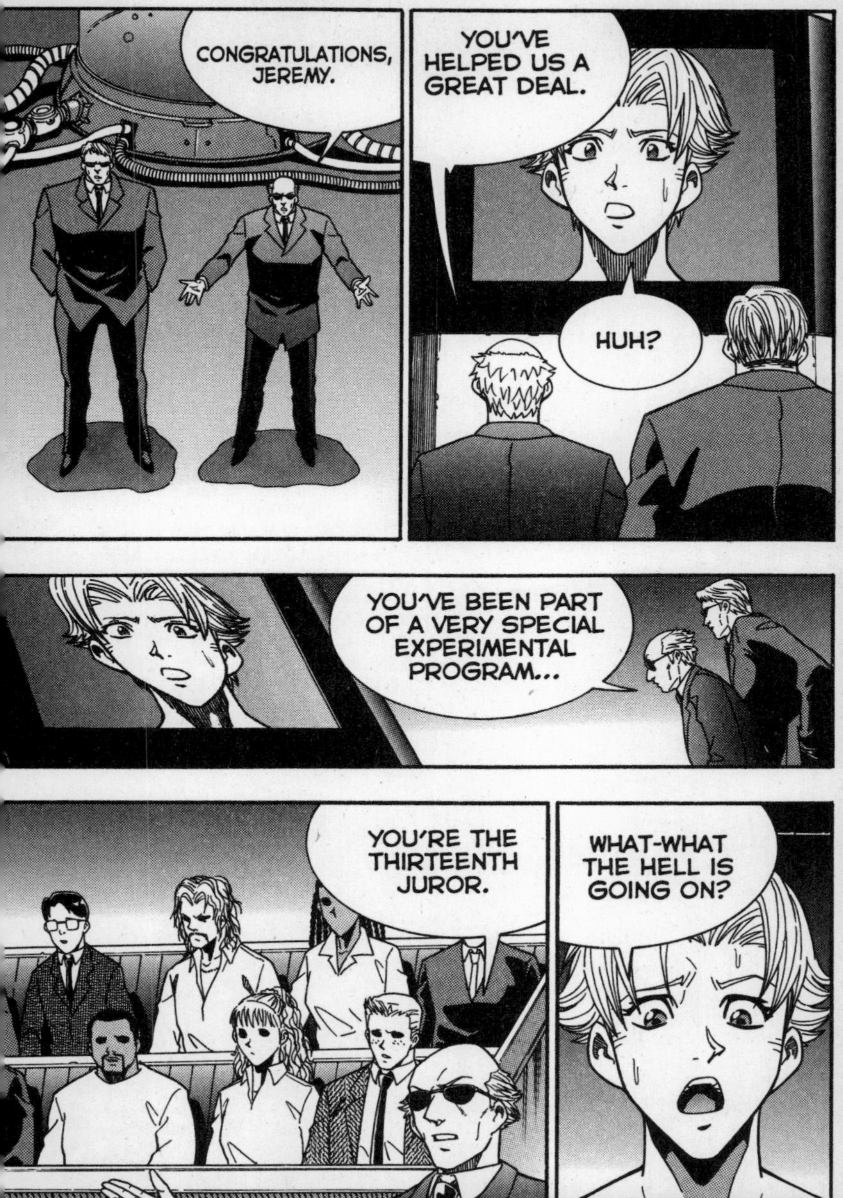
CONGRATULATIONS, JEREMY.
YOU'VE HELPED US A GREAT DEAL.
HUH?
YOU'VE BEEN PART OF A VERY SPECIAL EXPERIMENTAL PROGRAM...
YOU'RE THE THIRTEENTH JUROR.
WHAT-WHAT THE HELL IS GOING ON?

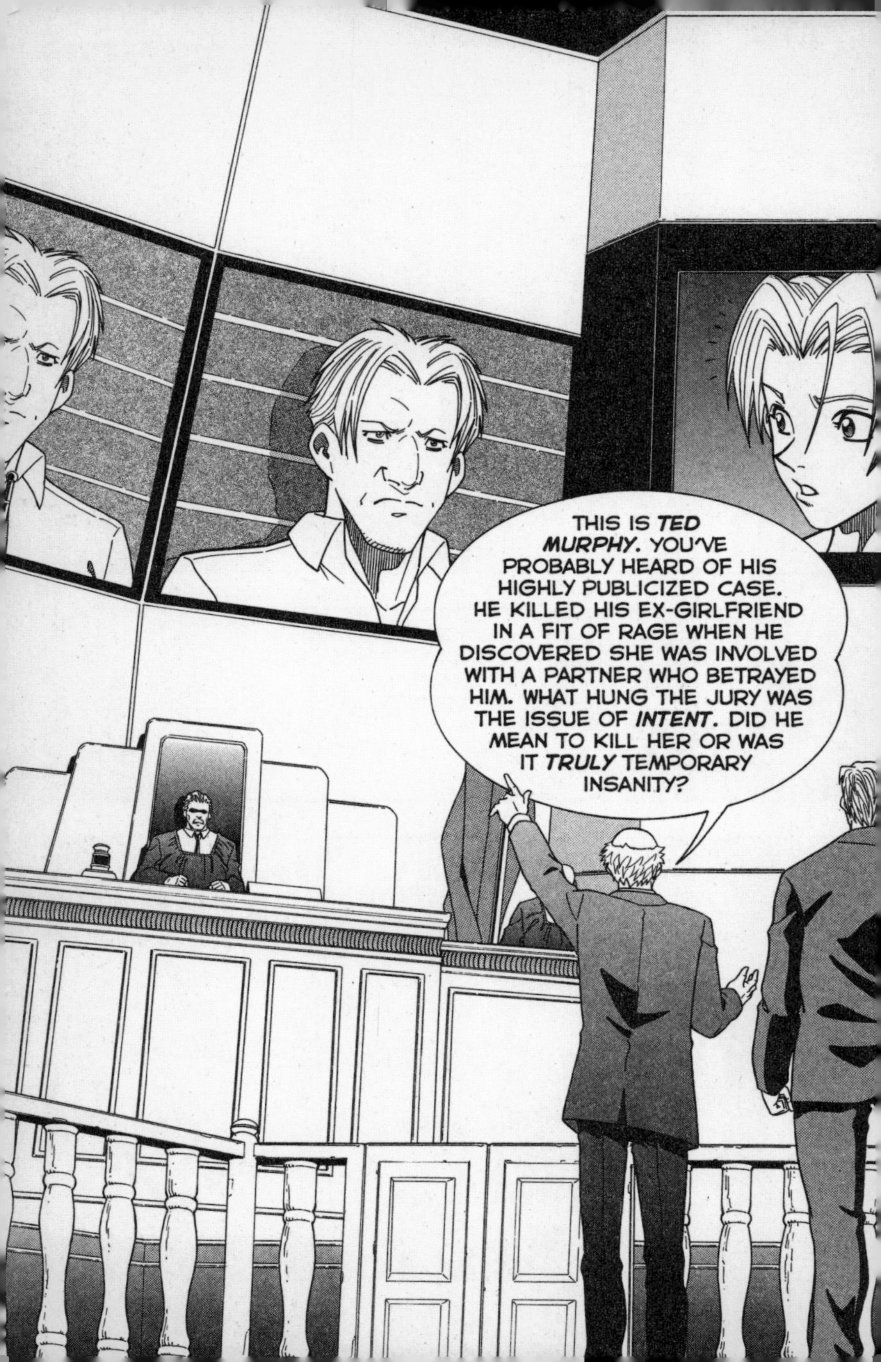
THIS IS TED MURPHY. YOU'VE PROBABLY HEARD OF HIS HIGHLY PUBLICIZED CASE. HE KILLED HIS EX-GIRLFRIEND IN A FIT OF RAGE WHEN HE DISCOVERED SHE WAS INVOLVED WITH A PARTNER WHO BETRAYED HIM. WHAT HUNG THE JURY WAS THE ISSUE OF INTENT. DID HE MEAN TO KILL HER OR WAS IT TRULY TEMPORARY INSANITY?

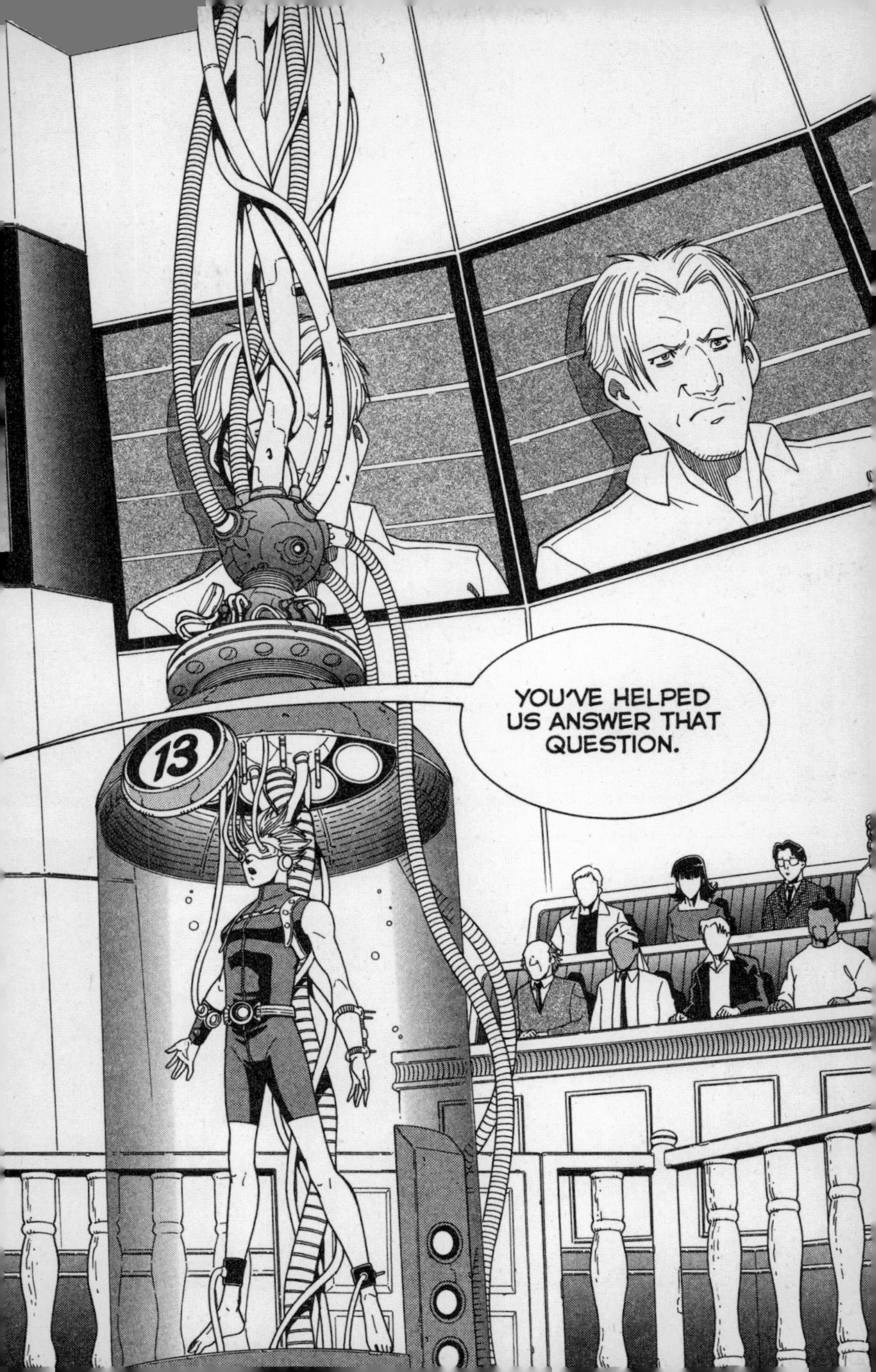
YOU'VE HELPED US ANSWER THAT QUESTION.
13

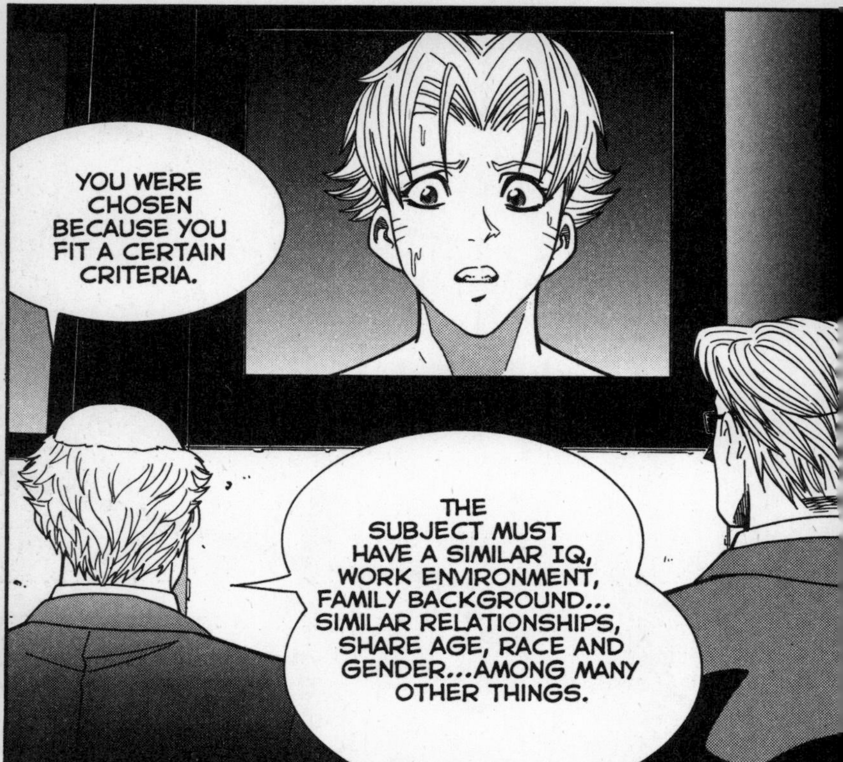
YOU WERE CHOSEN BECAUSE YOU FIT A CERTAIN CRITERIA.
THE SUBJECT MUST HAVE A SIMILAR IQ, WORK ENVIRONMENT, FAMILY BACKGROUND... SIMILAR RELATIONSHIPS, SHARE AGE, RACE AND GENDER...AMONG MANY OTHER THINGS.
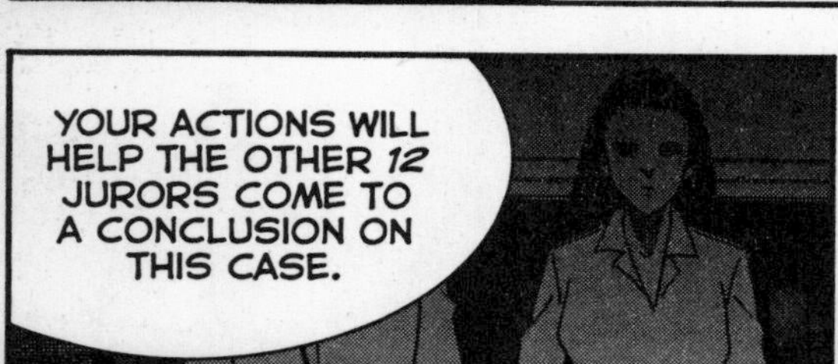
YOUR ACTIONS WILL HELP THE OTHER *12* JURORS COME TO A CONCLUSION ON THIS CASE.
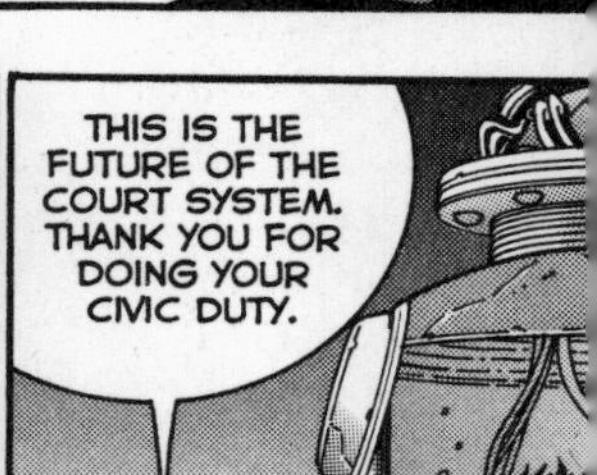
THIS IS THE FUTURE OF THE COURT SYSTEM. THANK YOU FOR DOING YOUR CIVIC DUTY.

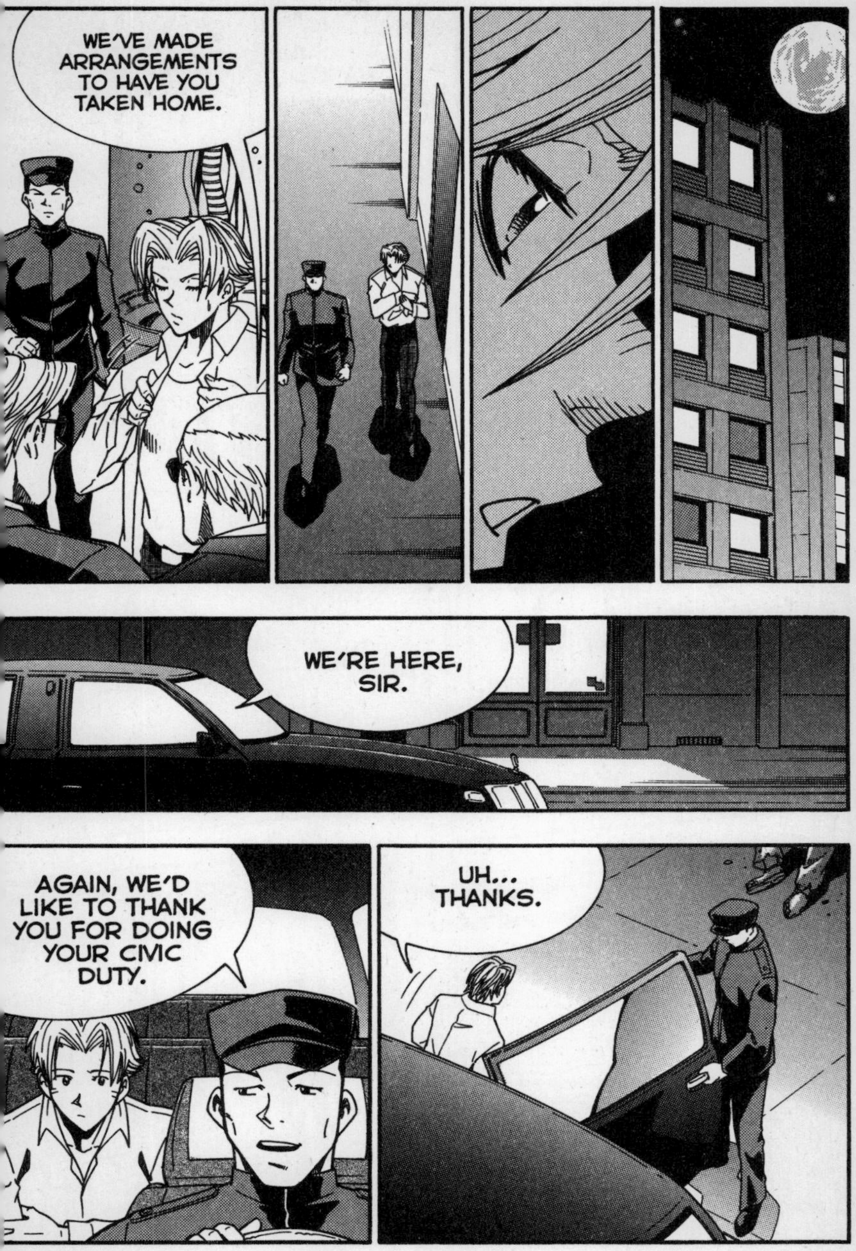

WE'VE MADE ARRANGEMENTS TO HAVE YOU TAKEN HOME.
WE'RE HERE, SIR.
AGAIN, WE'D LIKE TO THANK YOU FOR DOING YOUR CIVIC DUTY.
UH... THANKS.

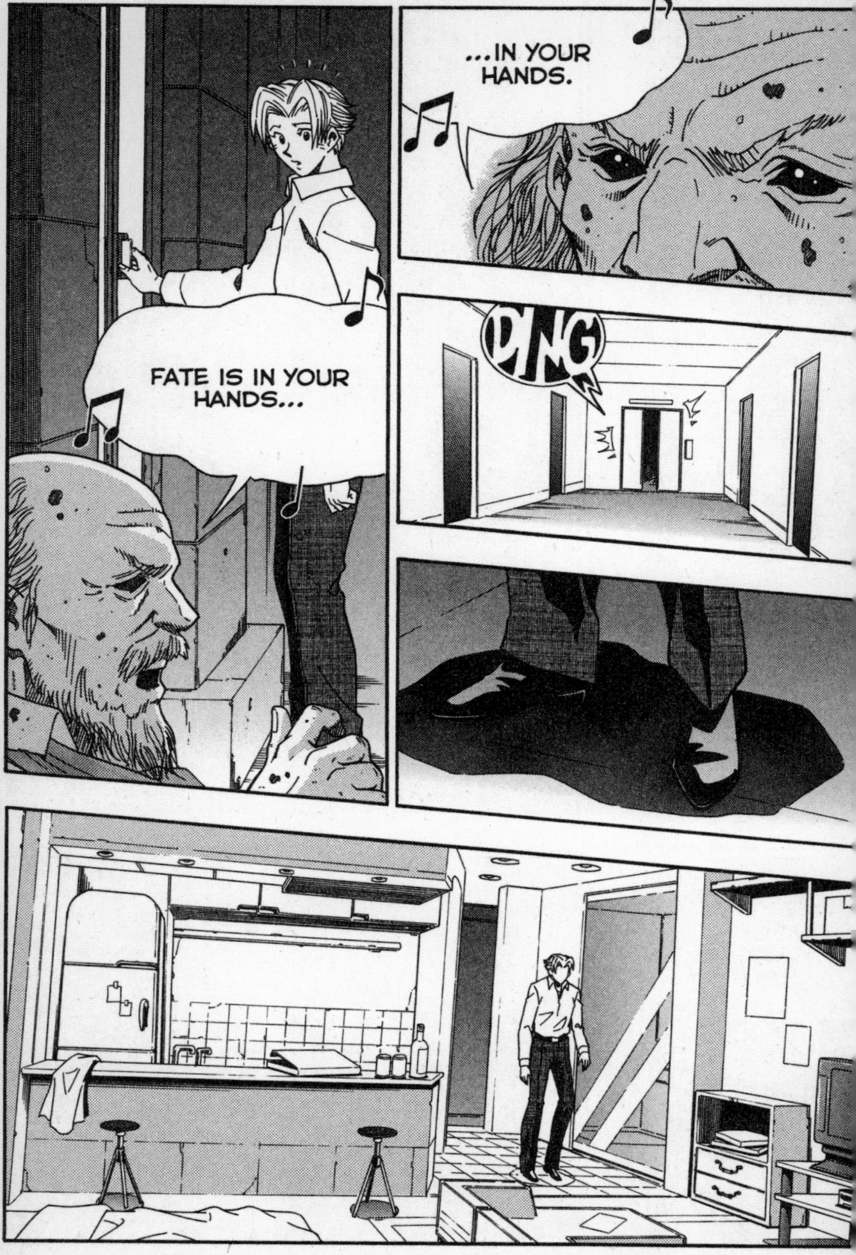
FATE IS IN YOUR HANDS...
...IN YOUR HANDS.
DING

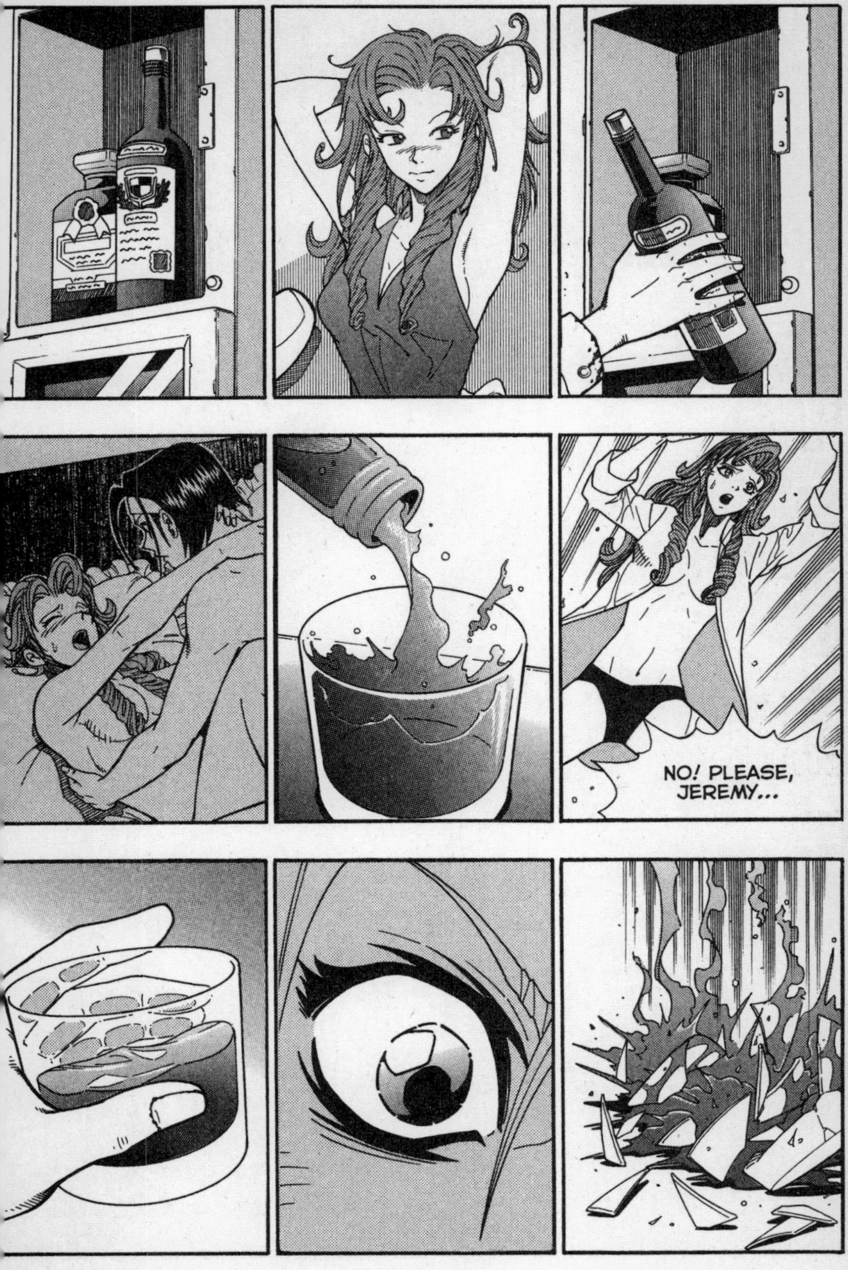
NO! PLEASE, JEREMY...

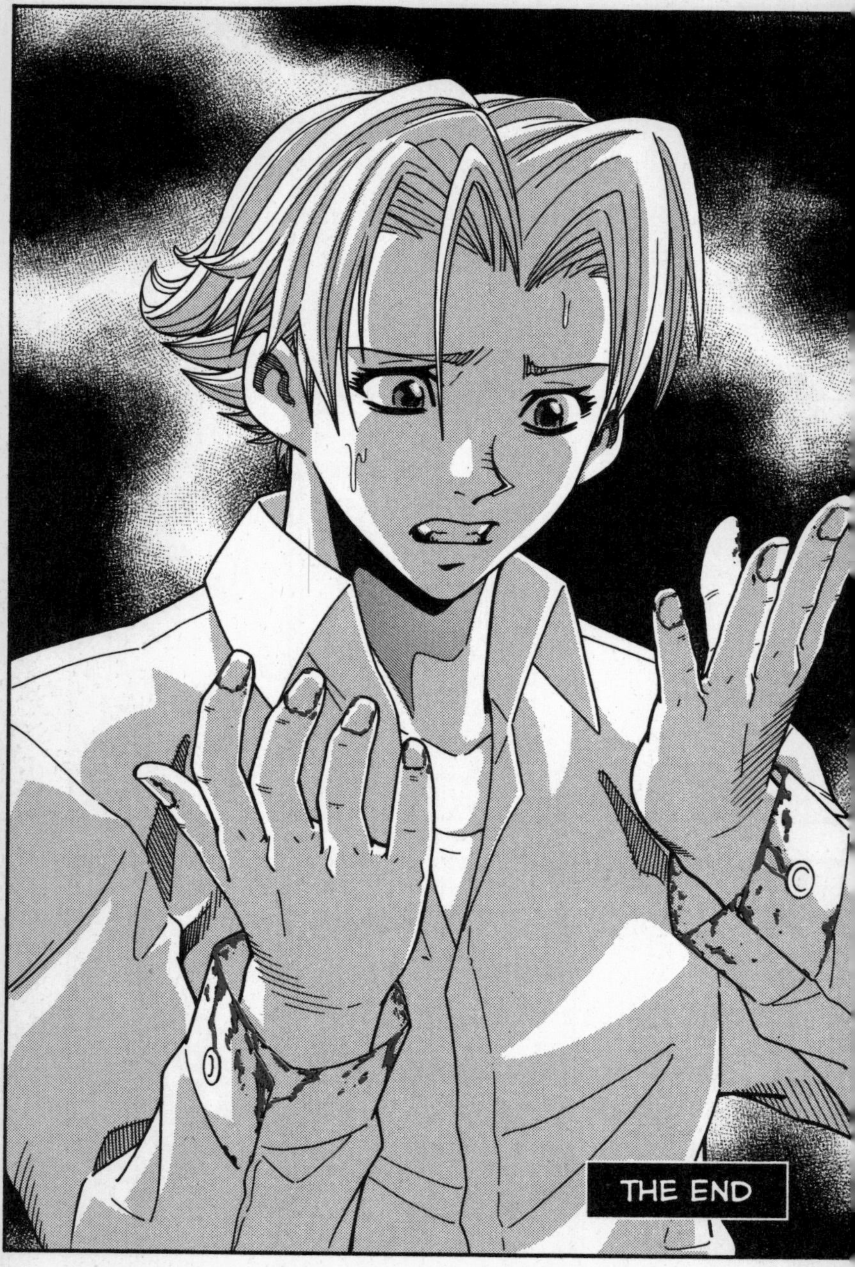
THE END

# JuRor 13

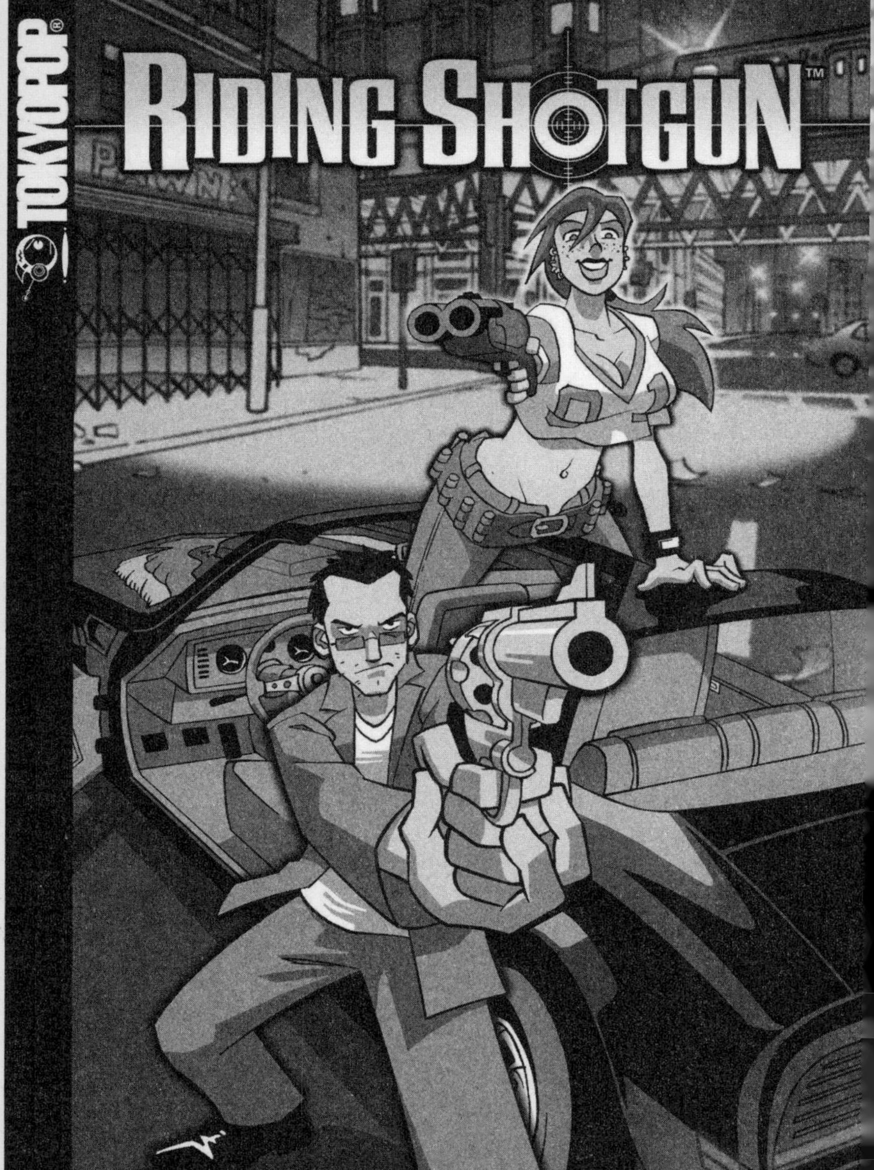
TOKYOPOP®
RIDING SHOTGUN™

# COMING SOON

# RIDING SHOTGUN

WRITTEN BY: NATHANIEL BOWDEN
ART BY: TRACY YARDLEY

THE GUN INDUSTRY HAS FINALLY MANAGED TO JUSTIFY THE EXISTENCE OF FIREARMS IN MAINSTREAM AMERICA...BY MAKING ASSASSINATION LEGAL. AND OF COURSE THERE IS AN ASSASSIN'S GUILD, GUIDELINES AND AN ASSASSIN'S ETIQUETTE THAT SHOULD BE FOLLOWED. NOW, DOYLE AND ABBY DON'T REALLY HAVE A LOT OF RESPECT FOR ANY OF THAT, UNTIL THEY FIND THEMSELVES BROKE, UNABLE TO LAND HIGH PAYING KILLS, AND BEHOLDEN TO THE NATIONAL ASSASSIN'S COMMITTEE TO EVEN STAY IN GOOD FAVOR WITH ANYONE. THE LAST THING THEY NEED IS FOR THEIR FIRST NAC HIT TO GO WRONG, BUT WHEN IT ENDS UP BEING DOYLE'S EX-GIRLFRIEND, ALL HELL BREAKS LOOSE. THIS IS AN ABSURD LOOK AT AN INCREASINGLY VICIOUS SOCIETY, BUT ALSO THE TOUCHING TALE OF TWO PEOPLE BROUGHT CLOSE BY GUN VIOLENCE.

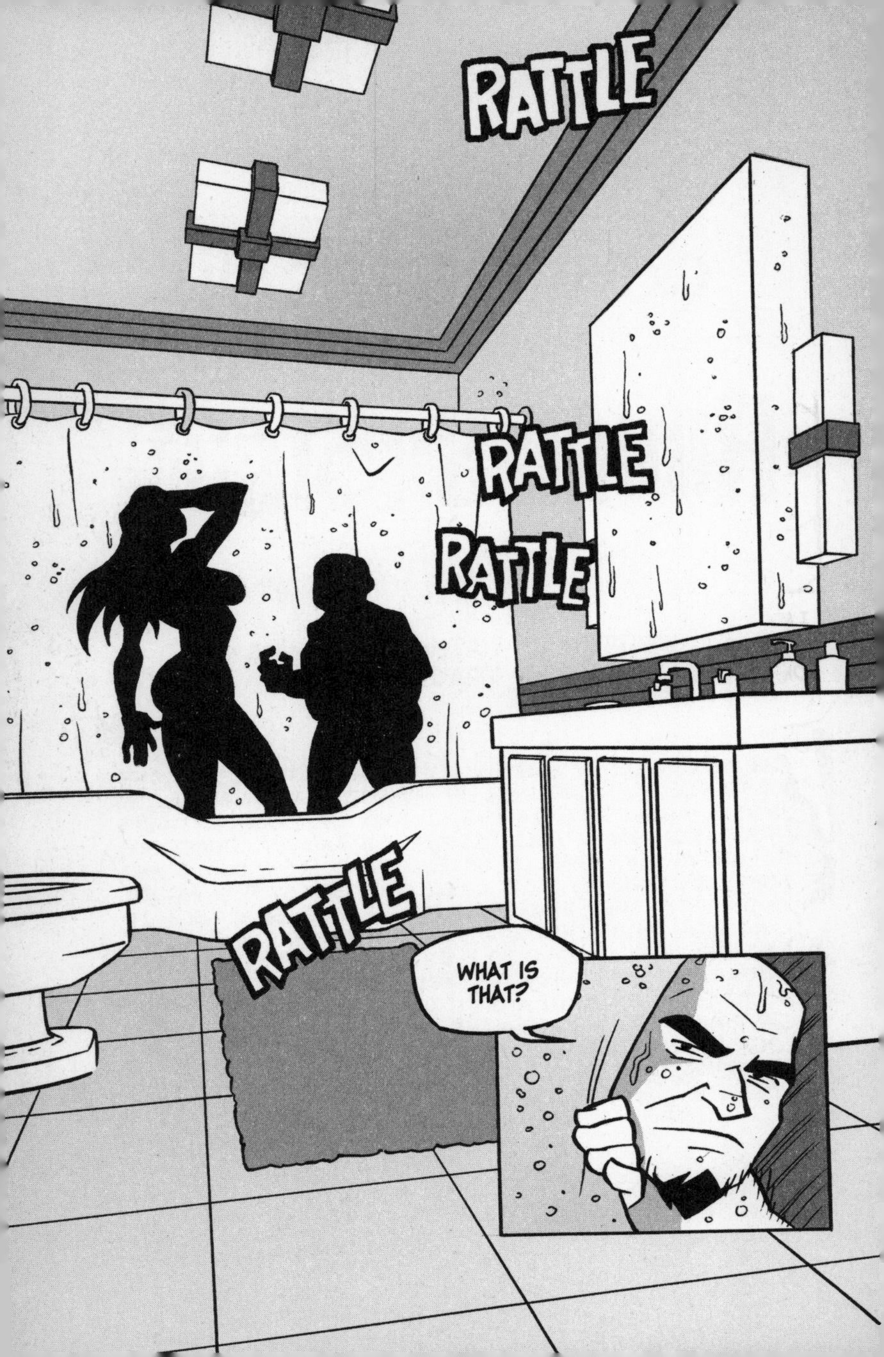
RATTLE
RATTLE
RATTLE
RATTLE
WHAT IS THAT?

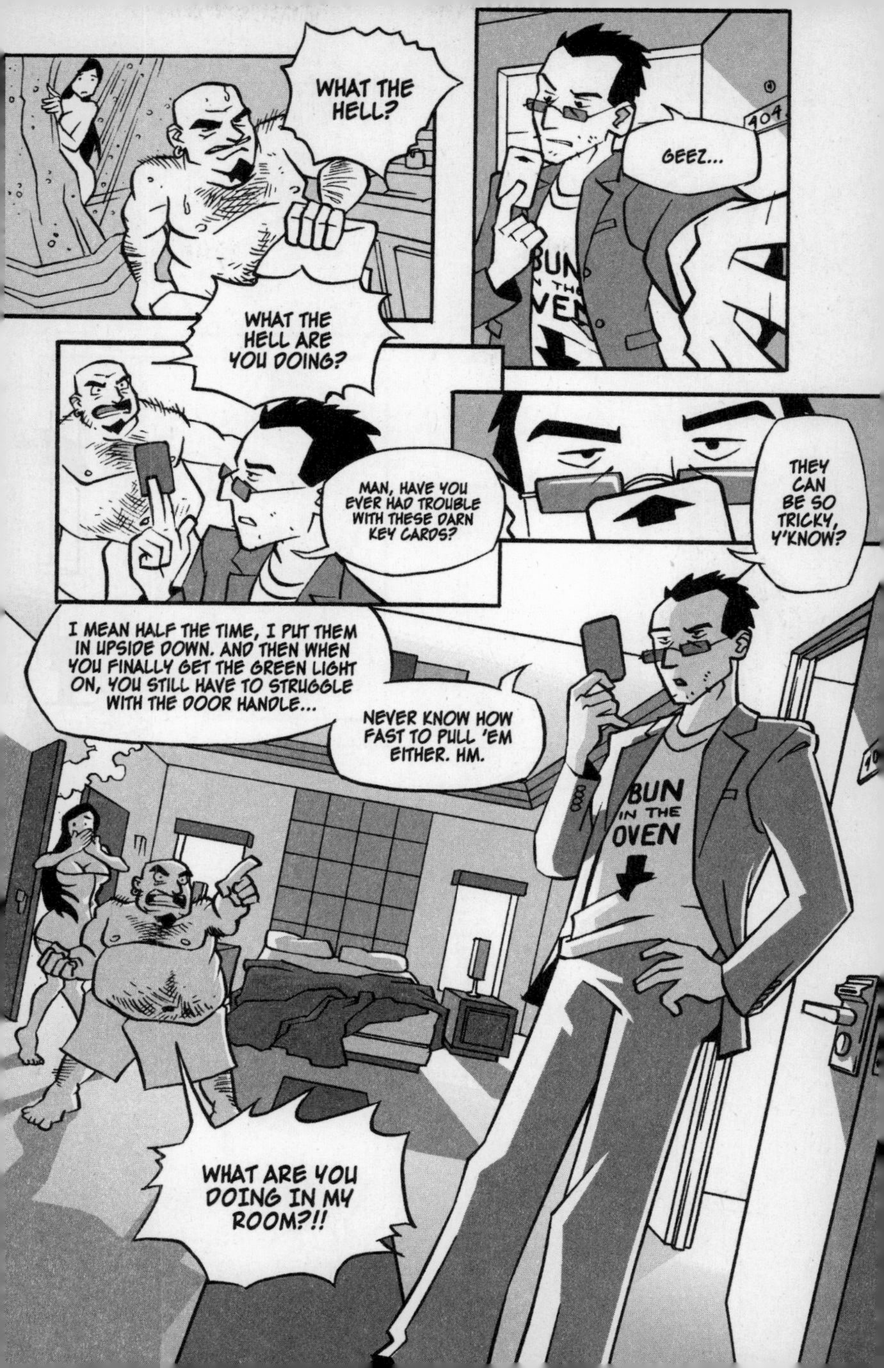
WHAT THE HELL?
GEEZ...
404
BUN IN THE OVEN
WHAT THE HELL ARE YOU DOING?
MAN, HAVE YOU EVER HAD TROUBLE WITH THESE DARN KEY CARDS?
THEY CAN BE SO TRICKY, Y'KNOW?
I MEAN HALF THE TIME, I PUT THEM IN UPSIDE DOWN. AND THEN WHEN YOU FINALLY GET THE GREEN LIGHT ON, YOU STILL HAVE TO STRUGGLE WITH THE DOOR HANDLE...
NEVER KNOW HOW FAST TO PULL 'EM EITHER. HM.
BUN IN THE OVEN
WHAT ARE YOU DOING IN MY ROOM?!!

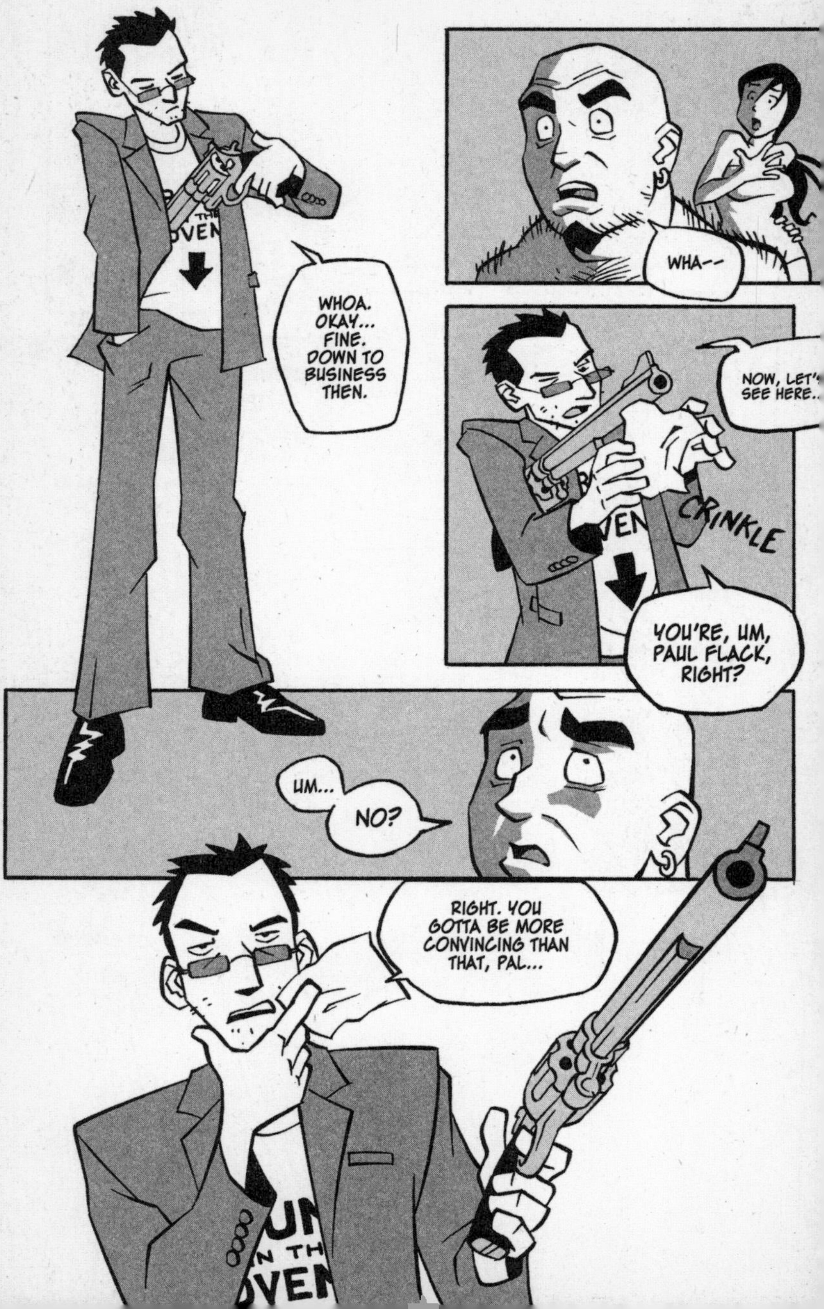
WHOA. OKAY... FINE. DOWN TO BUSINESS THEN.
WHA--
NOW, LET'S SEE HERE..
CRINKLE
YOU'RE, UM, PAUL FLACK, RIGHT?
UM...
NO?
RIGHT. YOU GOTTA BE MORE CONVINCING THAN THAT, PAL...

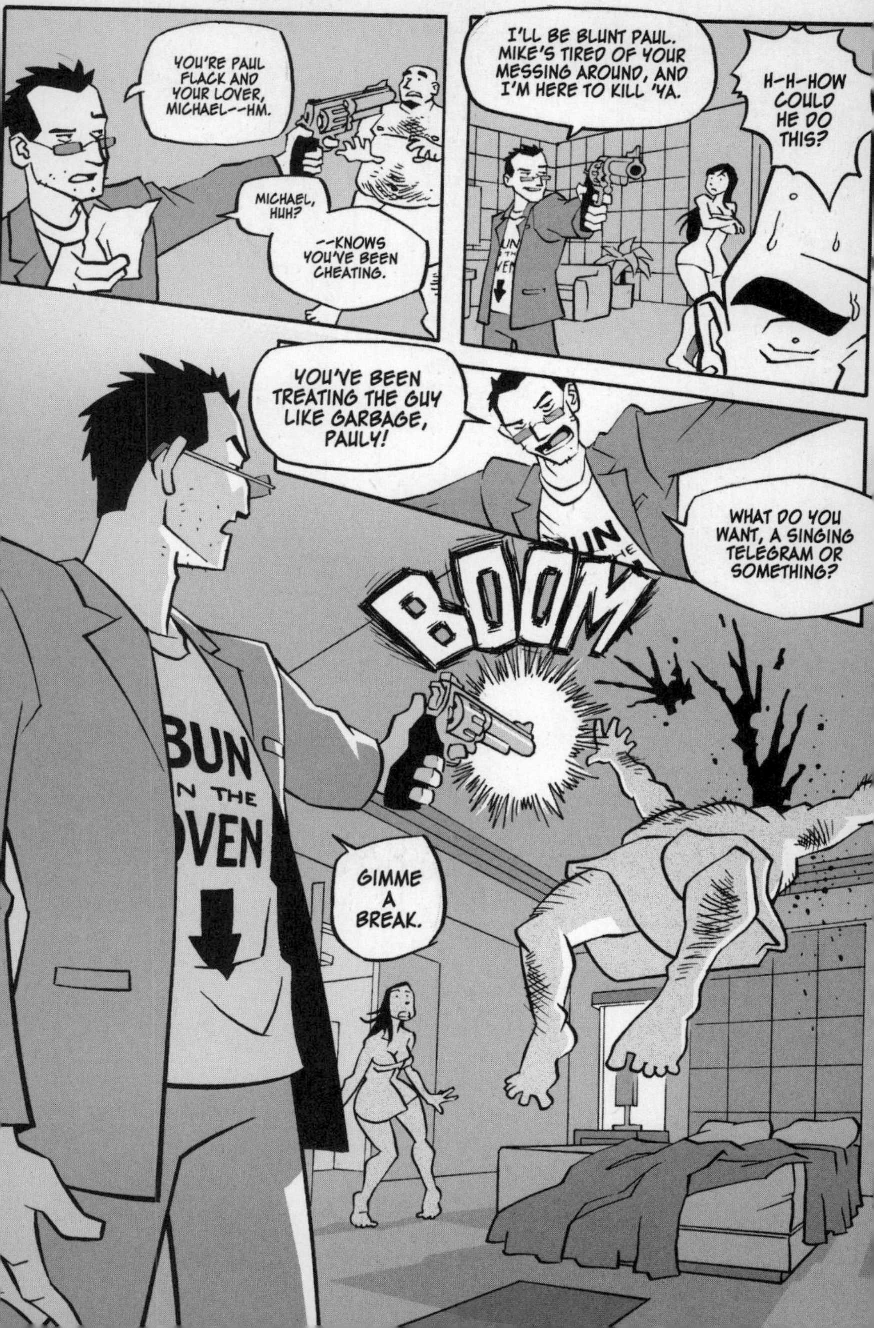
YOU'RE PAUL FLACK AND YOUR LOVER, MICHAEL--HM.
MICHAEL, HUH?
--KNOWS YOU'VE BEEN CHEATING.
I'LL BE BLUNT PAUL. MIKE'S TIRED OF YOUR MESSING AROUND, AND I'M HERE TO KILL 'YA.
H-H-HOW COULD HE DO THIS?
YOU'VE BEEN TREATING THE GUY LIKE GARBAGE, PAULY!
WHAT DO YOU WANT, A SINGING TELEGRAM OR SOMETHING?
BOOM
BUN IN THE OVEN
GIMME A BREAK.

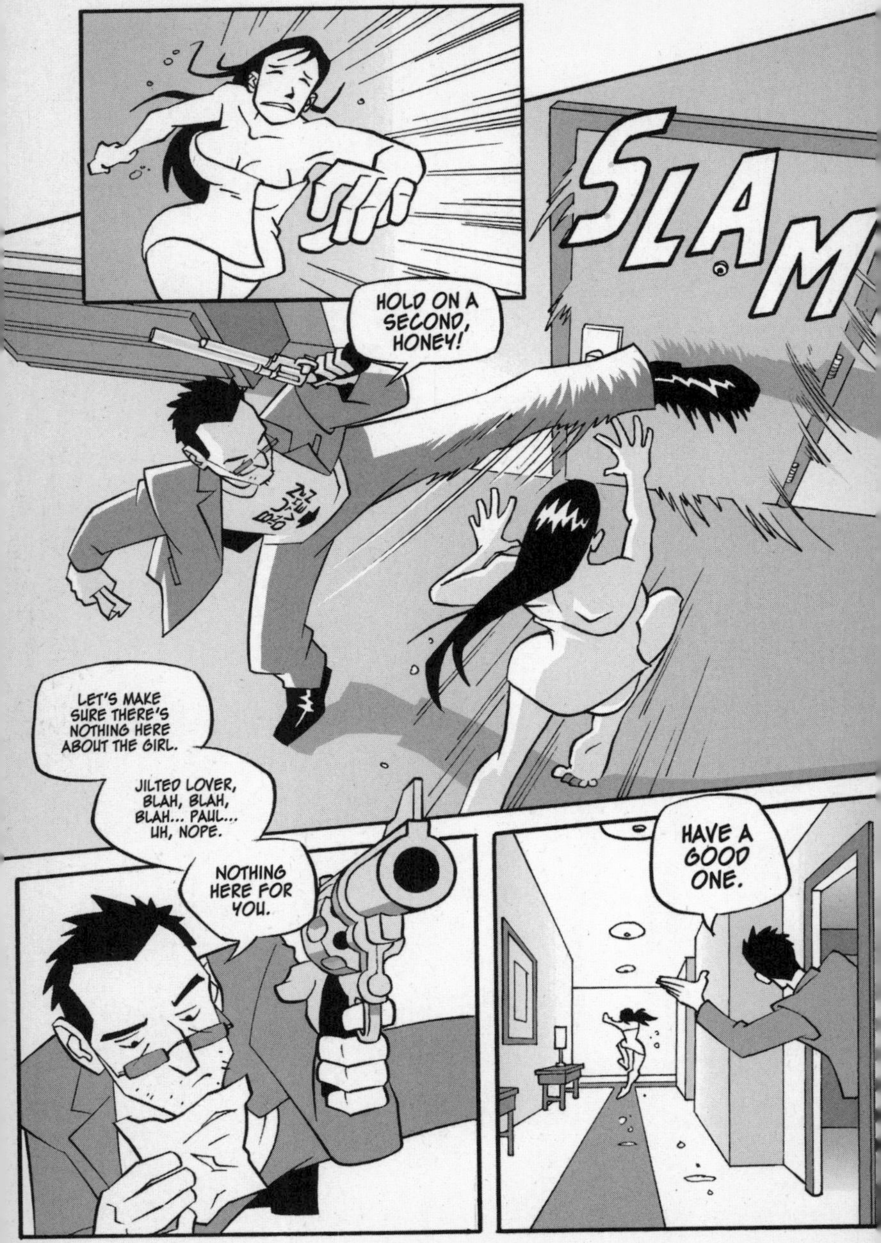
SLAM
HOLD ON A SECOND, HONEY!
LET'S MAKE SURE THERE'S NOTHING HERE ABOUT THE GIRL.
JILTED LOVER, BLAH, BLAH, BLAH... PAUL... UH, NOPE.
NOTHING HERE FOR YOU.
HAVE A GOOD ONE.

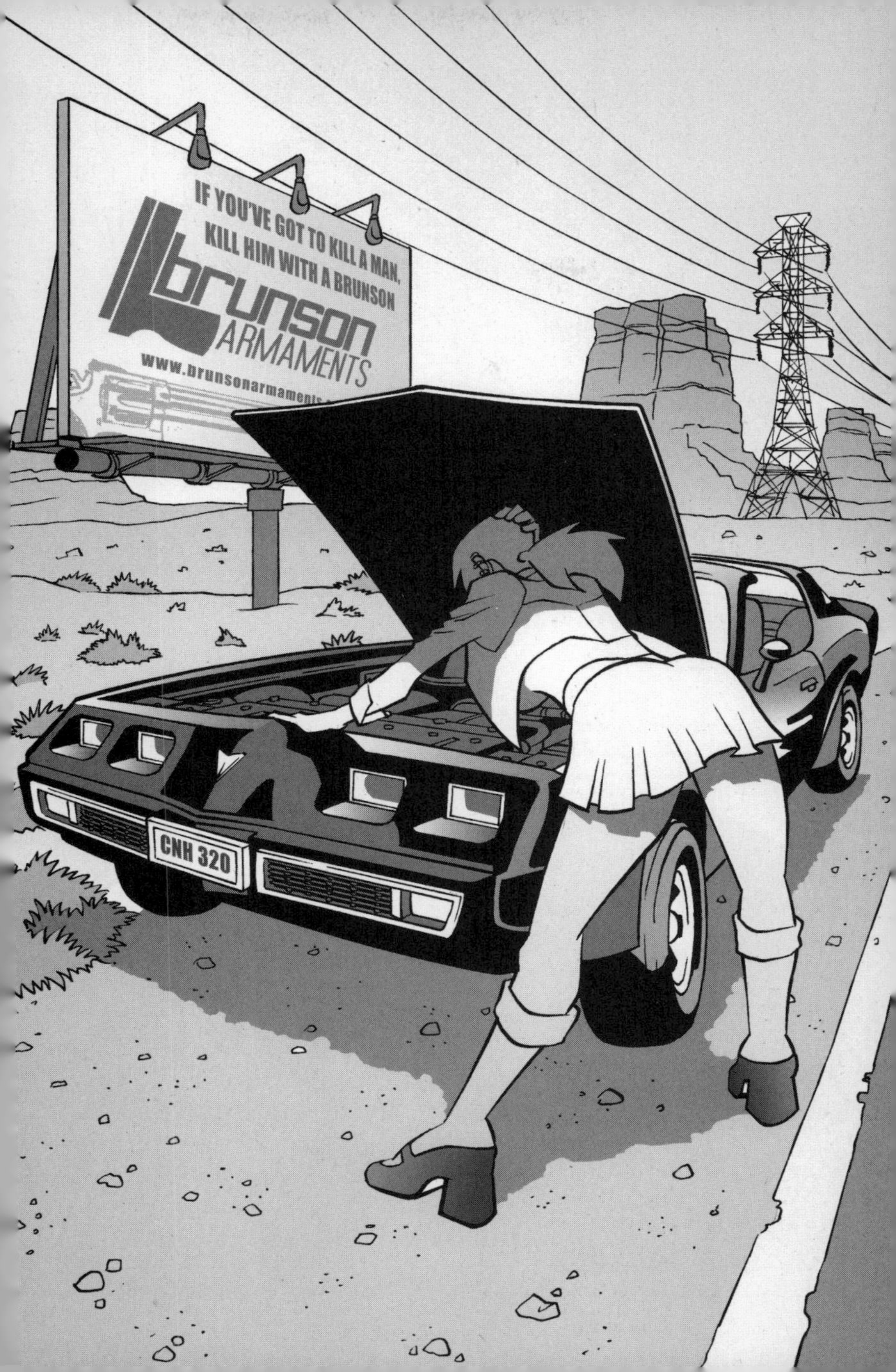
IF YOU'VE GOT TO KILL A MAN,
KILL HIM WITH A BRUNSON
brunson
ARMAMENTS
CNH 320

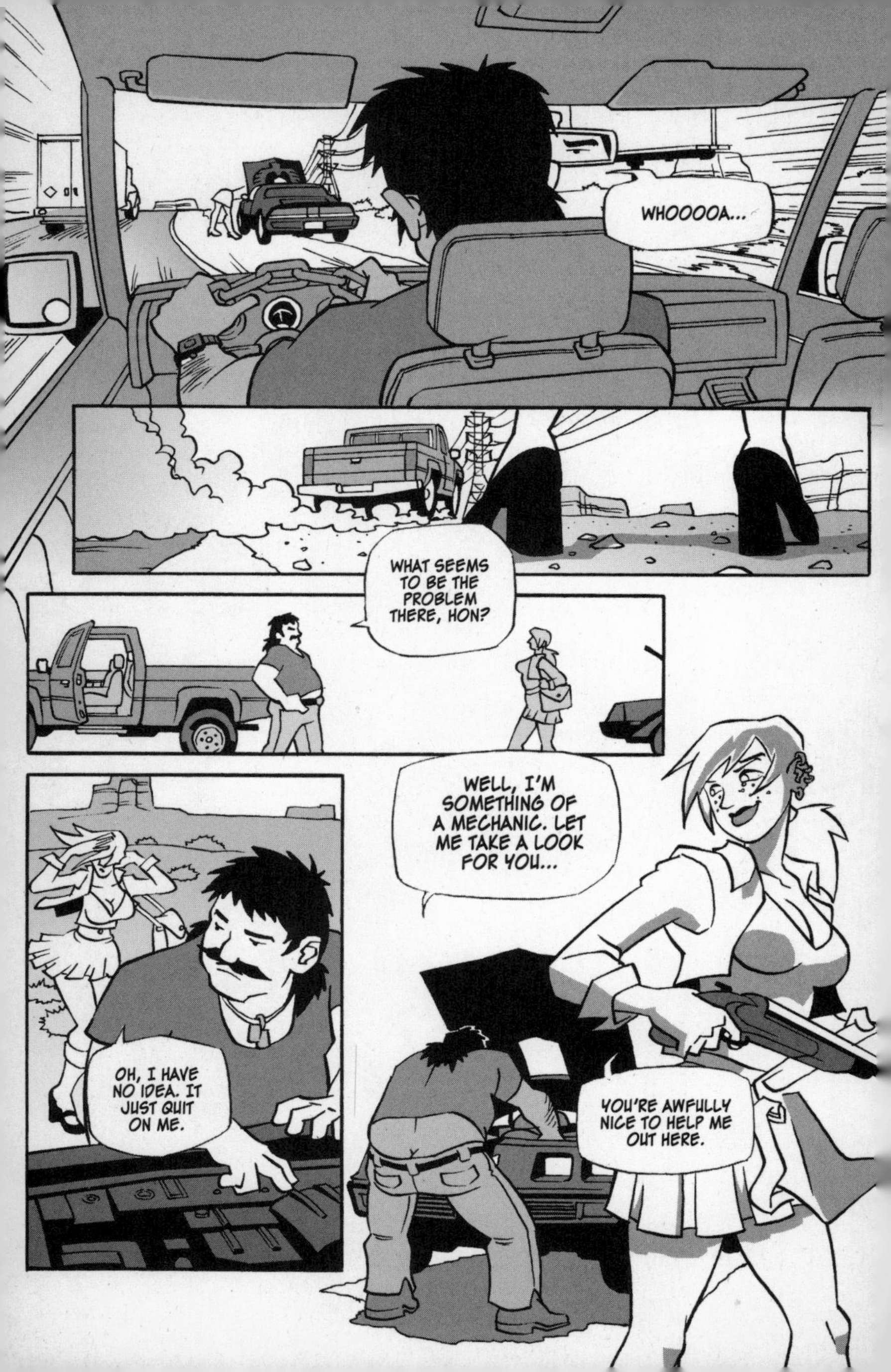
WHOOOOA...
WHAT SEEMS TO BE THE PROBLEM THERE, HON?
OH, I HAVE NO IDEA. IT JUST QUIT ON ME.
WELL, I'M SOMETHING OF A MECHANIC. LET ME TAKE A LOOK FOR YOU...
YOU'RE AWFULLY NICE TO HELP ME OUT HERE.

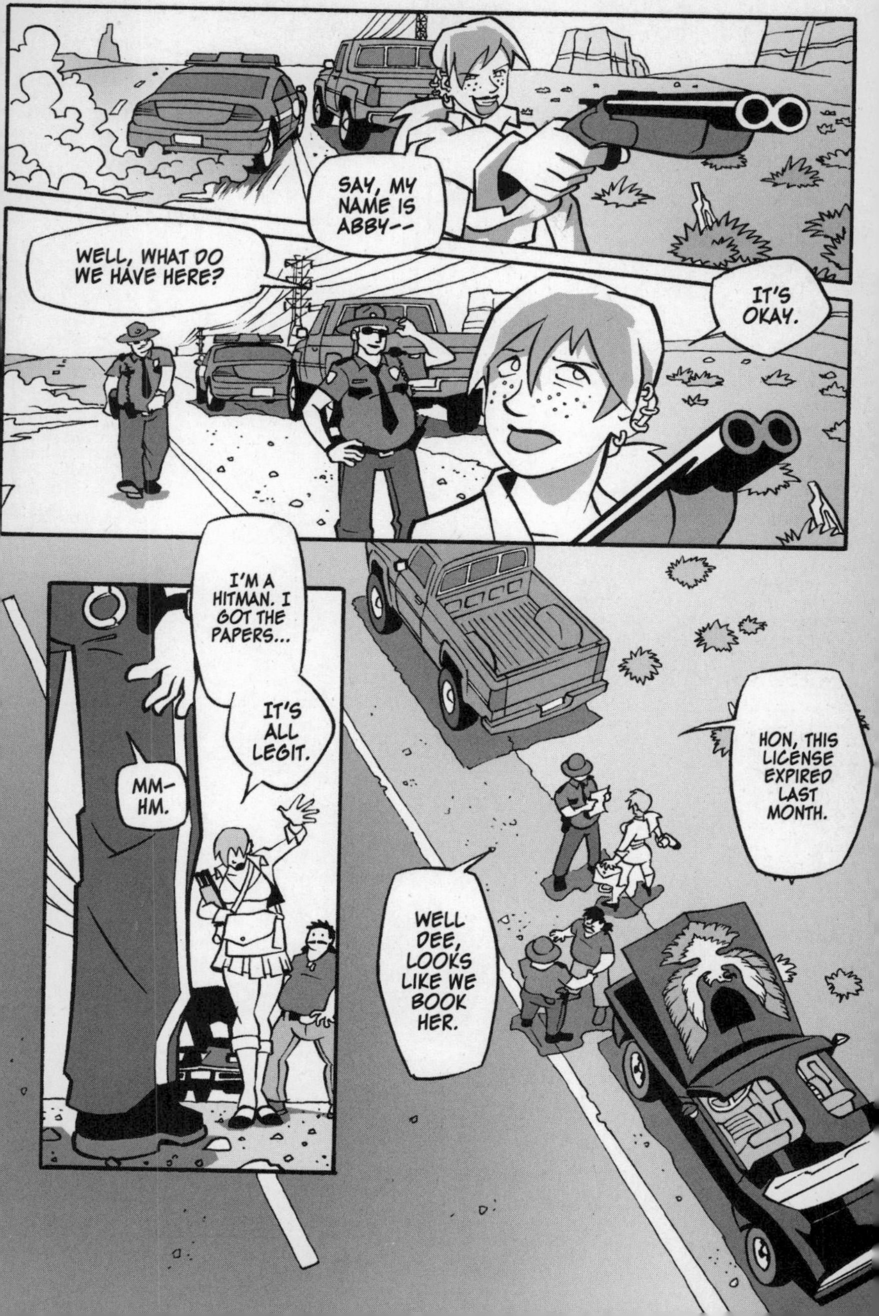

SAY, MY NAME IS ABBY--
WELL, WHAT DO WE HAVE HERE?
IT'S OKAY.
I'M A HITMAN. I GOT THE PAPERS...
IT'S ALL LEGIT.
MM-HM.
HON, THIS LICENSE EXPIRED LAST MONTH.
WELL DEE, LOOKS LIKE WE BOOK HER.

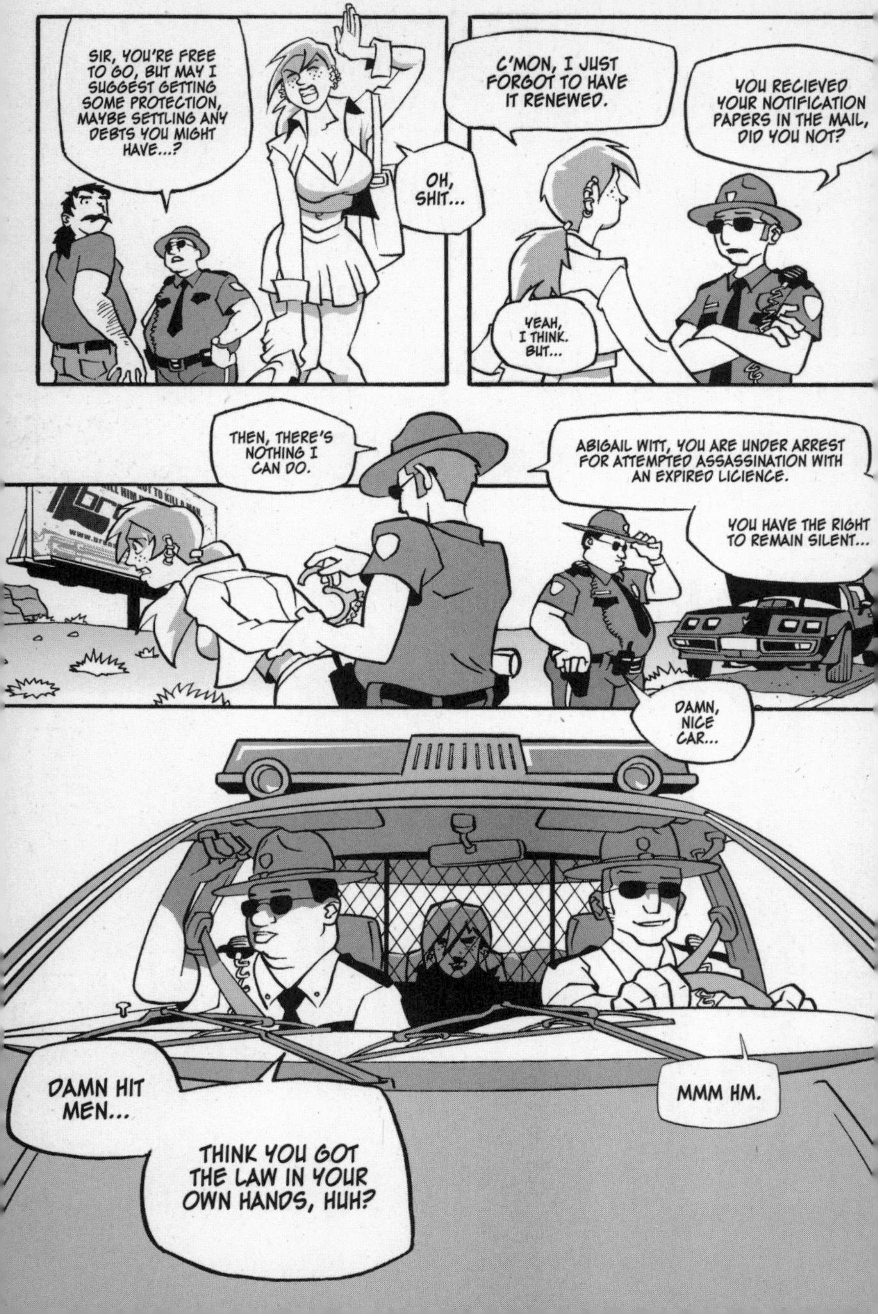
SIR, YOU'RE FREE TO GO, BUT MAY I SUGGEST GETTING SOME PROTECTION, MAYBE SETTLING ANY DEBTS YOU MIGHT HAVE...?
OH, SHIT...
C'MON, I JUST FORGOT TO HAVE IT RENEWED.
YOU RECIEVED YOUR NOTIFICATION PAPERS IN THE MAIL, DID YOU NOT?
YEAH, I THINK. BUT...
THEN, THERE'S NOTHING I CAN DO.
ABIGAIL WITT, YOU ARE UNDER ARREST FOR ATTEMPTED ASSASSINATION WITH AN EXPIRED LICIENCE.
YOU HAVE THE RIGHT TO REMAIN SILENT...
DAMN, NICE CAR...
DAMN HIT MEN...
THINK YOU GOT THE LAW IN YOUR OWN HANDS, HUH?
MMM HM.

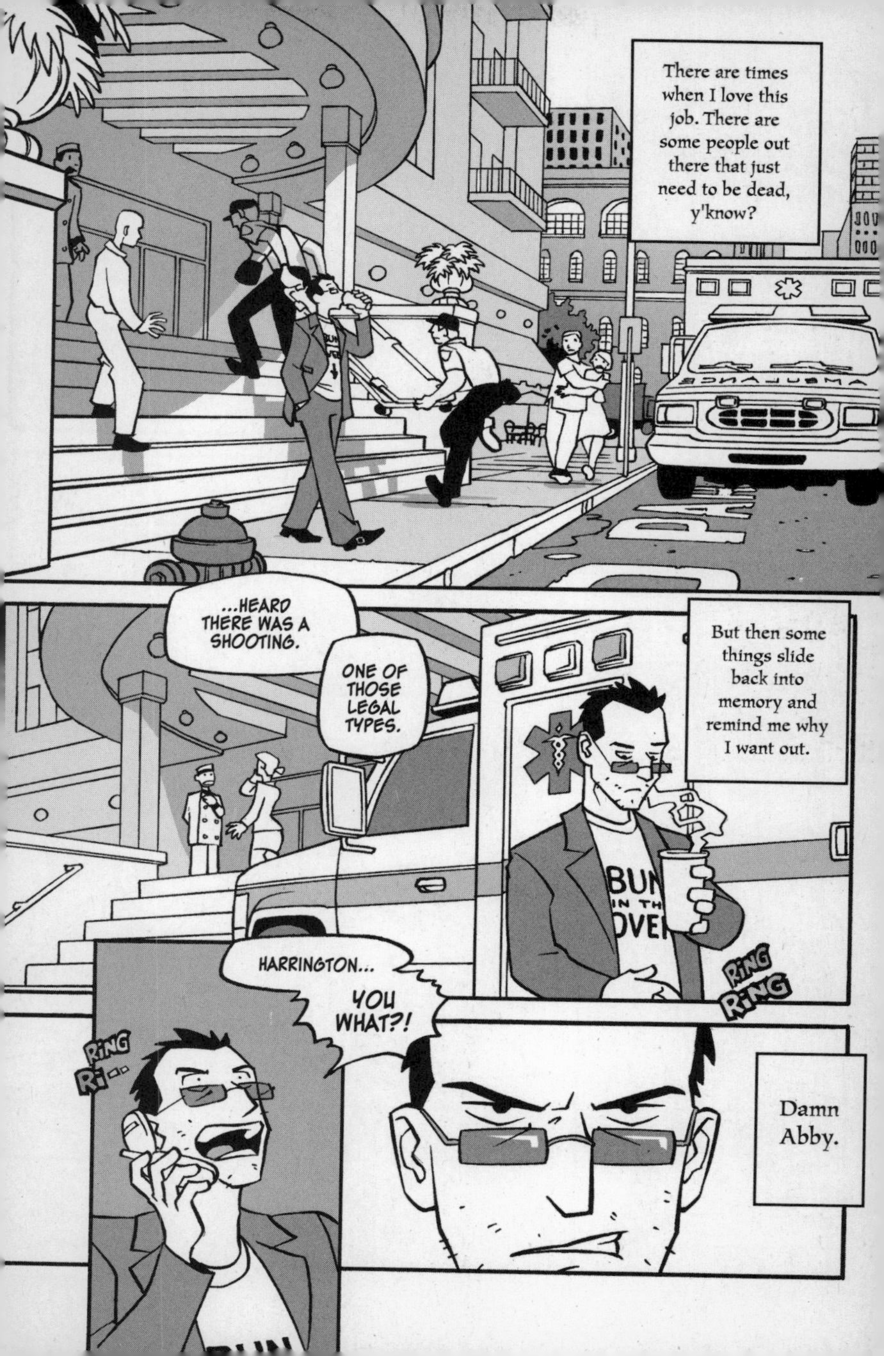
There are times when I love this job. There are some people out there that just need to be dead, y'know?
...HEARD THERE WAS A SHOOTING.
ONE OF THOSE LEGAL TYPES.
But then some things slide back into memory and remind me why I want out.
RING RING
RING Ri--
HARRINGTON...
YOU WHAT?!
Damn Abby.

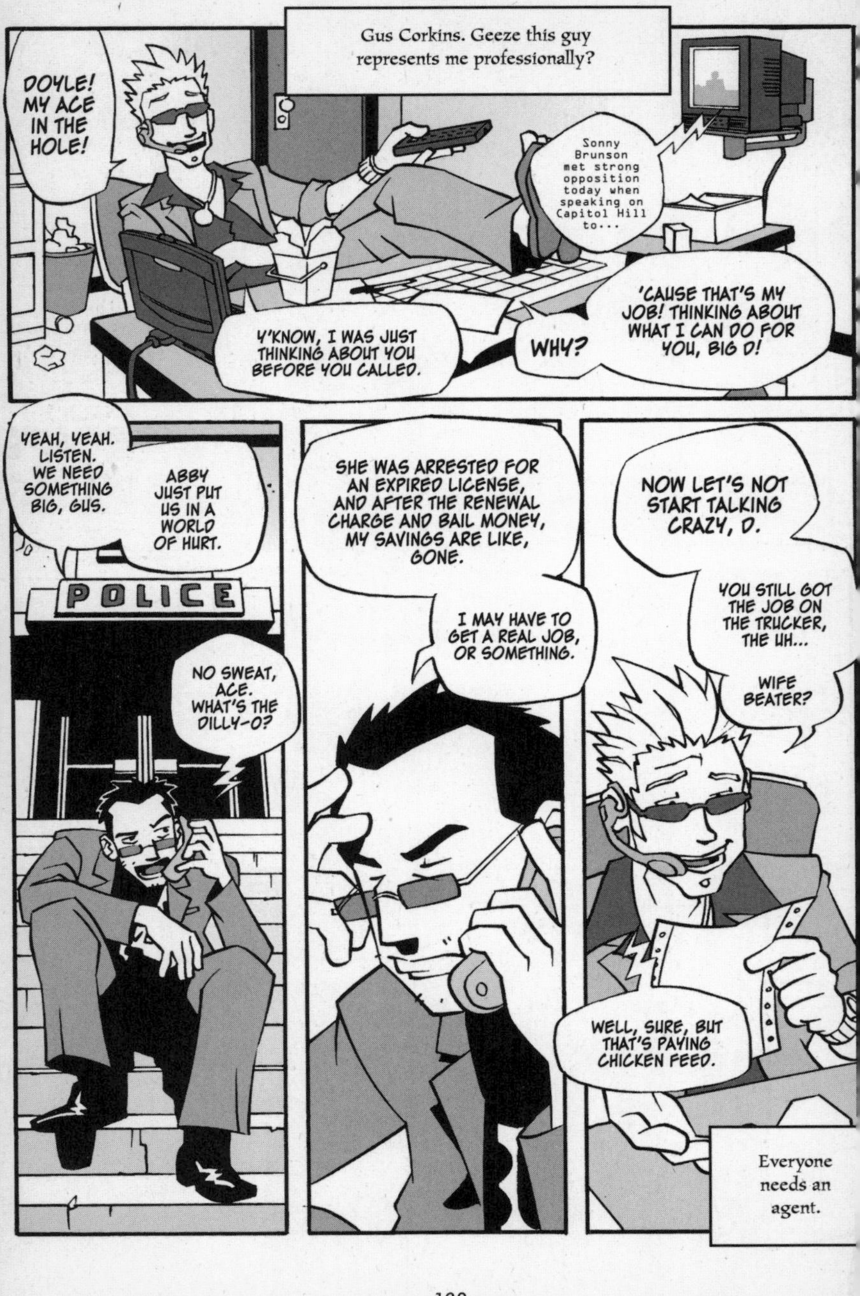

Gus Corkins. Geeze this guy represents me professionally?
DOYLE! MY ACE IN THE HOLE!
Sonny Brunson met strong opposition today when speaking on Capitol Hill to...
Y'KNOW, I WAS JUST THINKING ABOUT YOU BEFORE YOU CALLED.
WHY?
'CAUSE THAT'S MY JOB! THINKING ABOUT WHAT I CAN DO FOR YOU, BIG D!
YEAH, YEAH. LISTEN. WE NEED SOMETHING BIG, GUS.
ABBY JUST PUT US IN A WORLD OF HURT.
POLICE
NO SWEAT, ACE. WHAT'S THE DILLY-O?
SHE WAS ARRESTED FOR AN EXPIRED LICENSE, AND AFTER THE RENEWAL CHARGE AND BAIL MONEY, MY SAVINGS ARE LIKE, GONE.
I MAY HAVE TO GET A REAL JOB, OR SOMETHING.
NOW LET'S NOT START TALKING CRAZY, D.
YOU STILL GOT THE JOB ON THE TRUCKER, THE UH...
WIFE BEATER?
WELL, SURE, BUT THAT'S PAYING CHICKEN FEED.
Everyone needs an agent.

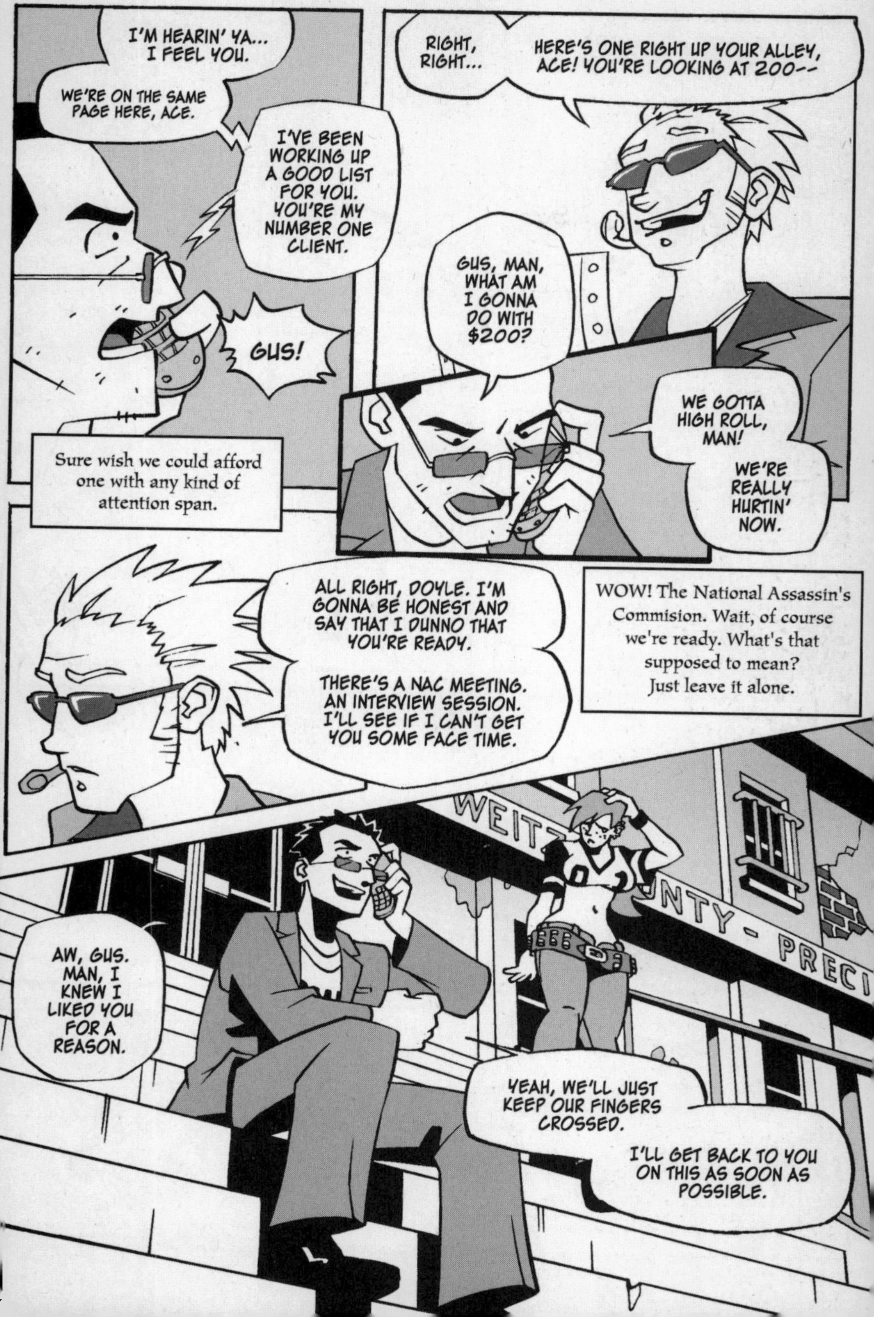
I'M HEARIN' YA... I FEEL YOU.
WE'RE ON THE SAME PAGE HERE, ACE.
I'VE BEEN WORKING UP A GOOD LIST FOR YOU. YOU'RE MY NUMBER ONE CLIENT.
GUS!
Sure wish we could afford one with any kind of attention span.
RIGHT, RIGHT...
HERE'S ONE RIGHT UP YOUR ALLEY, ACE! YOU'RE LOOKING AT 200--
GUS, MAN, WHAT AM I GONNA DO WITH $200?
WE GOTTA HIGH ROLL, MAN!
WE'RE REALLY HURTIN' NOW.
ALL RIGHT, DOYLE. I'M GONNA BE HONEST AND SAY THAT I DUNNO THAT YOU'RE READY.
THERE'S A NAC MEETING. AN INTERVIEW SESSION. I'LL SEE IF I CAN'T GET YOU SOME FACE TIME.
WOW! The National Assassin's Commision. Wait, of course we're ready. What's that supposed to mean? Just leave it alone.
AW, GUS. MAN, I KNEW I LIKED YOU FOR A REASON.
YEAH, WE'LL JUST KEEP OUR FINGERS CROSSED.
I'LL GET BACK TO YOU ON THIS AS SOON AS POSSIBLE.

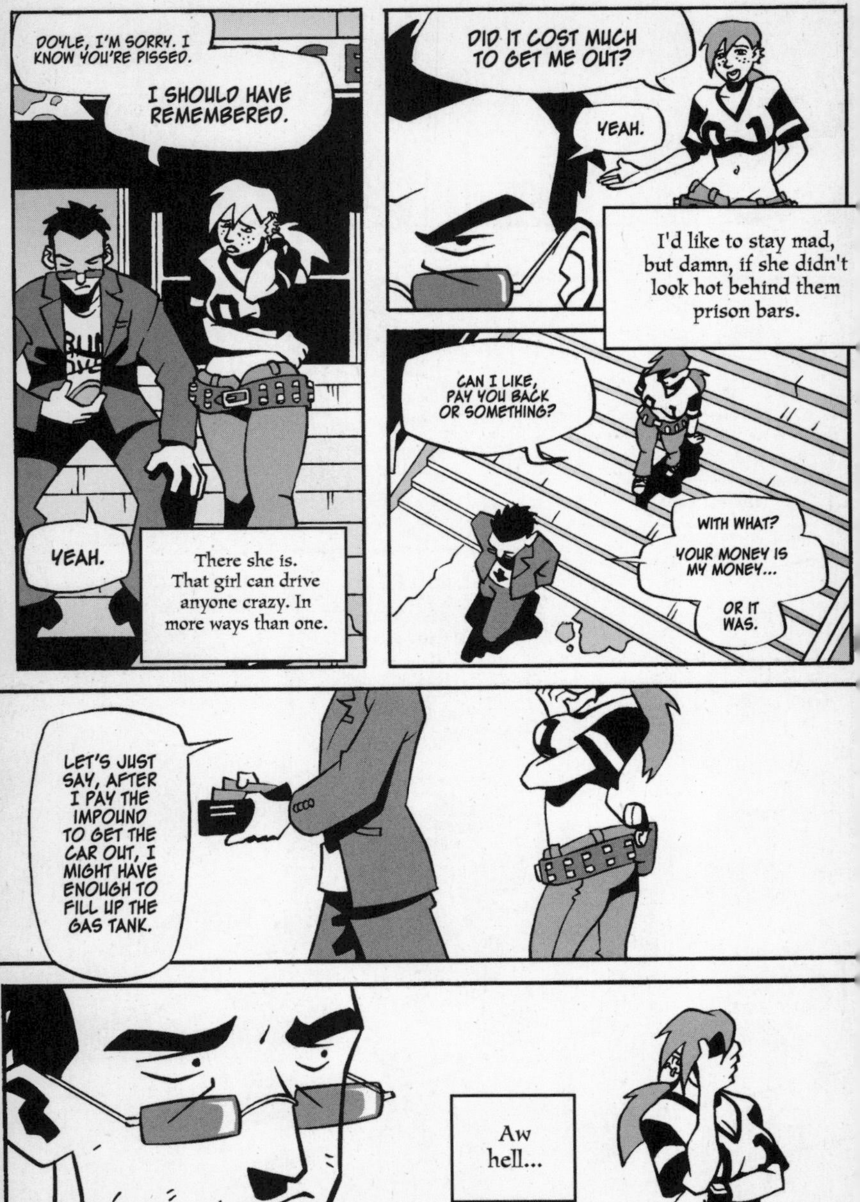
DOYLE, I'M SORRY. I KNOW YOU'RE PISSED.
I SHOULD HAVE REMEMBERED.
YEAH.
There she is. That girl can drive anyone crazy. In more ways than one.
DID IT COST MUCH TO GET ME OUT?
YEAH.
I'd like to stay mad, but damn, if she didn't look hot behind them prison bars.
CAN I LIKE, PAY YOU BACK OR SOMETHING?
WITH WHAT?
YOUR MONEY IS MY MONEY...
OR IT WAS.
LET'S JUST SAY, AFTER I PAY THE IMPOUND TO GET THE CAR OUT, I MIGHT HAVE ENOUGH TO FILL UP THE GAS TANK.
Aw hell...

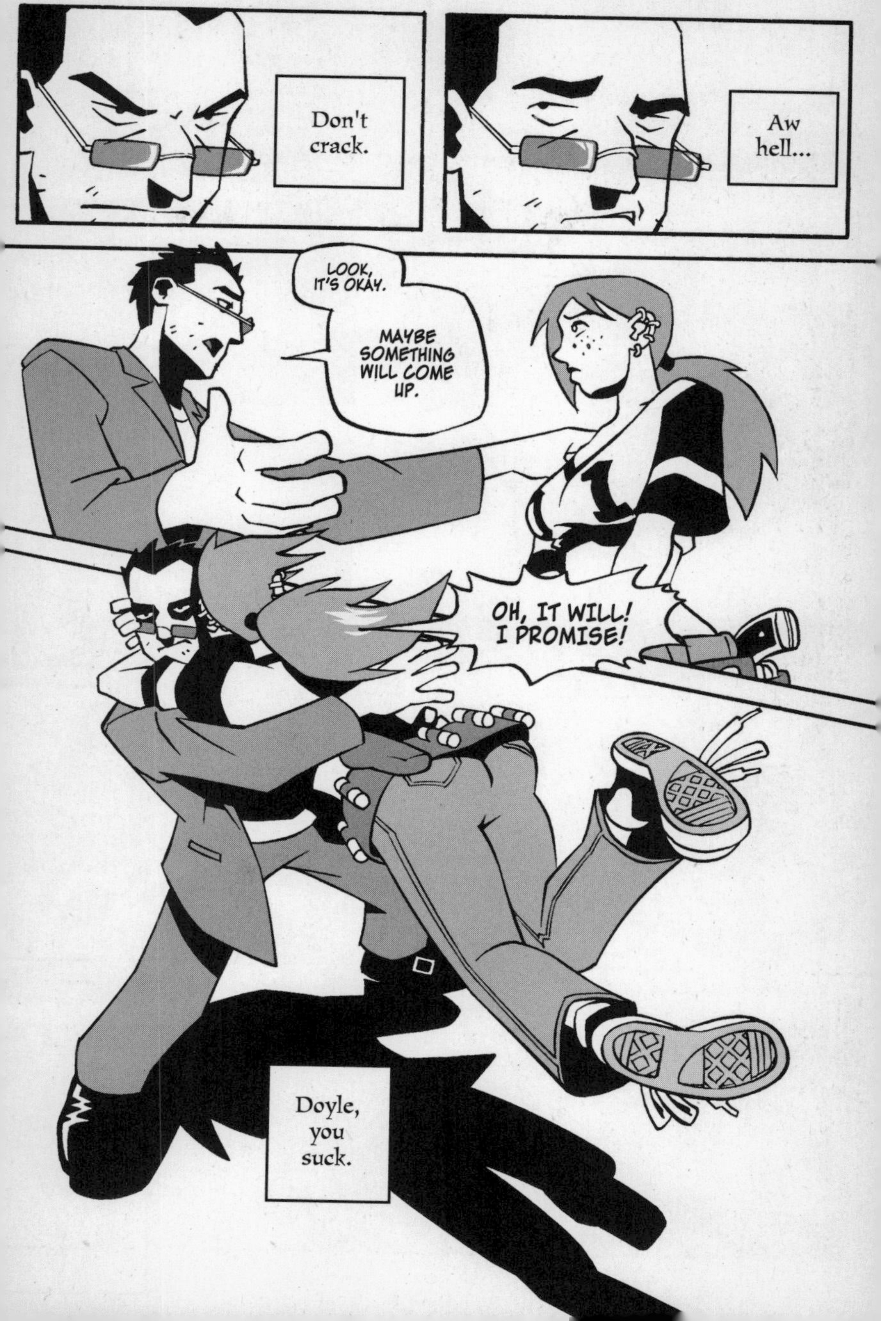
Don't crack.
Aw hell...
LOOK, IT'S OKAY.
MAYBE SOMETHING WILL COME UP.
OH, IT WILL! I PROMISE!
Doyle, you suck.

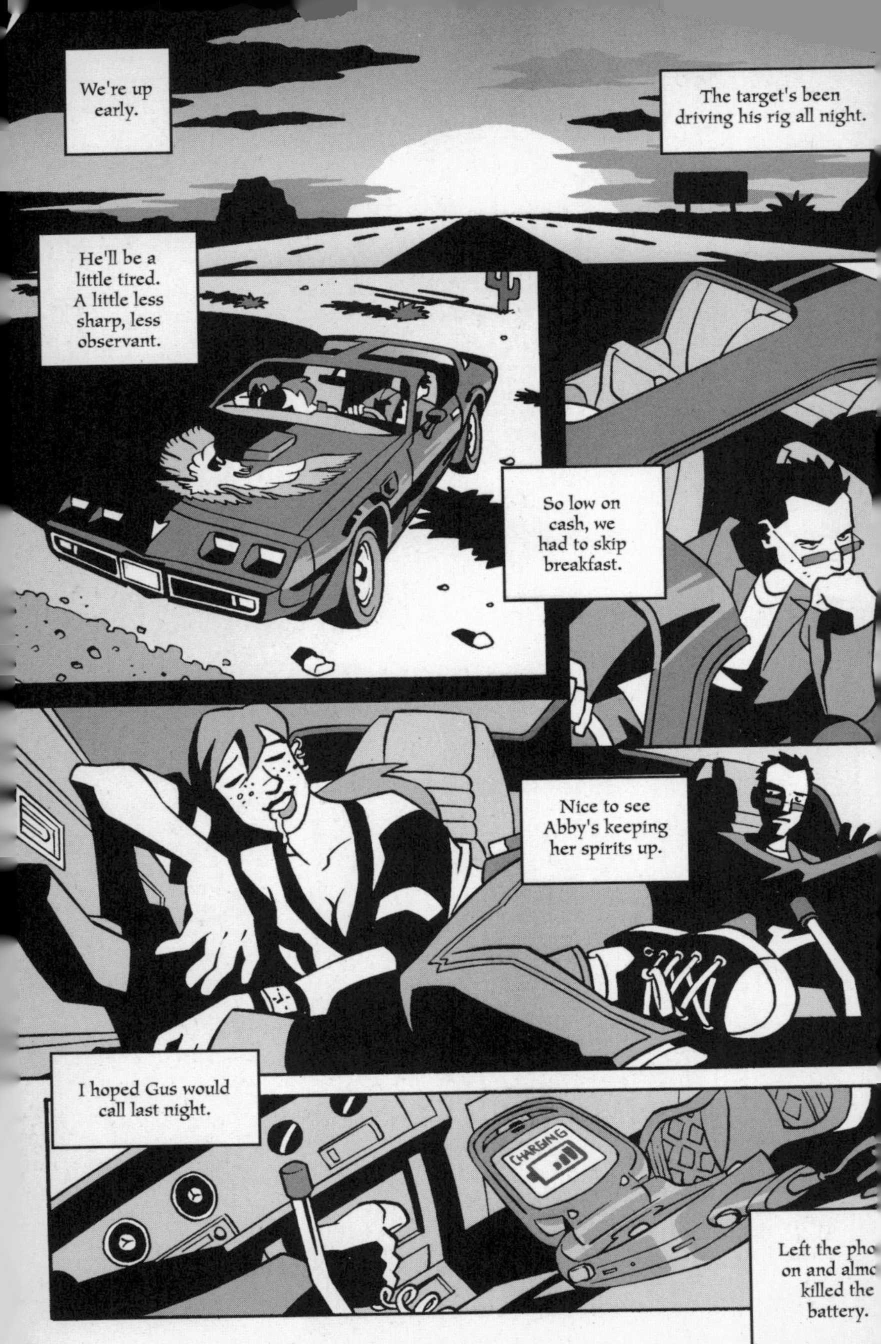
We're up early.
The target's been driving his rig all night.
He'll be a little tired. A little less sharp, less observant.
So low on cash, we had to skip breakfast.
Nice to see Abby's keeping her spirits up.
I hoped Gus would call last night.
CHARGING
Left the pho on and almc killed the battery.

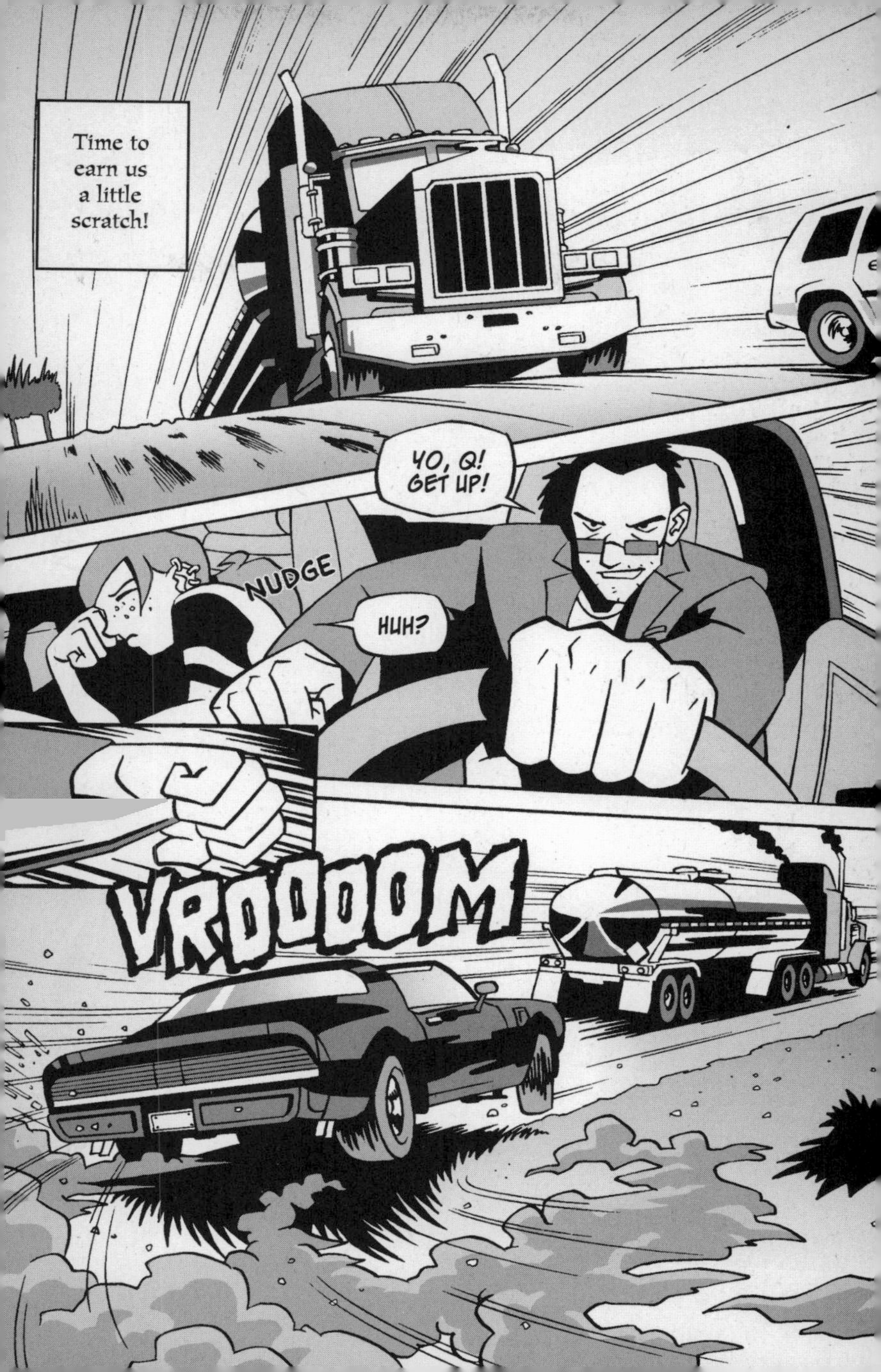
Time to earn us a little scratch!
YO, Q! GET UP!
NUDGE
HUH?
VROOOOM

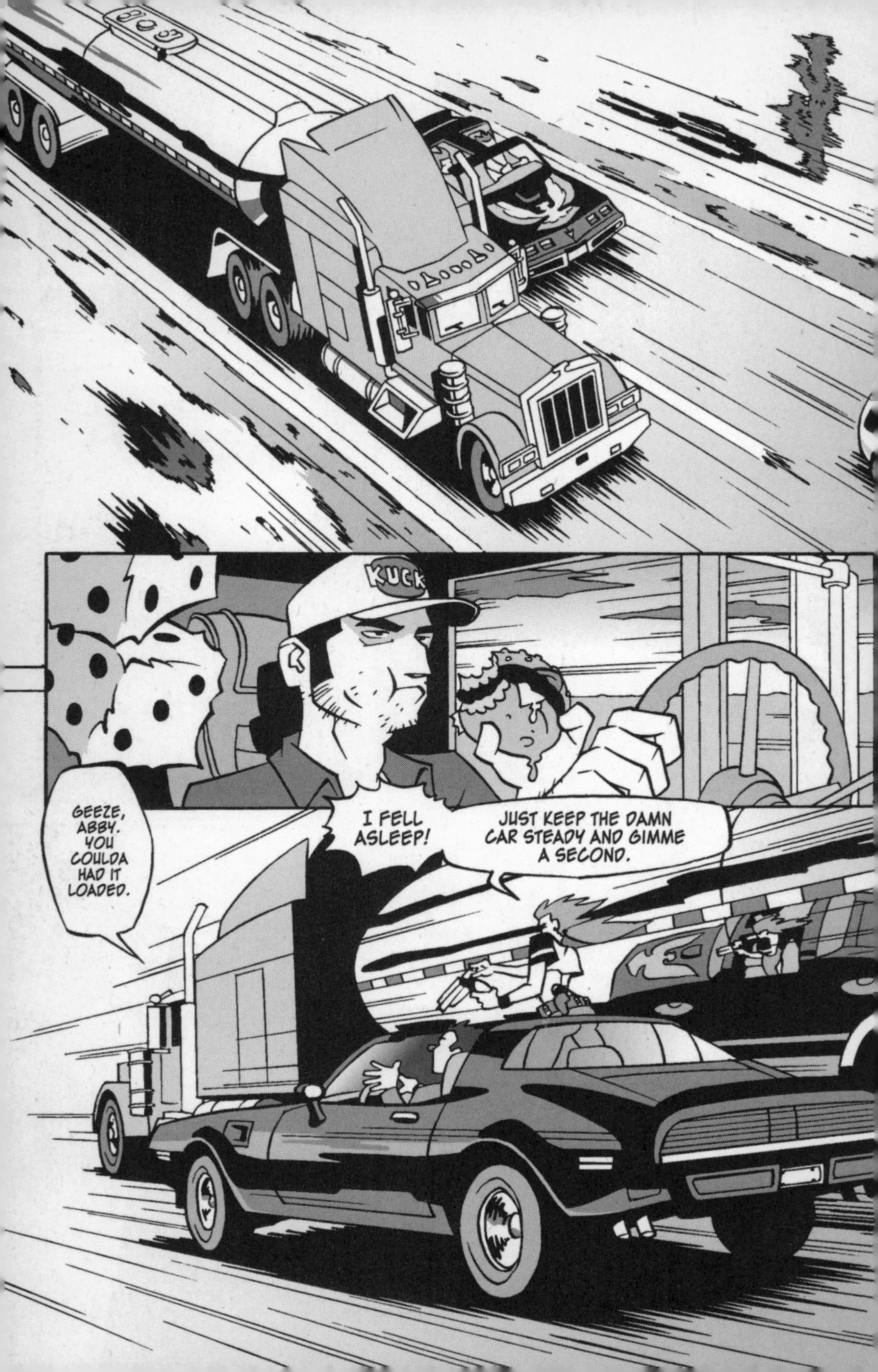
KUCK
GEEZE, ABBY. YOU COULDA HAD IT LOADED.
I FELL ASLEEP!
JUST KEEP THE DAMN CAR STEADY AND GIMME A SECOND.

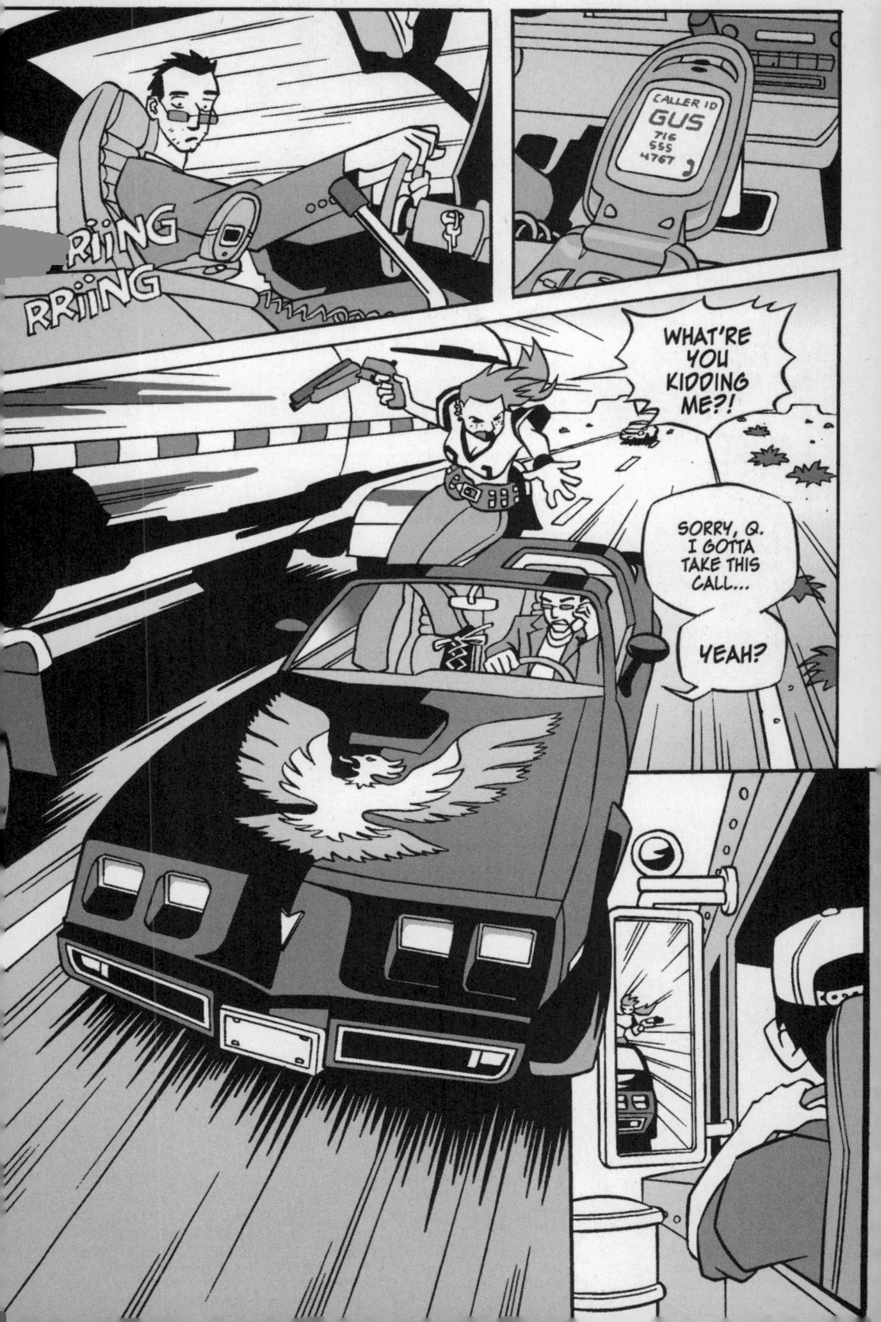
RIING
RRIING
CALLER ID
GUS
716
555
4767
WHAT'RE YOU KIDDING ME?!
SORRY, Q. I GOTTA TAKE THIS CALL...
YEAH?

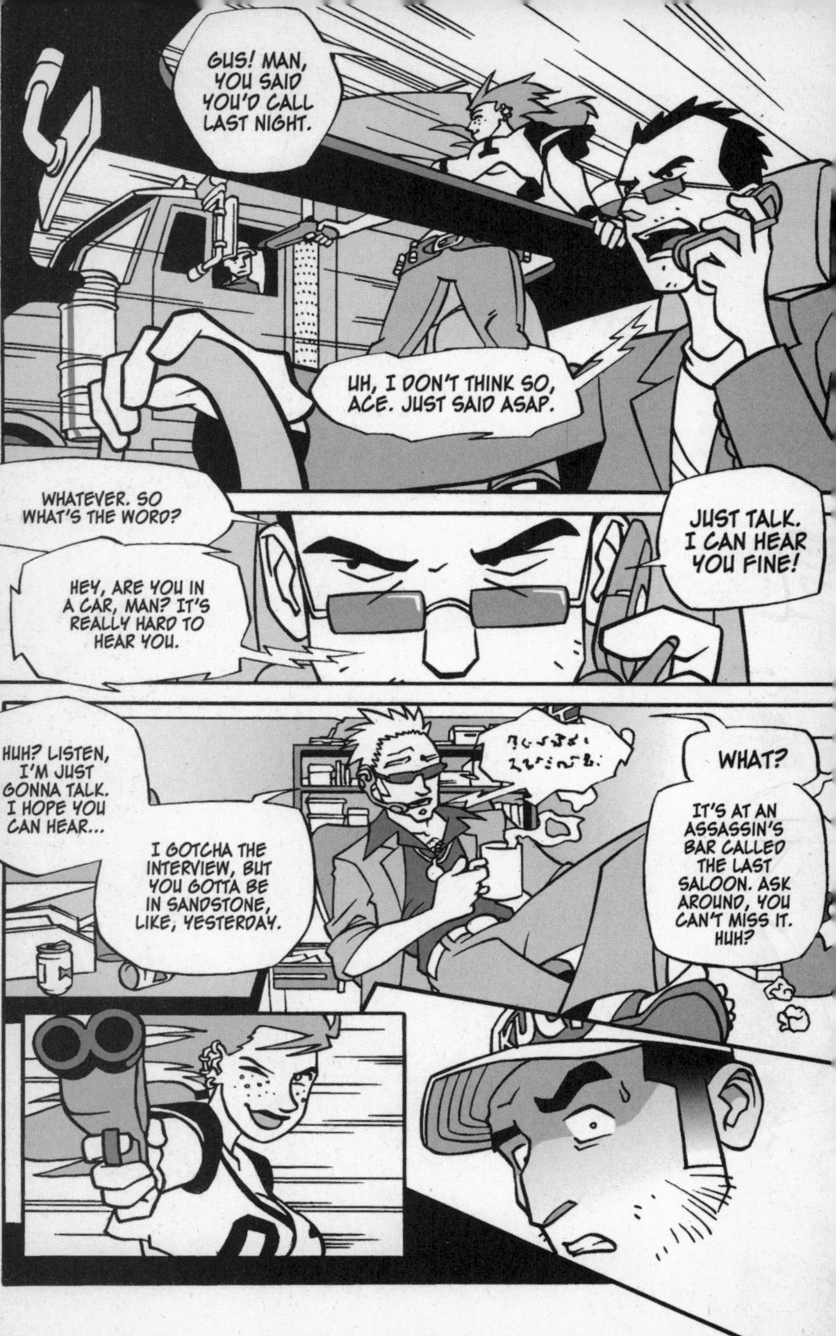
GUS! MAN, YOU SAID YOU'D CALL LAST NIGHT.
UH, I DON'T THINK SO, ACE. JUST SAID ASAP.
WHATEVER. SO WHAT'S THE WORD?
HEY, ARE YOU IN A CAR, MAN? IT'S REALLY HARD TO HEAR YOU.
JUST TALK. I CAN HEAR YOU FINE!
HUH? LISTEN, I'M JUST GONNA TALK. I HOPE YOU CAN HEAR...
I GOTCHA THE INTERVIEW, BUT YOU GOTTA BE IN SANDSTONE, LIKE, YESTERDAY.
WHAT?
IT'S AT AN ASSASSIN'S BAR CALLED THE LAST SALOON. ASK AROUND, YOU CAN'T MISS IT. HUH?

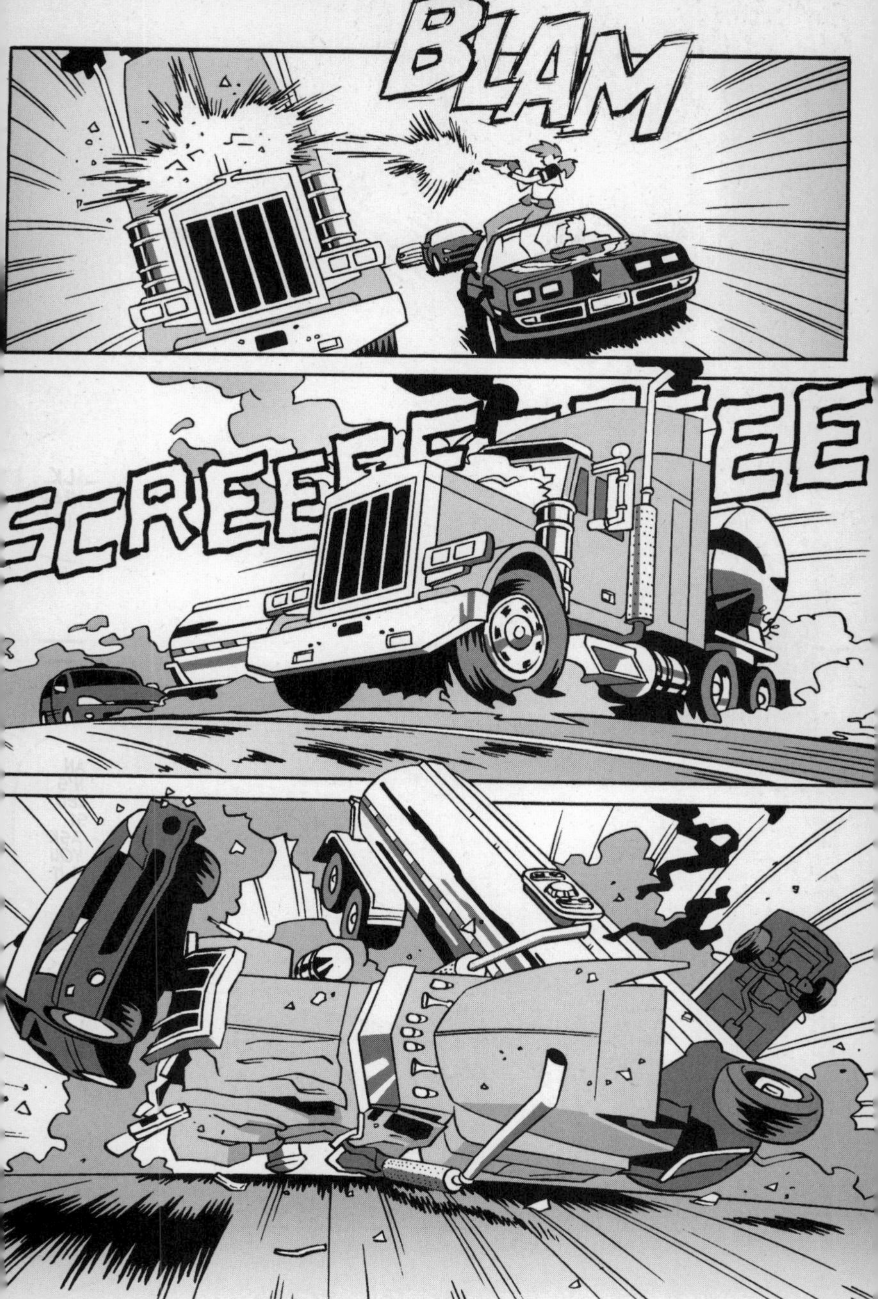
BLAM
SCREEE EE

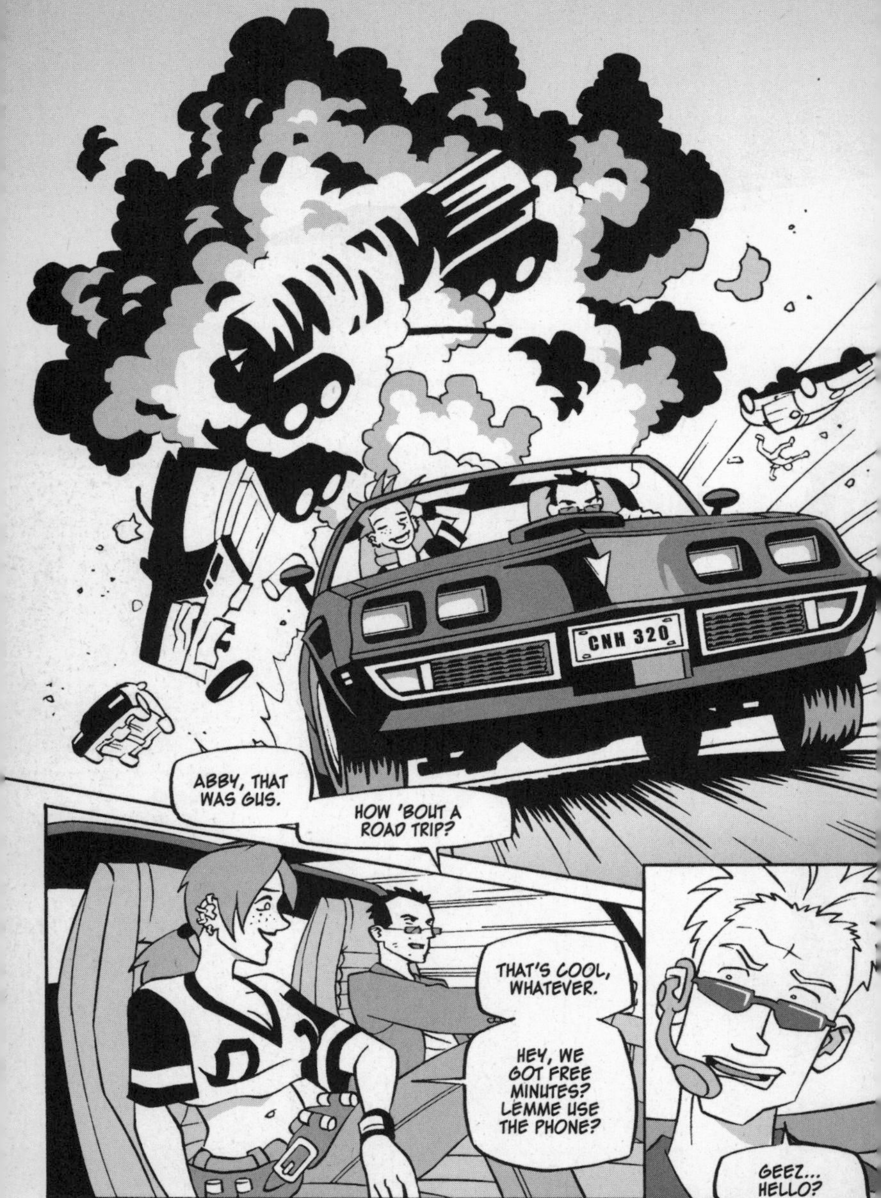
CNH 320
ABBY, THAT WAS GUS.
HOW 'BOUT A ROAD TRIP?
THAT'S COOL, WHATEVER.
HEY, WE GOT FREE MINUTES? LEMME USE THE PHONE?
GEEZ... HELLO?

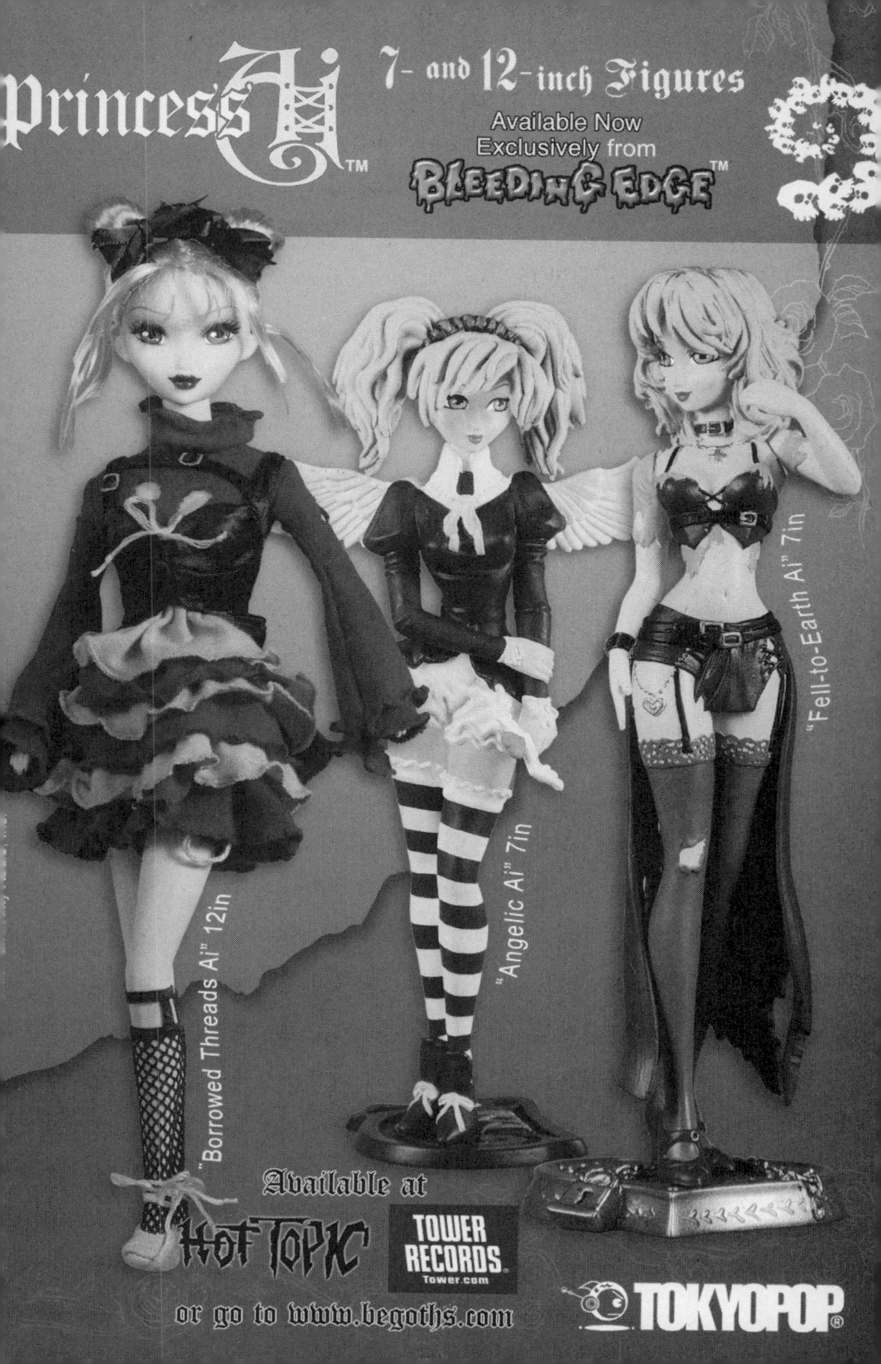

Princess Ai™
7- and 12-inch Figures
Available Now
Exclusively from
BLEEDING EDGE™
"Borrowed Threads Ai" 12in
"Angelic Ai" 7in
"Fell-to-Earth Ai" 7in
Available at
HOT TOPIC
TOWER RECORDS
Tower.com
or go to www.begoths.com
TOKYOPOP®

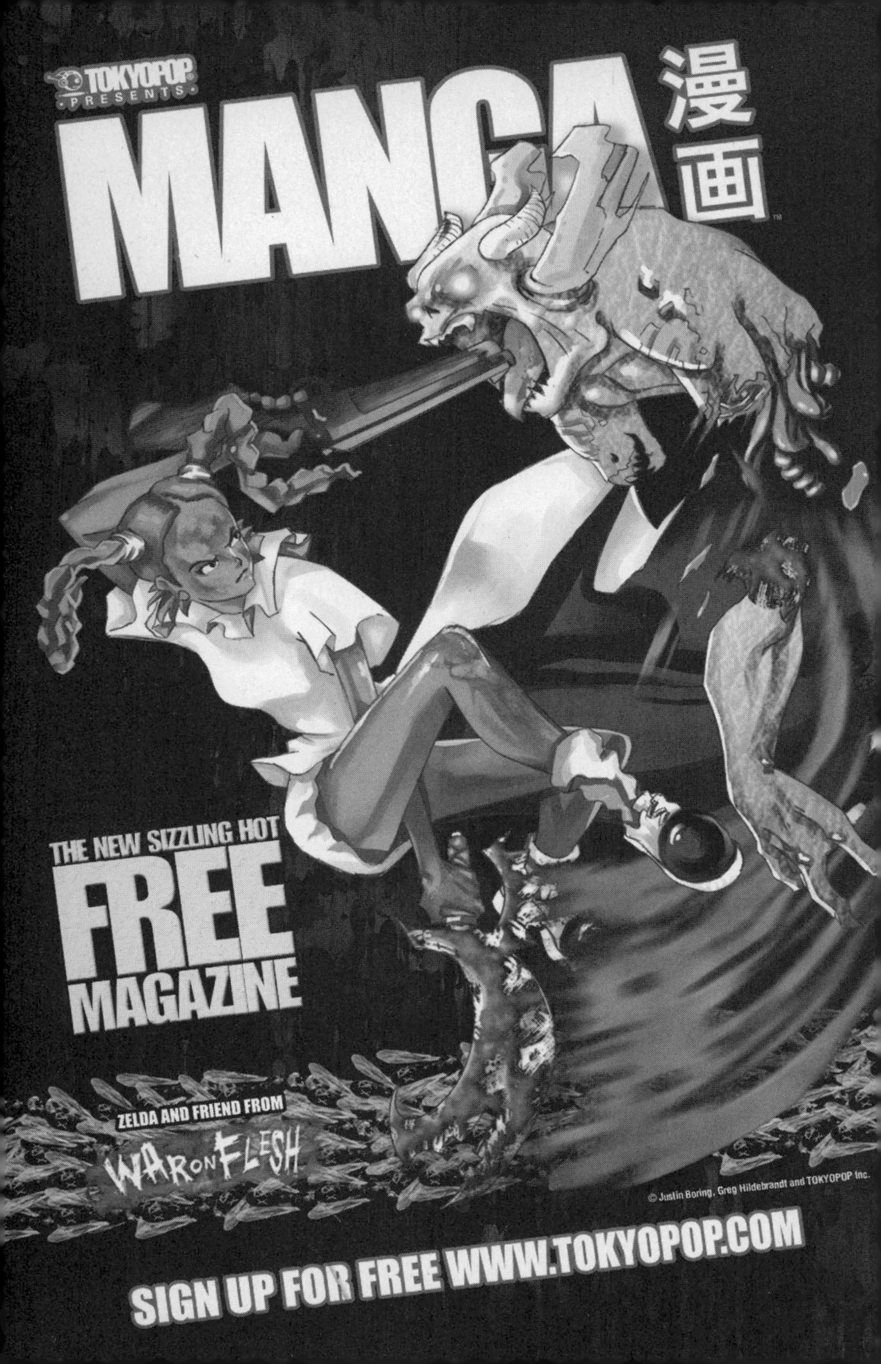

TOKYOPOP PRESENTS
MANGA 漫画
THE NEW SIZZLING HOT
FREE
MAGAZINE
ZELDA AND FRIEND FROM
WAR ON FLESH
© Justin Boring, Greg Hildebrandt and TOKYOPOP Inc.
SIGN UP FOR FREE WWW.TOKYOPOP.COM

# ROADSONG

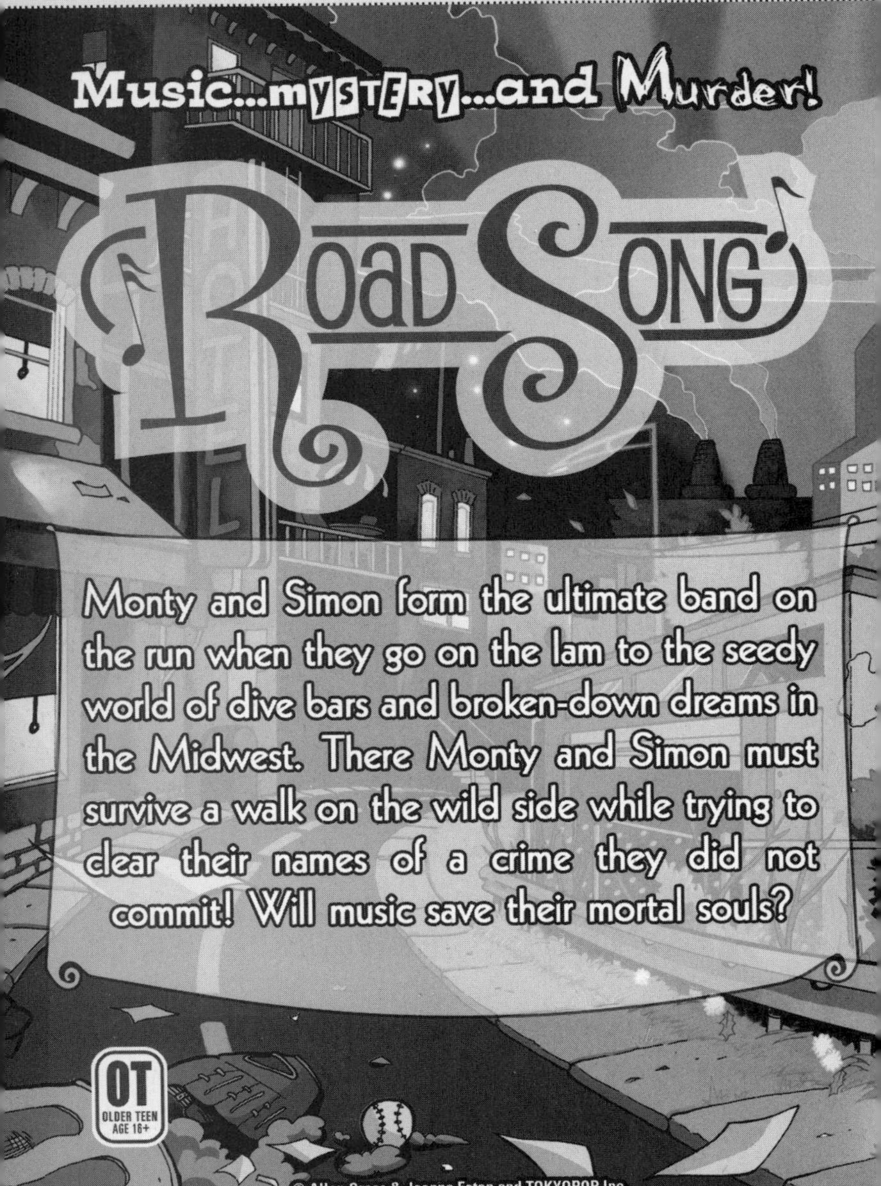
Music...mystery...and Murder!
RoadSong
Monty and Simon form the ultimate band on the run when they go on the lam to the seedy world of dive bars and broken-down dreams in the Midwest. There Monty and Simon must survive a walk on the wild side while trying to clear their names of a crime they did not commit! Will music save their mortal souls?
OT
OLDER TEEN
AGE 16+
© Allan Gross & Joanna Estep and TOKYOPOP Inc.

READ A CHAPTER OF THE MANGA ONLINE FOR FREE: